Gentrification and Schools

Education Policy

Series Editors:

Lance Fusarelli, North Carolina State University
Frederick M. Hess, American Enterprise Institute
Martin West, Harvard University

This series addresses a variety of topics in the area of education policy. Volumes are solicited primarily from social scientists with expertise on education, in addition to policymakers or practitioners with hands-on experience in the field. Topics of particular focus include state and national policy, teacher recruitment, retention and compensation, urban school reform, test-based accountability, choice-based reform, school finance, higher education costs and access, the quality instruction in higher education, leadership and administration in K-12 and higher education, teacher colleges, the role of the courts in education policymaking, and the relationship between education research and practice. The series serves as a venue for presenting stimulating new research findings, serious contributions to ongoing policy debates, and accessible volumes that illuminate important questions or synthesize existing research.

Series Editors

LANCE D. FUSARELLI is a Professor and Director of Graduate Programs in the Department of Leadership, Policy and Adult and Higher Education at North Carolina State University. He is coauthor of *Better Policies, Better Schools* and coeditor of the *Handbook of Education Politics and Policy.*

FREDERICK M. HESS is Resident Scholar and Director of Education Policy Studies at the American Enterprise Institute. An author, teacher, and political scientist, his books include *The Same Thing Over and Over: How School Reformers Get Stuck in Yesterday's Ideas* and *Common Sense School Reform.*

MARTIN WEST is an Assistant Professor of Education in the Graduate School of Education at Harvard University. He is an Executive Editor of *Education Next* and Deputy Director of Harvard's Program on Education Policy and Governance.

Ohio's Education Reform Challenges: Lessons from the Frontlines
    Chester E. Finn, Jr. Terry Ryan, and Michael B. Lafferty

Accountability in American Higher Education
    Edited by Kevin Carey and Mark Schneider

Freedom and School Choice in American Education
    Edited by Greg Forster and C. Bradley Thompson

Gentrification and Schools: The Process of Integration when Whites Reverse Flight
    Jennifer Burns Stillman

Gentrification and Schools

The Process of Integration When Whites Reverse Flight

by

Jennifer Burns Stillman

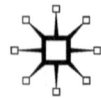

GENTRIFICATION AND SCHOOLS
Copyright © Jennifer Burns Stillman, 2012.
Softcover reprint of the hardcover 1st edition 2012 978-1-137-00899-2
All rights reserved.

First published in 2012 by
PALGRAVE MACMILLAN®
in the United States—a division of St. Martin's Press LLC,
175 Fifth Avenue, New York, NY 10010.

Where this book is distributed in the UK, Europe and the rest of the world, this is by Palgrave Macmillan, a division of Macmillan Publishers Limited, registered in England, company number 785998, of Houndmills, Basingstoke, Hampshire RG21 6XS.

Palgrave Macmillan is the global academic imprint of the above companies and has companies and representatives throughout the world.

Palgrave® and Macmillan® are registered trademarks in the United States, the United Kingdom, Europe and other countries.

ISBN 978-1-349-43591-3   ISBN 978-1-137-00900-5 (eBook)
DOI 10.1057/9781137009005
Library of Congress Cataloging-in-Publication Data

Stillman, Jennifer Burns.
    Gentrification and schools : the process of integration when whites reverse flight / by Jennifer Burns Stillman.
        p. cm.—(Education policy)
    ISBN 978–1–137–00899–2
    1. School integration—United States. 2. Gentrification—United States. 3. Migration, Internal—United States. 4. Whites—Migrations—United States. 5. Educational equalization—United States. 6. Educational change—United States. I. Title.

LC214.2.S76 2012
379.2'60973—dc23   2011052908

A catalogue record of the book is available from the British Library.

Design by Newgen Imaging Systems (P) Ltd., Chennai, India.

First edition: August 2012

To Andrew, my camerado through it all.

Contents

List of Figures and Tables   ix
Preface   xi
Acknowledgments   xvii

1   School Integration in Gentrifying Neighborhoods   1
2   School Preferences and the Process of Choosing   11
3   Starting the Integration Process   33
4   Solving the Collective Action Problem   51
5   Retaining the Innovators and Early Adopters   65
6   Attracting the Early Majority   93
7   Retaining the Early Majority, A Crucial Step   105
8   A Diverse School   115
9   Tipping In   127

Appendices   151
Notes   185
References   191
Index   197

Figures and Tables

Figures

9.1	Types of gentry parents	128
9.2	Stages of school integration	129
E.1	Stage 0 of integration: the school is segregated	177
E.2	Stage 1 of integration: the school is stagnant	178
E.3	Stage 1 of integration: the school is catalyzed	178
E.4	Stage 2 of integration: the school is changing	179
E.5	Retaining the early majority gentry parents: a crucial point in the integration process	179
E.6	Successful tipping in process: the school is diverse	180

Tables

2.1	School preferences of gentry parents	16
6.1	A demographic breakdown of schools gentry parents consider "Changing Schools"	93
8.1	Demographic breakdown of *zone schools* gentry parents consider "Diverse Schools"	116
8.2	Demographic breakdown of *progressive public choice schools* (PCS) gentry parents consider "Diverse Schools"	117

Preface

Shortly after my daughter was born, I was walking down the street in my gentrifying neighborhood, sleeping baby strapped to my body in a Baby Bjorn, pleasantly lost in thought, only to be jarred by the sound of someone shouting out the window of his car: "Your baby's arm is flapping!" I still have no idea what this was about or why he said it, and it crosses my mind often when I think about the cultural differences I have encountered as a white, middle-class, highly educated resident of three different gentrifying neighborhoods in New York City. Gentrification—the reinvestment of capital in poor, urban communities, a process that is designed to produce space for a more affluent class of people than currently occupies that space (Lees, Slater, and Wyly 2008, 9)—forces contact between people who do not typically interact, and this diversity of extremes (poor *non*whites mingling with middle- and upper-middle-class whites) brings with it humor, annoyance, and bafflement, undoubtedly on both sides, though I can only attempt to capture the gentry perspective.

Why is it a problem if a baby's arm flaps? No matter which way I attempt to interpret this yell of warning, I simply don't know. I also don't know why one of my nongentry neighbors thought someone was going to pee in my stroller when I left it locked up outside my apartment building, or why the nongentry typically don't allow their children to go in the sandbox at the playground. Perhaps these things are related. And, although I am supposedly the advantaged member of my community, my children's clothes never seem quite as nice as our poorer neighbor's, their overall appearance far more disheveled. I once had a panhandler tell me that my kids were "messed up" as he looked in disbelief at their dirty faces and my daughter's broken arm and quickly backed away from asking for money.

Another source of personal confusion is the profoundly different way the gentry and nongentry experience weather. My own gentry children are often in T-shirts playing side by side at the playground with nongentry children in winter coats. My husband and I jokingly call the nongentry infants wrapped in scarves and hats under plastic stroller covers on a warm spring day "bundle babies," never quite sure if we are underdressing our off-spring or if the nongentry are over-dressing theirs. I never say anything to them about overheating their kids, but they often say something to me about how cold mine must be, trying to shame me into pulling out the winter hats. Shame seems much more popular with the nongentry. I once let my three-year-old daughter run naked through the sprinklers at the playground, only to be told by a nongentry mother to put some clothes on her because she "doesn't want her sons to look at that," and my daughter "is going to be looked at the wrong way by boys when she is older and I'll know why." I was completely taken aback by what I view as the inappropriate sexualization of a child, but my casual mores were clearly offensive and shocking to her, and I both complied with her request and took a moment to question my own sense of right and wrong. As a minority in my neighborhood, I am never quite sure when to assert my individuality and when to adopt the ways of the local majority.

There are normed ways of living in poor, inner-city neighborhoods that are very different from those I have experienced elsewhere, in what would likely be called "mainstream America." As a nonparent, I observed the differences with something akin to spectator interest, imagining myself on vacation in a foreign country, joyously eating Trinidadian bake and doubles, only having myself to look out for. I could laugh as I regularly stepped on chicken bones mysteriously strewn across the sidewalk. I could feel the strange guilt of watching a bloodied man stumble down the sidewalk, fresh slash mark on his face, only to be ignored by the others on the sidewalk who seemed to view this sight as nothing out of the ordinary (I took their cue to do nothing, not wanting to reveal my outsider status any more than my skin color already did). And I could ignore the casual accusations of "having white people all up in my grill," spoken by angry cell-phone talkers, especially since most of my nongentry neighbors kept their opinions about gentrification to themselves and usually greeted me on the street with politeness. After having children, my reaction to difference has become more guarded. It is no longer me observing, it is my family interacting. Children have a way of bridging adults, forcing them to relate with each other in ways they would not do as singletons. Now, the cultural differences I regularly encounter feel like a question: will you stay in this neighborhood and find your niche as a minority, become a stakeholder in this community? Or will you return to a place where you are part of the cultural majority and life is simpler?

This question of staying or going is at the heart of this book, asked in the context of school integration in gentrifying neighborhoods. My own extremely mixed feelings about what to do when my first child reached kindergarten—send her to the racially and socioeconomically segregated school down the street or seek another option—was the starting point for my exploration of what it takes for gentry parents like me to send their children to their neighborhood school and integrate it through their own actions. I couldn't confidently answer the question of whether *we* should stay or go, tangled up as I was in my many selves: mom, educator, liberal, believer in equal opportunity. I knew gentry parents like me *should* stay and integrate. We are highly educated individuals intrigued by diversity and difference, able to tolerate the discomfort of our minority status, uninterested in conformity (Allen 1984; Florida 2004; Ley 1996), all characteristics ideal for integrating a school. But, my family couldn't integrate a school alone, as one white, middle-class child in a school certainly can't constitute "integrated." And I knew I wasn't comfortable having my child be the only white, middle-class child in the school. I had read too many books and articles about the detrimental effects of segregation, and I had also spent four years teaching high school in two different segregated New York City schools.

My urban teaching experience, especially when contrasted with my suburban teaching experience and own upbringing in diverse Las Vegas schools, unfortunately left me convinced that my own children wouldn't comfortably fit into this type of environment. The lower-than-average reading levels, poor attendance rates, and constant disruptions of disenchanted students can make urban classrooms incredibly challenging for even the most dedicated teachers. Beyond these basic hurdles, there is a surprising element of isolation that still exists in segregated schools, despite the technology that makes interconnectedness possible globally. I had students who had never left Brooklyn, even to take a ten-minute trip to Manhattan. I had students who expressed apathy about the 9/11 attacks, two days after, because they didn't feel any connection to the people living ten miles away. "Miss, did you *know* someone who died? Is that why you're sad?" was a refrain expressed by several students with a genuine sense of separation from the rest of America. I had students who believed whites were a racial minority in America, and *that* is why it is wrong that they hold many positions of power in our society. Since that was all they had seen with their own eyes, my presentation of the US Census map did little to convince them that whites are actually a racial majority in America, even if not for long. And when one of my students introduced me to her mother at graduation as "the teacher who made me stop hating white people," I was extremely flattered, but equally concerned that she was not alone in her hatred, and that the American race problem really hasn't been solved to the extent those living in comfortably nondiverse (or superficially diverse) communities would like to believe.

Thus, with the equally powerful convictions that integration is an important way to help improve the education environment of struggling inner-city schools (something I sincerely care about as an educator) *and* that I cannot send my own children to a segregated school and have them be the integration (something I am sincerely uncomfortable with as a mother), I began to contemplate the importance of gentry collective action in integrating a school in a gentrifying neighborhood, and set out to research how schools in gentrifying neighborhoods are able to successfully integrate. I interviewed dozens of gentry parents—white, middle- and upper-middle-class parents who are gentrifying their neighborhoods with their presence and wealth—about their school choice process to find out whether they sent their children to their local school and contributed to integrating a school as well as a neighborhood.

I will admit that we didn't do it. When we finally answered the question of whether we should stay or go, we went. My daughter was fortunate enough to win a lottery to attend The School at Columbia University, a K-8 school affiliated the university that allots 50 percent of its seats to the children of faculty, and 50 percent to community lottery winners. The community lottery is open to children living in districts 3 and 5 (the Upper West Side of Manhattan, Morningside Heights, and Harlem), and winners are guaranteed enough financial aid to make attendance completely feasible for all winners. I am reluctant to admit utilizing private school, having spent my life attending public schools, teaching in public schools, living as the daughter and granddaughter of public school teachers, and married to a public school teacher, but The School at Columbia's diversity, lottery admissions policy, and substantial financial aid dampen some of the elitist shame I am inclined to feel. In a segregated, stratified school system like New York City's, The School at Columbia is using its resources to create a socioeconomically and racially diverse neighborhood school. They are socially engineering the democratic ideal in a way the public schools cannot as easily do. As a gentry parent with a lottery ticket to this haven, I grabbed it and haven't looked back.

Perhaps because my family chose to avoid our neighborhood school, because we didn't choose to be integrators, I have a deep admiration for those gentry parents who do enroll their children in the neighborhood school and set the stage for the integration that is possible in gentrifying neighborhoods. I believe school integration remains an important societal goal, and I am glad to have met others who not only share this belief, but have the courage to do something about it. No one will ever consider them heroes, they definitively do not see themselves as heroes, and I realize it is controversial to even suggest that enrolling one's child as the first white, middle-class child in a segregated, inner-city school is a courageous act. Privileged people who simply do the right thing are not to be esteemed, and hero status only comes to those who take a real risk in the face of genuine hardship to do what is right. Gentry hardship is contrived. They could live elsewhere; they could make different choices. They know this, and they know that their integrating actions will rarely engender much admiration. The gentry position of relative advantage doesn't allow it. But, after spending months interviewing gentry parents about their school choice decision-making process, I offer them my sincere respect for taking actions to try and improve inner-city schools. It isn't easy. This is their story of integration.

Acknowledgments

I am indebted to the many parents who allowed me to interview them for this book. It is difficult to talk honestly and openly about race and class, especially in this era where we are supposed to be postracial and blind to difference. Taking the time to walk me through what was, for most, a difficult school choice process for their children took a willingness to trust that I would be fair in my compilation of their experiences. I hope this book meets their expectations. I am also grateful to my own children for forcing me to confront my prejudices and fears when it comes to determining who should be responsible for school integration. I could never make policy recommendations that I, myself, would be unable to buy into as a parent living in a gentrifying neighborhood. Additionally, my ideas throughout this project were shaped and developed under the aegis of three very supportive dissertation advisors: Dr. Jeffrey Henig, who has a wealth of knowledge about urban politics and education that is unmatched; Dr. Vicki Lens, who provided outstanding methodological guidance as well as regular support and encouragement that this project was worth doing; and Dr. Douglass Ready, who let me experiment with unconventional writing about my personal experiences as a gentry parent before bringing me back to the realities of academia, and who thus served as my most important sounding board. I am indebted to all three, and sincerely appreciative of their time and interest. Dr. Luis Huerta and Dr. Carolyn Riehl also served as important mentors on my dissertation committee, and I thank them for their thorough critique of my ideas. Finally, I am especially grateful to be married to someone who is always thinking about how to improve schools. My husband, Andrew, is a partner in many ways.

1

School Integration in Gentrifying Neighborhoods

Gentrification is changing the demographic makeup of neighborhoods across America. This reinvestment of capital in underprivileged, urban communities has the effect of putting the affluent and the poor on the same streets, and has the potential to do the same in schools. Racial segregation and concentrated poverty rarely breed an optimal environment for learning,[1] and the arrival of the children of the gentry[2] in urban schools offers the potential to improve them. For this to happen, however, the gentry must resist what their relative privilege affords them and choose to send their children to the local, nonwhite, high poverty, segregated school—an unlikely choice for white, middle- and upper-middle-class, highly educated parents with the means to find other options. Resisting the pull of white flight from a school with shifting demographics is one thing; starting the reverse process is quite another. Not only do the individual gentry parents (GPs) have to make this unlikely school choice, enough of them have to do it so that the schools actually become integrated—an unlikely course of action when the collective action required to make this come about is voluntary. "Tipping in," in contrast to what Schelling (1972) coined as "tipping out" to describe white flight from neighborhoods and schools, is the subject of this book, told from the perspective of the GPs who made improbable choices, and contributed to the school integration process in their neighborhoods.

The Gentry Internal Conflict

Choosing to integrate a school in a gentrifying neighborhood as the people of privilege is difficult, as the choice is wrapped up in both doubts about school quality *and* gentrification's tensions. While proponents exalt gentrification as neighborhood revitalization and reinvestment, a way to increase a city's tax base, and a public policy tool that can improve economic opportunities for the poor (Byrne 2003; Caulfield 1994), opponents call it forced displacement, colonization, and genocide by race and class (Lydersen 1999; Powell and Spencer 2003; Smith 1996). The gentry are very aware of this dichotomy, and it effects how they see themselves within their communities. There are few other situations in modern America, outside of gentrification, where whites intentionally insert themselves as a community's racial minority. Racial integration usually works in reverse, with Americans of color slowly bleeding into white neighborhoods and institutions. Gentrification's challenge to this norm appears to cause not only the *external* conflict between new and old that is well documented in the gentrification literature, but also an *internal* conflict for many gentry as they struggle to reconcile whether they are helping or hurting a community with their choices.

In my dozens of interviews with GPs, I asked them not just about their school-choice process, but also about what brought them to their gentrifying neighborhood in the first place, and how they saw themselves within their communities. These discussions revealed that the GP challenge is not just one of an urban parent finding a way to satisfactorily stay in the city and raise children (small space, no yard, etc.), it is also one of dealing with the internal conflict that accompanies being gentry, and thus being educated enough to know exactly what this means. GPs are very aware of the various critiques leveled against gentrification, and as a result many of the GPs in this study identified their place within their communities with an antigentry sentiment, despite being gentry, especially those who were living in the heart of gentrif*ying* neighborhoods as opposed to gentrif*ied* neighborhoods. Numerous GPs made clear to me in one way or another that they didn't want their own actions to in any way contribute to the story line of the gentry as insensitive frontiersmen, engaged in a class war, seeking revenge on the poor for ruining the city, hoping "to scrub the city clean of its working-class geography and history" (Smith 1996, 27). They didn't want to be seen as "yuppies"—upwardly mobile, selfish individuals who only care about their material well-being and not about the community that is currently occupying the neighborhood where they are moving (Lloyd 2006). They were very familiar with these tropes, and they framed their own stories in reaction to these scathing narratives, even though they knew that their conscious attempt to not be a gentry caricature wouldn't change the fact that many would still view them as intruders.

Carrie's[3] description of her family's decision to buy an apartment in their newly gentrifying neighborhood was typical of the gentry internal conflict, explaining how the technicalities of their purchase did not make them part of the gentrification problem, because the apartment was "being built on an empty lot." She continued, "I just had a thing with not wanting someone to have to move out in order for us to move in. So, even though I know it changes the neighborhood to build a new building, the lot had always been vacant, a building had not been removed." Kevin attempted a similar, conflicted explanation of his gentrifying behavior, explaining to me how the struggles waged around housing issues were less "brutal" in his neighborhood, because "much of the housing stock is owner occupied single-family homes." And in his neighborhood, you didn't see the sort of gentrification that "is really centered around rental housing, where you have a new landlord coming in and then using pressure to sort of harass out the existing low-rent paying tenants, and replace them with higher paying tenants." Kevin went on to describe *that* kind of gentrification as taking on "a very very sort of destructive and divisive form." Then, admitting that maybe he was "in la la land on this," he explained that his perception of his neighborhood "was that it's been kind of a less destructive dynamic, because it's owners selling, and not that there is not a lot of rental, and not that all of the violence in gentrification, all the sort of cultural violence doesn't happen, but it's happening in kind of a slower way." He concluded with an ode to his internal conflict, lamenting that "it will be really unfortunate" when he wakes up five years from now to find a thoroughly gentrified neighborhood.

Loren's similar internal conflict was fascinating in its ability to prevent him from judging whether he is a good neighbor. When asked if he was involved in improving his community in any way since he didn't send his children to the zone school, he responded, "Yeah yeah, I'm not particularly officially involved in any way, I mean the most I can say I do is spend a lot of time with the kids on my block because I'm home during the day. Particularly in the summer, there are all these kids with nothing to do. So I just sort of do some stuff with all these kids, kids that live near me, and I have kids, and I'm around." After earnestly describing this engagement, he immediately backtracked, saying, "So, we're complete failures in that department, we're not doing anything to make it better, other than being there. I don't know, that's pretty arrogant, I don't know if that even counts."

There are no clear rules about what counts in terms of community engagement, nor are there clear rules about who should be seen as a gentrifier. I devised a definition for "gentry parents"—white,[4] middle- or upper-middle-class, highly educated parents who are gentrifying a neighborhood with their presence and wealth—but many of my interviewees clearly did not agree with this categorization. Margaret, for example, shunned my label, and went so far as to deny gentrification was even happening in her neighborhood. She explained how "the neighborhood has always had a mix of classes, so it's not *really* gentrification," and categorized herself as "working so hard to prevent gentrification from meaning what it's come to mean." She then highlighted the ways she has worked to build up her community for all residents, proving she wasn't a gentrifier, because that word implies the destruction of something. With another neighborhood GP, Margaret started the Community Supported Agriculture (CSA) in the neighborhood, a program that delivers boxes of seasonal produce from local farms to CSA members each week during the farming season. These two GPs started this program because, as Margaret explains, "When we moved in, there were no grocery stores, no vegetable stands, no farmers market." They saw "people living off fast food and bodegas," and wanted to help put a system in place so that fresh food would be available not just for their families, but for all neighborhood families. They established a sliding scale for the CSA, "so people who could afford could help subsidize those who couldn't," and they made sure that it took food stamps. Margaret saw herself not as an interloper, but as part of the neighborhood she was continually working to improve for all residents, new and old.

Katrine was similarly blind to seeing herself as a gentrifier, suggesting gentrifiers, by definition, want to change something, and she doesn't. She put it this way, "I try really hard to be part of the community, not just to be some white family who has moved in here and wants to take over and change the world. Because that's not what we want at all. We live here, we knew what it was when we came, and yet we still came, and we want to be part of the community." But wanting to be part of something, and being accepted as part of something, are two different things, and the reaction of the nongentry to the gentry was part of what contributed to their ongoing internal conflict. Lisbeth best captured this struggle to find a comfortable place of existence in the neighborhood. She is a writer, and is planning to title her article about her experiences trying to integrate her neighborhood school, "My Year as a Racist," because, as she candidly articulated, "You're damned if you do and you're damned if you don't. As a white parent who is perceived as having a certain amount of power...like the first day of school with my three year old daughter, parents are saying, 'Look, they're trying to take over!' So you have this, if you come in and invest in your neighborhood school, you're trying to take over. If you go to a different school, you're running away. So, it's like you're a racist if you go and a racist if you don't go."

The Promise of Equality in the Face of Hierarchy

The typical lack of social mixing between gentry and nongentry is partially the reason why these dynamics exist and persist. If the neighborhood gentry are made to feel like racists who are ruining the neighborhood's authenticity whenever they attempt to become more interconnected with their nongentry peers, they are unlikely to continue trying. And if the nongentry are made to feel like they should be grateful for social mixing because it is somehow supposed to benefit their lives, they are equally as unlikely to try. This problem cannot be easily rectified, even in a school situation where all the parents theoretically enter on equal grounds. As Blomley (2004) aptly summarizes the basic problem with social mixing in gentrifying neighborhoods, "…it promises equality in the face of hierarchy." And as blind as the gentry try to be to their own privilege out of respect for their new neighbors, something many GPs in this study tried to do with their repeated antigentry sentiments, both sides know where they fall in society's hierarchy.

Thus, as GPs contemplate whether they should attempt to integrate their local schools, they cannot ignore their internal conflict over gentrification, which is regularly exacerbated by nongentry resentment—sometimes subtle, sometimes not—directed toward their existence. The social hierarchies that exist can't be eliminated simply by disregarding them. GPs can't will them away by simply taking a stance against themselves. This means that GPs, when faced with choosing a school for their children, will likely choose something other than their zone school if they perceive this to be the easiest way to ameliorate the external conflicts stemming from gentrification. If, as Lisbeth put it, "you're a racist if you go or a racist if you don't go," you might as well not "go." If GPs believe that they help maintain neighborhood harmony *more* by staying away from the local school and not trying to impose their white, middle-class values upon the school, then they will likely stay away. However, to further complicate matters, *even if* GPs believe that entering the local school will dampen down gentrification's external conflicts and ease some of the tensions that exist in their neighborhoods over race and class, they will still exercise their privilege as the need arises and do what they perceive to be in the best interest of their children. Kevin, among the most conflicted of my interviewees, still made the point that "this is not a moral question. No one is going to be judged whether you send your kid here or you don't…you have to do what is right for you kid in the end."

While Kevin's assessment that "no one is going to be judged" might hold truth among GPs themselves as they grapple with their school-choice dilemma together, others will likely judge these GPs harshly for viewing themselves as being in a difficult situation. They are clearly not victims in the way poor families of color are victims of society's inequities, and it is a stretch to frame them as such. But, in the context of gentrification, when the *non*gentry can *always* be framed as the victims—victims of poverty and segregation *or* victims of a takeover and displacement—the gentry are boxed into a psychological bind where they feel the confusion of being damned if you and damned if you don't. In this state of mind, they simply don't know what to do. They don't know what is right. They know they are not victims, but they also don't see an easy path to school choice. And in this indecisive, conflicted state, they sometimes seem condescending and self-serving for generally erring on the side of protecting their privilege.

A Fear of Falling

As Kelly (2008) concludes in his contribution to *The Way Class Works*, "The great contradiction of education in the modern era is that it is both an avenue for upward mobility, as well as the main social institution in which social status is reproduced from one generation to the next." GPs know this, and they don't want to inadvertently move themselves and their children down the social ladder by *making themselves victims*— sending their children to schools where the education is not as good as an education they could very likely access elsewhere—when they are not, *currently*, the victims. Ehrenreich (1990) would call this a "fear of falling," a "rational fear" held by the middle class that their children will not also be middle class if they don't instill them with the right education and work values. She argues that unlike the lower or upper classes, where class is simply transmitted through birth, middle-class professionals cannot simply pass down their middle-class status to their children. The steep educational barriers to enter middle-class professions—law, medicine, engineering, business, and so on—keep out those who lack discipline and a willingness to delay gratification, something parents can't simply give to their children. The only thing middle-class parents can do "...is attempt, through careful molding and psychological pressure, to predispose each child to retrace the same long road they themselves once took" (Ehrenreich 1990, 83). If they fail in this task, their children could fall down the social class ladder. A child's school experience is key to this careful molding process, with peer effects viewed by middle-class parents as equally important to parental pressure.

This fear of falling is real. It is why even some GPs who sincerely believe in integration would tell me, "There is always a 'but,' I could do the noble thing and integrate my local school, but..." The unspoken "but," which GPs didn't feel the need to speak, is the obvious parental choice to never purposely give your child less than you are capable of giving them. If larger equalizers are not present in society—and they generally aren't in the American, decentralized, fragmented education system of roughly 15,000 public school districts and thousands of additional private schools, where every family jockeys for the best position it can get within their means—parents will not disadvantage their children for some larger, abstract sense of doing the "right" thing, especially in communities where this action has the potential to incite hostility and accusations of a gentry takeover.

Meaningful Social Mixing Changes the Debate

In spite of these challenges and others that will be described throughout this book, school integration in gentrifying neighborhoods is happening. And if it becomes the norm instead of the anomaly that it currently is, it could change the terms of the debate over gentrification. The social mixing occurring in schools between gentry and nongentry children complicates the opposition's stance that gentrification is bad for a neighborhood. Meaningful social mixing between people of different racial and socioeconomic backgrounds has, arguably, been the missing link in finding common ground between gentrification's proponents and opponents. Without it, it is easy for opponents to vilify white people and those of a higher social class who are moving into a poor, minority neighborhood as only caring about their own personal economic benefit as gentrifiers, with little concern for improving the neighborhood for those who already live there. Without social mixing, it is difficult for proponents of gentrification to make a compelling case that the arrival of a more advantaged group is doing anything more than displacing those who are already living there. Without social mixing, the theoretical benefits of gentrification have not been realized, the hypothetical middle-class "peer effects" that some espouse as justification for deconcentrating the poor (Goetz 2003) have been elusive, and the theoretical arguments in favor of gentrification are not accepted as valid.

School integration in gentrifying neighborhoods makes social mixing a reality. If segregated schools are "savagely unequal" (Kozol 1992), then whatever displacement is necessary within a neighborhood to bring a more racially and socioeconomically diverse group of children into a school might be worth the price.[5] In an ideal world, the trade-offs between one good and another wouldn't be necessary. In our world, there is a gray space where gentrification might both help and hurt families simultaneously. This book lives in the gray, exploring gentrification's potential while remaining acutely aware of the many hurdles that prevent tipping in from becoming a widespread reality.

Plan for the Book

Tipping in appears to be a process that involves four different stages of integration, and the book is organized to take the reader on a journey through each stage, from a Segregated School to a Diverse School. The research methodology employed to create this book, grounded theory, is laid out in Appendix A. This section also includes a description, but not identification, of the three New York City (NYC) neighborhoods that backdropped this study, as well as an explanation of the quantitative and qualitative methods used to select the 52 GPs I formally interviewed. Chapter 2 sets the stage for understanding tipping in through the perspective of GPs by giving an overview of their school preferences, explaining why schools in gentrifying neighborhoods are usually unable to match each preference, and taking a look at the way GPs go about choosing a school. Chapter 3 identifies the elements necessary for a Stage 0, Segregated School to attract the first wave of GPs, the Innovators.[6] Chapter 4 is devoted solely to explaining how Innovator and Early Adopter GPs go about solving the collective action problem when contemplating their entrance into a Segregated School. Chapter 5 explores why Innovator and Early Adopter GPs often leave their Stage 1, Catalyzed Schools before their presence takes root, highlighting a roadblock I call the gentry/nongentry culture gap. Chapter 6 delves into the way Innovator and Early Adopter GPs entice the Early Majority into their schools through staging elaborate school tours and stirring up a buzz in the neighborhood. Chapter 7 explains why the Early Majority GPs often leave their Stage 2, Changing Schools, in effect stalling the integration process. Retaining the Early Majority is a crucial element of a successful integration process. Chapter 8 looks at the culmination of tipping in, exploring what it means to be a Stage 3, Diverse School, and why achieving this goal doesn't necessarily mean things are easy. Chapter 9 summarizes the school integration process in a gentrifying neighborhood, frames the tensions that will inevitably hamper school integration efforts, and closes with policy recommendations to facilitate tipping in, specifically the introduction of Urban Education Cooperatives.

Explicating the school integration process in a gentrifying neighborhood may make it easier for GPs contemplating their options and weighing their own agency in integrating their neighborhood schools to determine if engaging in this process is for them. It may also help urban school leaders interested in diversifying their schools avoid some of the pitfalls that make tipping in so difficult. My hope is that this book helps to make tipping in the norm in gentrifying neighborhoods. Without neighborhood gentrification leading to school integration, an opportunity for harnessing the social capital that the gentry bring to their neighborhoods is being lost. Gentrification need not remain a divisive either or proposition—the great salvation of the poor or the devastating annihilation of a neighborhood. Gentrification might not be either of these things.

2

School Preferences and the Process of Choosing

Tipping in is the process of school integration in a gentrifying neighborhood through the compounding choices of many gentry parents (GPs). To understand why this process is so difficult to even start, much less complete, there are three factors that require a detailed examination: (1) What GPs prefer in a school, (2) Why the zone public schools in gentrifying neighborhoods are usually unable to match each preference, and (3) Why the GP process of choosing a school usually leads GPs even further away from considering their zone neighborhood school. All three aspects of school choice are roadblocks to integration, as is the unusual overall context in which GPs enter the school marketplace. As members of a cultural minority in their neighborhoods, but part of the American cultural majority, GPs have to contemplate their education preferences within a neighborhood that usually can't meet them, knowing that it wouldn't take much to have those preferences met elsewhere. They are *not* minorities who realize that because they are minorities they are very unlikely to have their preferences met, as would, for example, an Italian family living in Ekalaka, Montana, who wants an Emilio Reggio education facilitated in the Italian language. GPs are minorities who know they probably *can* find what they are looking for in a school if they simply leave their immediate neighborhoods. This is a very different reality than being a minority *everywhere* you go in town, and this fact hovers over all the other aspects involved in the GP school-choice process: how they choose, what they are presented with, and what they would prefer to choose.

Public School People

Before exploring the specific school preferences of GPs, it is first important to note that these preferences will typically be searched for within the constraints of public school options. When asked what brought them to their gentrifying neighborhoods in the first place, the GPs in this study mostly expressed a desire to find housing that was relatively low cost and conveniently located to their places of employment. When compared to their highly educated New York City (NYC) peers (all of the GPs interviewed for this study had bachelor's degrees, with many holding advanced degrees as well), peers who use their college degrees to make a lot of money on Wall Street or in affiliated industries, GPs tend to be relatively poor. The career choices of most of my 52 formal interviewees tended toward "creative" and "meaningful" professions—graphic designers, museum curators, comedians, chefs, artists, writers, magazine editors, college professors, K-12 teachers, human rights attorneys, nonprofit workers of all stripes—professions that allow for a decent, solidly middle-class or upper-middle-class life, especially if both GPs in the family are working, but not a life of opulence. Thus, GPs tend to end up in their gentrifying neighborhoods in part because it is the only place they can afford to live in a space large enough to make raising children tenable *and* remain in New York City. Likewise, these "creative" and "meaningful" career choices prevent access to private schools, which can cost up to $30,000 annually in New York City. Thus, by choice or by necessity, GPs tend to be self-described "public school people."

Most of the GPs in this study attended public schools themselves, and this fact oriented them toward "believing" in public schools as a democratic good. For many, it was expressed almost as an ideology. Lisbeth explained this general sentiment very well, first by labeling herself as "a public school kid," continuing with, "I believe in public school, I feel like it's like jury duty. It's where you go to meet people who are not like you and form consensus. And you build a better society in public school, especially in an urban school environment." Having a public school belief system appeared to keep GPs both grounded in their financial reality and able to feel good about sending their children to public schools.

GPs appreciated the irony that their nongentry neighbors seemingly view the gentry financial reality as "rich," a characteristic they definitely do *not* see in themselves. One GP I interviewed, Brigitta, was very amused by my term "gentry parent," because of her self-perception as being middle class and struggling to make ends meet. She laughed wholeheartedly when I asked her to describe the school buzz she was hearing among her gentry parent friends and said, "I love it! Gentry parent friends, makes me feel like I ride horses or something! If we were true gentry, we wouldn't be in public schools." Leslie also laughed about the economic divide between her and those New Yorkers *she* perceives to be rich, recalling a conversation about schools with a coworker where she thought to herself, "You guys make enough money to send all three of your kids to private school? Well that's a whole different world than the one I'm living in!" She went on to explain how parents "of my grouping" all *have* to send their kids to public school, which is "why the *good* public schools are so competitive, you can't get into them, because everybody wants to go to these schools."

In New York City, where there is a flourishing private school industry offering a tremendous variety of schooling options for the very wealthy, and a public school system serving 1.1 million children, roughly 75 percent who are considered poor, the "good" public schools for those in the middle are perceived to be scant. GPs are typically *as* educated as the very wealthy, so they have a certain sense of entitlement to a great education for their children. As Lisbeth put it, "We don't have any money, but we're part of a power culture." GPs' position within the power culture complicates their reality that they can't afford to buy a private school education, even though they have more in common with the types of families at these schools than with the poorer, less educated families who are typical of the majority of public school enrollees. Most scholarships at private schools are reserved for "diversity," and these white GPs will not be eligible. The few GPs I interviewed who ended up in private schools had biracial children, who qualified for diversity scholarship money, or the GPs were assisted by their parents. And those who were able to make the private school choice did so very reluctantly, believing that their GP peers would look at the decision as some kind of moral failure. Amber, for example, found it "very hard to admit" that she sends her children to private school, "because there is such an impetus, such a strong, such value attached to changing these public schools." She admired her GP friends for "taking their energy and putting it into their local public school," and "hung her head in shame" whenever the question of school choice came up.

Public Elementary School Options in New York City

Despite the fact that most GPs are not financially able to access the private school world (nor would they necessarily want to even if they could), they still all believed that they had a choice about how their children are educated. Not a single GP in this study was resigned to his child's school situation as unchangeable or inevitable. Armed with their various college degrees, GPs are used to navigating their way through the world on their own terms, and not a one started and ended their school choice process with their zone school. Even those GPs who enrolled their children in their zone school saw it as a choice, a choice they made at the end of a search process. In New York City, there are many options for public school people. GPs all believe they have choices, in part because they really do. The New York City Department of Education (NYCDOE) offers a variety of schooling alternatives for those savvy enough to figure out what exists beyond the zone school.

There are roughly seven categories of schooling a GP can access, depending on district or borough of residence. First, every child has access to his or her zone school. All a parent has to do is go to the NYCDOE website, enter their address, and a school will pop up on the screen, the school their child is eligible to attend simply because they live at that particular address. There are many zone schools that are considered "good" by those who are in the business of rating schools, and what most of these schools have in common is their racial and socioeconomic diversity, and their location in New York City's more affluent neighborhoods. They are typically the nonsegregated schools in the city that have both a large middle-class presence in the school, a substantial white *and* nonwhite student population, and an engaged, active parent body. When I talk about the goal of tipping in, the goal is for the zone school in a gentrifying neighborhood to become one of these diverse neighborhood schools. They need not have a *majority* of their students from the white, middle class; they simply need to have a strong enough white, middle-class presence that the schools are *perceived* to be diverse, middle-class schools, and are considered a desirable school option for a GP. For a family that is zoned for one of these "good" schools, the school choice is usually an easy one. Many families with means move simply to live within the zone lines of these schools.

A second option for NYC children entering elementary school is to try to get an extra seat at another zone school in the same district. Principals are allowed to enroll children from outside the zone if there are spots left once all zoned children are enrolled. Some districts hold lotteries to raffle off the extra seats at individual schools to lucky families unhappy with their own zone school. Some districts and individual schools use more informal methods.

A third option is to enter the lotteries for the various public choice schools in the city. These are schools that are not restricted by zone lines for admittance, because they supposedly offer something unique, like a "progressive" education (more on this type of education later). In Neighborhood C, all of the schools are "choice" schools, and students do not have a zone school, making the GP choice process in Neighborhood C uniquely different from the process engaged by families in Neighborhoods A and B. All parents are able to rank their school choices out of the available options, and they are then assigned by lottery and rankings.

A fourth option is to apply to public choice schools that do not employ a lottery system, but instead interview families or screen children to determine whether they are a good fit for the school, for example, The Special Music School of America, which identifies musically gifted four-year olds, and both Central Park East 1 and 2, which are extremely progressive, and they want to make sure families are committed to this style of education.

A fifth option is for families to have their child tested for gifted and talented (G&T) programs. All children are able to take the test for free, which is currently part Bracken School Readiness,[1] part OLSAT.[2] Children scoring in the 97th percentile or above are eligible to enter the citywide gifted programs lottery. Children scoring in the 90th percentile or above can enter their district-wide gifted programs lottery. Families that rank every single G&T program available to them are guaranteed a spot. Conversely, families that do not rank every option are not guaranteed a spot.

A sixth option for families in Manhattan only is to apply to Hunter College Gifted Elementary School, a state-run public school. The screening exam, the Stanford Binet IQ test,[3] costs approximately $300, and the top 200 scorers make it through Round 1. Round 2 involves parent observations, as reported on a form, and a play observation session conducted by school psychologists. At the end of this round, the top 25 girls and 25 boys are accepted.

A seventh and final public elementary school option is to enter the lotteries for charter schools in the city. Charter schools are publically financed but privately governed, and offer some sort of unique program to children who win the lottery, for example, longer school days and longer school years allowing for more enrichment and tutoring. What an NYC family chooses, or tries to choose, depends in part on who they are and what they prefer their child's education to look like.

School Preferences

The school preferences of all of the GPs I interviewed were remarkably similar. Almost every GP in this study expressed a desire for schools that are diverse, and the majority preferred schools that are on the progressive end of the pedagogy and school culture spectrum. Almost two-thirds were also opposed to G&T programs. Table 2.1 displays the school preferences of the interviewed GPs. GPs who explicitly expressed a preference were given a "yes" or "no" for each preference. A "neutral" was ascribed to those GPs who didn't explicitly care one way or the other about the school attribute. With regard to pedagogy, most of the GPs who were neutral

Table 2.1 School preferences of gentry parents (n=52)

	Racial diversity preference (%)	Progressive pedagogy preference (%)	Gifted and talented preference (%)
Yes	86	54	18
No	12	30	60
Neutral	2	16	22

were families whose number one preference was a dual language program, and thus their pedagogical preferences were focused primarily on how a school's dual language program was implemented. Each of these preferences will be explored in detail in light of how neighborhood public schools in gentrifying neighborhoods are usually unable to match each preference.

School Preference One: Racial Diversity

GPs of all types—Innovators, Early Adopters, Early Majority, and Late Majority—expressed a preference for schools that are racially diverse. The few who didn't care about racial diversity were the Innovators, who had no problem being the only white family in a school, usually foreign GPs, which will be discussed further in the next section. In New York City, the phrase "diverse," among GPs, takes on a completely different meaning than it does when white parents talk about "diversity" in the suburbs. Instead of measuring a school's diversity quotient by how many children of color attend a school, GPs measure diversity in terms of how many white children attend the school. When a GP would tell me, as they often did, that their neighborhood school was "not diverse," they meant that there were few to zero white children. "White counting" (my term) was regularly employed by GPs to gauge the extent of a school's diversity. GPs either brought up the white count themselves, or when asked by me to provide one, they were easily able to do so. If the numbers were low enough that "white counting" was possible, the school would not be considered diverse by most GPs, and thus unable to meet this preference.

"Diverse" was *not* code language for wanting a predominantly white school. GPs repeatedly made the claim that they "wouldn't want to send my kid to an all-white school either," expressing a belief that "all of anything is not healthy." Sharon chose one school for her daughter over another because, although she would have been one of the only white children at either school, the school she chose had an almost even mix of black and Hispanic children, whereas the other school was "all African American," and that "bothered" her, "not because they're African

American," but she thought, "No, too much of one, and she will stand out so much, too much." Trista shared Sharon's concern about "standing out," and expanded on why it was especially important for her son, who is half Indian: "I don't want him to stand out anywhere. Like, right now he does not stand out in his class. I wanted him to stand out in other ways, but not because of his...his racial features, and so, you know, it's hard to say that, but it's true. So it's why I wouldn't want him in an all-white school, I wouldn't want him in an all-black school."

Many GPs tied this desire for school diversity to their choice of New York City as a home. Marcia explained that she "lived in New York City for a reason, and I don't want my kid in this all-white school, because I want her to be exposed to different backgrounds and everything and it just makes for an interesting place." Robert also said that he "wanted to come to New York to live in a place that was more bi-cultural," and he differed from many of his work colleagues who were sending their kids to "private, white schools." That *isn't* what he wanted. He wanted his daughter "to experience something that is a little bit more multicultural. And have that real experience, that real New York experience, to grow to appreciate all of those differences."

Many GPs also considered diversity to be a key component of their child's education, embracing what their children would learn from other children coming from different backgrounds. Eduardo explained that he wants his children "to be exposed to the full range of society" because he thinks that "many of the issues of difference that are challenging to society are because people have really isolated segments of society, and we can't understand each other." He went on to explain how his own upbringing in a class-mixed environment enables him to comprehend difference more than just "intellectually, because most of these thing are emotional reactions—words or body language or levels of communication or how close you speak to each other. These are things that, you can understand them intellectually at a certain level, but not be able to emotionally react to them appropriately." He continued, clearly convinced that he held an important truth: "I've seen this over and over again with highly educated peers who just weren't raised in that environment. Like, they can abstract it and say, 'Yeah, I understand that in X culture they take the snot and throw it on the floor so everybody sees that they're healthy, and that is considered a good thing.' And it's one thing to think about it and say, 'Yeah, it's just a cultural or anthropological thing,' and another thing is to actually be there and not be grossed out by it."

Laura also saw the basic educational value of diversity, and was "thrilled" that her daughters would just "have that," that knowledge of what it means to live in a diverse environment, and "they won't have to learn it later," something Laura felt like she had to do because she didn't grow up within a diverse community. Laura also thought diversity was preventing her kids from compartmentalizing the world the way her peer group does. She proudly described how her kids, "to this day, don't...they don't know a difference. They don't see it...they don't see it that way. It's just kind of like, if they're describing a friend, it might be, like, she has peach skin, and curly hair." Astrid had similar hopes for her own daughter growing up without the same "ridiculous grids we've set up as adults." Her daughter currently had "no concept," and Astrid believed that "if she grows up without a concept, then maybe she'll live as an adult without a concept."

The strong preference for diversity, expressed by GPs in many different ways, suggests that Clotfelter's (2004) hypothesis of "white avoidance," which states that, "...other things being equal, white parents prefer not to send their children to racially mixed schools and, among racially mixed schools, prefer those with the lowest proportions of nonwhite students" (78), does not hold true for GPs. GPs *do* prefer racially mixed schools, and are *not* seeking schools with the lowest proportions of nonwhite students. The public schools GPs usually ranked as their first choice were extremely diverse, with whites usually comprising less than 50 percent of the school population.[4] GPs are *not* avoiders of diversity; indeed, it is their preference for diversity that keeps them from entering the neighborhood school. If their child were to be the only white child in the neighborhood school, that demographic reality would not be considered sufficiently diverse. Thus, gentrification's initial impact on the demographic makeup of the neighborhood school is usually nonexistent. The neighborhood school is usually racially and socioeconomically segregated, and GPs don't want their child to be in that nondiverse school environment. Accordingly, GPs typically seek out other public school options, choosing one of the other possibilities for their child beyond their own zone school.

Foreign GPs and Their Role in the Integration Process
There is one distinct group of GPs who appear to think about diversity differently than their GP peers: white foreigners, usually of European descent.[5] These foreign GPs still value diversity, but *racial* diversity is not as important. White foreigners feel like minorities whether they are surrounded by light faces or dark faces, and their ability to "not care" about being the only white family in a school stood in sharp contrast to American-born GPs. Katrine, whose son was the first white child at her segregated neighborhood school (though *not* her zone school, which she described as not being a place she wanted to send her child due to the way the kids from that school acted on the playground, and her accordant

intuition that "that's not where I'm supposed to be"), surmised that being a foreigner, "being removed from all of that stuff that you grow up with in American society," allowed her to easily enroll her son without considering the racially segregated nature of the school. She clearly was discerning in other ways, as evidenced by her rejection of her zone school, but racial isolation didn't matter.

Fran, another foreign GP, similarly described her racial lens, "But for me, for example, I never, maybe because I'm European, I'm never really like, I never make the distinction between white and black, I don't really see it strongly." Astrid, although married to an American white man, echoed the sentiments of her European peers, "You're already an outsider, it doesn't really matter where you're an outsider, you're already used to that kind of discomfort. So, it's not as threatening. And we have not lived through that kind of segregation in that way. We're in some ways we're blind to some of the ingrained things that other people have to struggle with. We have other hang-ups that our culture brought." Even several nonforeign GPs recognized the role foreigners were playing in shifting the demographics of their school, admiring their ability to shed racial concerns. Amanda, a nonforeign GP, specifically remarked on the ease the "Europeans" show toward her racially segregated neighborhood school, describing them as "being like, 'What are you worried about? It's perfect!'" Lisbeth, another nonforeign GP, was similarly struck by the way "foreigners" are so much more relaxed about the school situation in her gentrifying neighborhood, observing that they "are less freaked out about it. It's a whole different world."

This "whole different world" seems to be much less constraining when choosing a school. Without "white counting" automatically entering the mind, as it appears to do for most nonforeign GPs, foreign GPs perceive many more options for their children. Eduardo, for example, enrolled his son in a school *he* considered diverse but was avoided by other nonforeign GPs in this study, who specifically labeled it as "not diverse"(i.e. no white children), because he thought of diversity primarily in terms of class or country of origin. He saw tremendous variety in the school's social class composition and ethnicity, and wasn't bothered by the fact that there weren't other "white" children. Astrid was somewhat enraged by the failure of nonforeign GPs in her neighborhood to see the diversity that *she* saw at her school, because she was tired of being asked about the school by potential gentry families who were interested in her experience in a school that "wasn't diverse." She would say to them, "It *is* diverse! There are people from Senegal, there are people from the United States, there are people who are rich, there are people who are poor, it's a diverse group of people, they just have the same skin color! They're just as diverse as any group of white people, no one would ever call a white group of people 'not diverse,' just because they're white! You know, and there are different religions, there are kids not allowed to eat meat, there are kids allowed to eat meat, there are kids who wear scarves on their heads, there are kids who don't. There's a huge diversity in that school, it just happens to be that they share the same skin color!" This greater mental freedom exhibited by foreign GPs often leads them to be part of the first group of GPs entering a racially segregated school.

School Preference Two: Progressive Education

"Progressive" education is also highly valued by GPs, second only to the GP preference for diverse schools. GPs repeatedly identified themselves and their peers as "on the more progressive end of the curriculum spectrum," which loosely means they favored a "child-centered, problem-oriented, interdisciplinary, and multi-cultural" (Brantlinger 2003, 62) teaching style. In a progressive classroom, "...the teacher is no longer the authoritarian figure from whom all knowledge flows. Rather, the teacher assumes the peripheral position of facilitator, encouraging, offering suggestions, questioning, and helping to plan and implement courses of study" (Semel and Sadovnik, 1999, 8). Progressive education has come in and out of favor with reformers over the past century, ever since John Dewey started writing about and applying the idea at his Lab School in Chicago in the early 1900s. Critics view progressive education as allowing students too much freedom at the expense of academic rigor; thus, its advocates often use language other than "progressive" to describe similar educational goals.

In 1990, the Network of Progressive Educators drafted a contemporary description of progressive education that mostly steered clear of the term. It is interesting to look at some of their goals and see how closely these goals map with the value of diversity, GPs' first school preference. For example, not only do they advocate for meeting a child's individual interests in the classroom, they also press for the "school's embrace" of the "home cultures of children and their families," stating that classroom practices should "reflect these values and bring multiple cultural perspectives to bear." They further assert that schools should be models "...of democracy and humane relationships, confronting issues of racism, classism and sexism." In essence, progressive educators want schools that instill in children the value of diversity, in part through a diverse pedagogy that reflects that diverse community (Semel and Sadovnik, 1999, 18).

The Coalition of Essential Schools, another modern organization dedicated to progressive education, similarly advocates for "...an in-depth, intra-disciplinary curriculum respectful of the diverse heritages that encompass our society" (Semel and Sadovnik, 1999, 19). Valuing progressive education seems almost synonymous with valuing diversity, so it should come as no surprise that the progressive schools, at least in New York City, are where diversity can be found. The self-proclaimed progressive elementary schools in New York City also all happen to be among the most racially and socioeconomically diverse in the city. Since diversity is such an important preference for GPs, it could just be that they naturally gravitate toward progressive schools because they know this is where they will find diversity.

All of the explicitly progressive schools in the city are *not* zone schools, but choice schools, which is partly why they are able to achieve diverse student populations. These schools are not bound by zone lines in selecting children. Parents have to enter lotteries or complete another type of screening process to access these schools, and they are the most competitive schools among GPs, further enhancing the school's perceived quality. As Leslie, a GP working in mass media, pointed out, "information is privilege, right? If I don't know what a progressive school is, I probably won't pursue this option for my child. People are self-selecting on many, many levels." By selecting progressive schools, GPs are able to self-select into both a more diverse school than the neighborhood school as they surround themselves with fellow GPs who share their progressive preference, and into what is likely a more educated group of nongentry parents. The poor children of color who attend these progressive schools have parents who have to make an effort to seek out this alternative, which likely means these parents are relatively more educated and more assertive about the quality of their child's education than those who stick with the zone school (Wells 1993). When parents have to make some effort, it has a noticeably positive impact on the student body, and GPs take advantage of these slim pockets of choice.

Segregated Neighborhood Schools Not Perceived as Progressive
Because progressive education is an explicit desire, GPs are unlikely to choose their segregated zone school simply because it is perceived as not being progressive, in addition to not being diverse. This perception seems to be based on stereotypes about urban schools, generated in part from the media attention given to "successful" urban charter schools. Charter schools, because they are free to govern themselves as they wish despite garnering public funding, have more freedom to experiment, and the media likes to highlight the intense structure found in these schools, and

the dedicated teachers and administrators devoted to longer school days and school years to get *these* children—poor, nonwhite children—on par with more affluent children. Headlines citing the "Miracle" (Matthews 2006), or the "Dream" (Headden 2006), introduce articles that marvel at the ability of an urban school to achieve such high test scores with such disadvantaged children. For a GP following these stories, the image of these schools is that they are not appropriate places for *their* children. GPs tend to be highly educated, and they generally follow the advice of child development experts: reading to their children every day, providing their children with appropriate stimulation and educational experiences. Enrolling their child in a "successful" urban school that appears geared toward remediating home deficits does not make sense to a parent whose child is not deficient. These schools may be engaged in excellent pedagogy that *is* progressive, and would be appealing to GPs, but this aspect of the school, if it exists, does not appear to make its way into the media.

Thus, these urban charter schools rarely make it on to GPs' lists of school options. And the segregated neighborhood zone school, if it has a decent academic reputation, usually gets automatically lumped into the "not progressive" camp, perhaps because of the similar demographics to the charter schools highlighted in the media. Louisa, a GP whose zone school had an excellent academic record, hesitated to send her child there because she was "concerned about the intense test prep," and she didn't want her son to be a part of a school that "focused so much on testing." This was a common way GPs described their zone school—"too traditional," "too much test prep." Test scores seem to be a double-edged sword in the urban school-choice process. If a segregated urban school has bad test scores, it is a bad school. If a segregated urban school has good test scores, it must be doing too much test prep. When asked why a charter school with a great reputation was not on a GP's list of options, Genevieve's response was typical, "I've just heard they do too much skill and drill." Martha, an acclaimed artist, posed it as a question, "Don't they do a bunch of skill and drill?" asking me, because I am a teacher and education policy researcher. "I just want something more interesting for my child," she continued. "I don't care that the school doesn't have white children, I just want a school where interesting things are happening." Kevin, though not working in a creative profession, substituted the term "creative" for "interesting" as he attempted to describe what he thought his segregated zone school was like in contrast to what he wanted: "So, for people who wanted kind of a very structured and somewhat more conservative, kind of middle-of-the-road education, it was good. It was not a failure in any way. It was a good, solid, reasonable school that was a perfectly good option. It just was not one that we thought had enough of the kind of creativity or emphasis or energy that was the kind of school we wanted to send our kid to." This type of perception of the neighborhood zone school's pedagogical practices, whether true or not, gives GPs an additional reason to cross them off of their list of public school possibilities—not diverse, not progressive.

School Preference Three: Not Gifted and Talented

The third school preference expressed by a large majority of GPs in this study was a negative preference. They generally do *not* want their child enrolled in a G&T program. Although many GPs end up enrolling their children in G&T programs, it is rarely because this option is a preference. Some GPs were open to the idea that some children really are gifted and need to be separated for accelerated schooling, but far more erupted against this sorting process of the very young. Margaret, a GP notable for her successful efforts to eliminate the G&T program from her school, called it "a crime" to test four-year olds and determine who is gifted and who is not. She believed it was "all smoke and mirrors," nothing more than "a tracking program," something "completely ridiculous" when children are four. She practically shouted during our interview, "But why are we tracking them at four years old and saying, you're smart, you're smart enough and you're not smart enough, I mean it's a crime! I think it's an absolute crime! It's a joke!" Faith, though much more mild mannered and passive about the state of public schools than Margaret, also used the term "ridiculous," questioning how it was remotely possible to determine, at four, whether a child is gifted.

Kate, a GP from a working-class background, had a sickeningly negative feeling toward G&T programs, explaining, "I can't describe the gut feeling I get when I think about gifted education, it's the same feeling I get when I talk about home schooling. You know, it's like, it's just wrong, it's just so wrong! And I can't put my finger on why, but kids who are not as advanced need somebody to look up to, and everybody has something to offer, so the kids who are advanced and better behaved need to be mixed in with everybody so that you can see, grow up dealing with everybody. You're not going to be surrounded in your life by just the best and the brightest, you need to deal with everybody." Erich, a GP who is gay and adopted his son, echoed Kate's sentiments, explaining, "I want my son to have a well-rounded life. I don't want him segregated from the crowd. I want him to be with kids who are smarter and dumber than him, who are less capable, whatever the word is I'm supposed to use. And I don't think it is good to have one class of three be the gifted class, because then kids who are in the one that is gifted feel one way, and the kids who aren't...it's just wrong, stupid!" Marcia simply stated that "the whole thing is crazy;" Ivy derided the G&T program as "a designer handbag"; and Cindy, more diplomatically, described G&T as "this kind of weird, false thing."

Many GPs used less contemptuous language, instead explaining that they were simply philosophically opposed to dividing the kids up. They "didn't believe in G&T programs." They thought it was "wrong to tutor a four-year-old in test taking." Carrie, a GP who works in education, tested her son and then deeply regretted it, telling me, "I wished I hadn't done it...I mean, it was fine. He totally thought it was fine, and he did fine and everything, but...I don't really believe in that program, and yet, I, like, compromised myself that day and was just like, 'Never mind, I don't care, my kid has to get into school!' And we went to the test and then later, the more I thought about it I was like, I just...I don't want him to be a part of that." She then told me she didn't think there was anything wrong with it, probably because she knew I was testing my daughter, and she knew that if she hadn't won the lottery of her choice, she might have ended up enrolling him in a G&T program, despite her passionate opposition. This is common.

G&T Programs: Why They Are an Option Even if They Are Despised
The majority of GPs in my study were opposed to G&T programs, but they almost all still had their child tested for these programs, and many enrolled their children in these programs. GPs consider it their obligation as parents to keep all remotely acceptable public school options open, even those that are far from their ideal, because, as Sharon explained, "You *have* to, you've got to do everything." They don't *prefer* G&T programs, but they often end up in them for one of two reasons. First, in a hierarchical system, they don't want to be on the bottom of the pyramid. Meredith's reasoning was common among those who eventually succumbed, first labeling G&T programs "ridiculous," then going on to explain that " if you're going to have a G&T program, I want them to be in it rather than not." Or, as Kate put it, "I'm very much against gifted classes. On the other hand, if everybody else is going to be in a gifted class... [voice trails off as if no further explanation is necessary]." Within a school with a G&T program, no GP wants his or her child to be left out of what is clearly being labeled the better class of children with the better teachers. If their neighborhood school has a G&T program, *of course* they want their child to be a part of it. Brooke, a single mother, acknowledged that "the whole G&T thing is kind of a scam, but if it is a scam that I can take advantage of, then I will." GPs

will not disadvantage their own children even if they have disgust with the G&T concept.

Second, G&T programs are often a GP's *only* way into another option outside of their zone school. After Marcia sheepishly admitted testing her daughter for G&T despite her opposition, she went on to say, "Oh, well you have no choice if you want another opportunity to go to a different school. If that's what they're using to get into schools, then of course she's gonna take it, you know, just to give us opportunities and choices." Winning a lottery into a preferred diverse, progressive school may not happen, and the G&T option is at least an option. For a GP, their only other public school choice might be their segregated neighborhood zone school. And since diversity is a strong preference for GPs, G&T programs must be kept on the table, although this option often *also* keeps them from having their diversity preference met, since G&T programs in New York City tend to be much whiter than the general school population. White and Asian students comprise a significant majority of G&T seats despite their roughly 30 percent combined demographic number in the overall system (Winerip 2010).

G&T Programs: A Different Kind of Segregation
GPs are very aware of the segregated stigma placed on G&T programs, the opposite kind of segregation than what they find at their neighborhood school. And they are tremendously uncomfortable with this stigma, another reason they do *not* prefer G&T programs. Elizabeth described the "segregation problem" with the G&T programs, recalling how on school tours, "you go into the G and T classrooms and they're one ethnicity, and you go into the general education programs and they're another." She went on to explain that this was "one of the reasons why I really didn't want my son to go there." Melanie was also "very uncomfortable" with the G&T option, hating that "it's so segregated," and she did everything possible to find another option, even though her child tested in. Sheila, too, searched hard for a non-G&T option, explaining how she and her friends call P.S.____ "the apartheid school," and they "don't want to be in a school like that where there is one track for one group and one track for another group."

The racial segregation condemnations usually extended to a class segregation critique as well. Trista, for example, called the G&T programs "notoriously middle-class white families, who aren't all that gifted and talented, they just passed a test." This observation, that "passing a test" is simply a skill middle-class white families are good at, was shared by Brooke, who found the segregated and "elite" nature of the programs inevitable, because "everything is elitist, because the people who are the most educated and have the most resources are the ones who have the ability to figure this stuff out." Marjorie came to the same conclusion, calling the G&T screening "tests for parents," because they were basically testing a child's vocabulary and whether the parent has been reading to their child.

The NYCDOE has attempted to temper this alleged built-in middle-class advantage for children testing for G&T programs, standardizing the testing process and making it free for all interested families, whereas there used to be a fee involved that was paid to private testing agencies, and individual schools had their own standards for admissions. These efforts, thus far, have basically been unsuccessful. The standardization has made the entrance process even more test dependent, and principals have much less leeway to accept children who don't test well, often leading to less diversity. The latest statistics (Winerip 2010) show black and Hispanic children in gifted kindergarten programs dropped to 27 percent under the test-only system, from 46 percent under the old system, despite the fact that roughly 65 percent of city kindergartners are black or Hispanic. Thus, despite systemic efforts to reduce the G&T racial inequities, the apartheid schools persist, and are frequently disparaged by GPs, both those who enroll their children and those who do not. Few GPs seem comfortable with this situation. As Elizabeth lamented, "I was like there is no way I'm sending my kid to that school, I definitely did not want a school with a G and T, but...that's where we are." Her choice, and the choice of many GPs like her, is simply the inevitable result of having to choose between two extremes.

The Choice between Polarized Extremes
Schelling (1978) explores this idea of having to choose between polarized extremes in his investigation of individual behaviors that lead to segregated situations. He explains that "people who have to choose between polarized extremes—a white neighborhood or a black, a French-speaking club or one where English alone is spoken, a school with few whites or one with few blacks—will often choose in the way that reinforces the polarization. Doing so is no evidence that they prefer segregation, only that, if segregation exists and they have to choose between exclusive association, people elect like rather than unlike environments" (146). This seems to be what is happening as GPs choose white, segregated G&T programs over nonwhite, segregated neighborhood schools. It is not necessarily a racist decision, as some might accuse them, it stems from the desire for their children to be comfortable in "like" environments if the diverse environment they seek is not available.

Exclusive situations can be especially difficult to consider entering as a minority when they involve intimate relationships. Being a minority in a neighborhood, where street relationships are definitively casual, does not typically push the boundaries of discomfort that diversity can cause too far. GPs can casually experience what Jane Jacobs (1961) describes as "the sidewalk ballet," where an assorted group of characters in a community can dance with each other, each with their own "distinctive parts which miraculously reinforce each other and compose an orderly whole" (50), and simply escape to the privacy of their home if the "ballet" becomes disorderly or unpleasant. Maggie's husband, a GP and longtime Neighborhood A resident before having children, was called "a slave-owning blah blah blah," and she had objects thrown at her by neighborhood children, but neither incident caused her gentry family to consider exiting the neighborhood. While "not pleasant," she didn't feel like the neighborhood was "dangerous," and she was able to brush off these negative sidewalk experiences as "kind of funny." Heather, who had a can of white paint thrown in her small backyard, coating all of her flowers and plants, also found humor by labeling the experience "a gentry hate crime, because the paint was white," and likewise didn't feel danger. Katrine described "addicts in the corner shooting up," and we laughed together during our interview that these "public characters" (68) would be good at deterring our own children from trying hard drugs. Not a single GP I interviewed had yet experienced any kind of truly frightening crime.

But the light heartedness GPs muster in reaction to bizarre, hostile, or disturbing sidewalk encounters, even if they are not criminal, is difficult to extend into a school where their children won't be able to simply head inside when things get uncomfortable. In a school setting, the relationships are intimate. Children form their friendships here, as do parents. And the "sidewalk ballet" in a gentrifying neighborhood doesn't necessarily make GPs want to continue the dance on more intimate terms. Peter, a GP who was part of an integration plan as a child attending school in the 1970s, was very frank about his hesitation to enrolling his son in the segregated neighborhood school, explaining: "I have my doubts about integration. It's supposed to be about building understanding, but I find that it just makes people want to be even further apart." Similarly, John, who is a social justice attorney and has developed many intimate relationships with his nongentry clients over the years, was wary of school integration based on these experiences. When his daughter didn't get into the middle school "that everybody wants to get into," he confided to Ellen, a fellow GP and vocal community activist, that "he didn't know if he could send her to the school she got into because she'd be one of three white girls." Ellen couldn't believe this reluctance was coming from someone whose life work was committed to equal justice for the less fortunate. But, when the setting is intimate as it is in a school, and when polarized extremes are the only two choices available, GPs often end up enrolling their children in the white, segregated G&T program instead of the black and/or Hispanic, segregated neighborhood school. It is not what they prefer, they prefer diversity, it is simply perceived as the less bad option when their preference is not available.

The Process of Choosing a School

Because all of the GP preferences generally lead them away from considering their segregated neighborhood school, tipping in will not happen easily or quickly. In addition to having school preferences that do not obviously mesh with the neighborhood school, the process that GPs go through in choosing a school also takes them further from this option. As Leslie reflected on her own choice process, she conceded that "maybe we're deluding ourselves, thinking we're making individual decisions, we're actually, you know, behaving like the herd." A herd mentality was, indeed, on display as GPs recounted the ways in which they had gone about choosing schools for their children. GPs all read the same books, went on the same tours, and went to the same website, *insideschools.org* to learn about what schools were considered good public options in New York City. *Insideschools.org* is a website developed by the nonprofit organization, Advocates for Children of New York, to rate schools, list demographic data and average test score performance, provide a narrative description of the school's strengths and weaknesses, and make available a forum for parents, teachers, and students to post their own comments about schools. GPs also all talked extensively with people in their own peer group about what was considered acceptable, peers who had the same school preferences. Their segregated neighborhood school, of course, was not on anyone's list.

Different Groups Have Different School Cohorts

The list of acceptable options seems to vary in New York City depending on who you are. One of the first GPs I interviewed introduced me to this idea of the perceived school cohort, and its impact on school choice. Margaret was describing the varied perception of her own neighborhood school, depending on demographics. She thought that nonGPs considered her neighborhood school as "the best of that cohort of schools," with "that cohort" described as containing the various segregated schools in their district. Her neighborhood school had a G&T program that was not chosen by white families but instead utilized by children of color, and one of her work colleagues who had graduated from this school "trekked her kid" to the school from a distant neighborhood because "she thought that it was the best school that her child should be in." Margaret went on to explain that for *her* friends, "obviously it's a different, we're in a different position." She then listed the schools she would put in her group's cohort of acceptable schools, and the G&T program at her neighborhood school wasn't even on that list, even though it was considered "the best choice" for someone in a different cohort.

After listening to Margaret's cohort theory, I started tracking each of my interviewee's hierarchy of choice, and identifying which schools were in their cohort of acceptable schools. Neighborhood by neighborhood, the same schools were in every GP's cohort. The order of preferences varied, but the GP cohort was fairly consistent. It was extremely rare for there to be a school on one GP's list that wasn't on every other GP's list in the same neighborhood. This finding makes sense in light of Jellison-Holme's (2002) qualitative study of the school choice decision-making process of "high-status" parents in the suburbs. The "high-status" parents she interviewed seemed to rationalize their school choice almost entirely on the opinions of other "high-status" parents. What other parents of the same social stratum thought about a school was more important than whatever school data was available. The "high-status" parents, through conversation, reinforced each other's beliefs about what was, and was not, an acceptable schooling option, primarily based on whether other "high-status" children attended a school, even though they believed they were rationalizing their decisions as based on school quality.

Saporito and Lareau (1999) similarly found that the school choice decision-making process varies depending on one's sociodemographic background, and is not simply a matter of picking the best school based on empirical data. Whites in their study used one process that was heavily influenced by the demographic makeup of a school, blacks used another process much less influenced by the student body. There was no standardized selection process like the one choice advocates assume. As Leslie put it, people tend to behave "like the herd," taking their movement cues from those who appear to be the same.

The Difficulty of Considering New Options

Within this herd mentality, it is not easy to insert a new school option onto the neighborhood GP list of acceptable schools and get GPs to consider this new option. It seems to be harder for GPs to imagine a *new* option, a school *not* already on the list of good schools, than for them to imagine a way to get their child into a school that *is* already on the list. Emily, whose plan was always to "find the school that worked for you and figure out a way to get in," is emblematic of GP confidence. GPs know the good public schools are competitive, but they are part of the "power culture," they believe there is always a way. Shawn's pep talk was typical of the attitude GPs had toward conquering the public schools. She assured me, a worried GP on my own public kindergarten quest, that if I waited until mid-October (i.e. almost two months into my daughter's kindergarten year), I could find a spot in any public school I wanted, because schools need to meet certain enrollment numbers to get their full funding.

This kind of inside knowledge of how things work, and mastery of the various angles one can take to obtain a spot in a coveted public school, was common among my interviewees. Every GP knew that they were supposed to harass schools, day after day, as a way of showing their love for that school, just in case a spot opened up. Carrie was reassured by her GP friends with older children that if she didn't get a lottery slot at her desired school, "You just have to wait it out and pursue the school over the summer, and you'll get in by the first day of school. If you let them know that you want that school, there's so much shifting that happens when people go to G and T, or people decide to move, or whatever, that spots come open and they don't keep calling people. They don't call anybody. They might say they keep a waitlist, but they don't. They say yes to the people who keep showing up, or the people who write them a letter, or the people who keep calling." Avery was given the same advice, that "the more times you call, the more times they check your name in a box on a spreadsheet," but she refused to play this game out of principle. She believed that if her name was on a waiting list, "calling shouldn't change where you are on that list." Avery's child didn't get a spot at her preferred school. Carrie's child did.

Every GP also knew how to borrow a childless friend's address to fake their way into a "good" zone school where they themselves couldn't afford the real estate. Jeremy, humorously, suggested maybe I should turn off the recorder when he admitted that people in his neighborhood often use the "standard solution," which is "getting an address," as if he was revealing a dangerous secret that the authorities, that is, the Department of Education, were unaware of. The authorities know, as was evidenced by Astrid's fear that they might lose the kindergarten spot they faked their way into with her husband's work address because "the school said that this year they were going to thoroughly check that you live in the apartment that you have registered. They made the parents sign a thing saying 'I am aware that my address will be checked, and I have to live there.'"

Not knowing anyone to borrow an address from, and not convinced that the harassment strategy would bear fruit, my family moved six blocks south and two avenues east the summer our daughter turned four so we could position ourselves in a better school *district* with more options. We couldn't afford the real estate within a good school *zone*, but we at least purchased the right to be eligible for extra seats and lotteries that always preference children who live within the district first. Kevin aptly referred to all of these types of maneuvers by GPs as "finagling their way in," and he summed up what appears to be the truth about GPs: "they are people with options."

Due to the difficulty of getting GPs to consider a new option when they feel confident that they will conquer all roadblocks to existing acceptable options, GPs collectively integrating a segregated school in a gentrifying neighborhood is unlikely. Brie's observation that GPs "start with the assumption that they shouldn't go to their neighborhood school" appears to be the default mind-set of nearly all GPs. In this sense, Ellen's (2000) "race-based neighborhood stereotyping" hypothesis appears to hold true for most GPs when it comes to the specific realm of schooling for their children. They automatically assume schools that are *not* diverse, that is, there are no white families, must not be good enough, or are deficient simply because they are not diverse. So, although their residential choices do not appear to be heavily influenced by stereotypes about nonwhite families, they have trouble not stereotyping the schools. They place the burden on the segregated neighborhood school to somehow prove that it is not guilty of being unacceptable. And this is extremely difficult for a school to prove.

Despite the obstacles, however, GPs have managed, collectively, to integrate their neighborhood schools, or at least start the process of integration. Throughout the course of my investigation, I interviewed not only families who were attending the schools identified quantitatively as in some stage of tipping in, but also families who were just starting the process of integrating other schools that, as of 2008, had shown no signs of increased white enrollment. The circumstances that appear to be necessary for the tipping in process to unfold will be examined in detail in the following five chapters.

3

Starting the Integration Process

This chapter explores the beginning of the tipping in process: attracting the first wave of gentry parents (GPs) to a segregated school. For the purposes of this study, a Stage 0, Segregated School is defined as having zero gentry children in attendance, as *perceived* by the GPs who were interviewed. While there may have actually been gentry children enrolled, if the GPs believed that their children were "the first" or among the first white children in the school, I classified those schools as Stage 0 prior to their entry, and classified the GPs as Innovators. Once a gentry child is enrolled in a Stage 0 school, the school becomes either Stage 1 Catalyzed or Stage 1 Stagnant (defined in detail at the end of this chapter). Every school in this study was, at some point, segregated in the last ten years using this definition, with the exception of some of the schools with Gifted and Talented (G&T) programs, where only the non-G&T classes were perceived as having zero white children. The segregated schools in this study ranged from being demographically almost 100 percent black to being roughly a 50/50 mix of black and Hispanic families. Poverty rates exceeded 70 percent in all of these racially segregated schools, making them both racially and socioeconomically segregated. To attract the first wave of GPs, the Innovators, to a Segregated School, there are characteristics unique to the neighborhood, the school, and the GPs themselves that facilitate the start of the integration process. Each of these three facets will be explored in detail below.

Neighborhood "Desirable" Public School Options Have Reached Capacity

For a segregated school to attract the first wave of GPs, there is one major neighborhood characteristic that must be in place: the neighborhood's desirable public options, as defined by the school-choice websites and books that make these determinations in tandem with the buzz coming from families on the ground, must have all reached capacity. The "neighborhood" is loosely defined as the larger school district that encompasses the GP's place of residence (there are 31districts within New York City), as preference for admittance to a public school is based on either zone of residence or district of residence. Neighborhood could also include a geographically adjacent school district if a school within that district is conveniently enough located to the gentrifying neighborhood, and the school hasn't yet reached a point of popularity that enrollment is limited to only residents of that district. The six or seven different types of public school options available to GPs were outlined in chapter 2, and the number of specific desirable schools that fit within these various options varied by neighborhood.

As also explored in chapter 2, GPs typically feel confident in their ability to "finagle their way in" to their desired public school. The school-choice plan of the typical GP is rooted in this confidence. However, there comes a point when the sought-after options reach capacity. Popular zone schools eventually entice enough families (with the assistance of eager real estate agents) to move within the zone boundaries rendering "extra seats" nonexistent for nonzone families. And, the sought-after progressive schools—both lottery and application—also reach a point where the school becomes so wildly popular that getting a spot is extremely unlikely. Many of the GPs I interviewed still vividly remembered their crushingly long-shot wait-list numbers for their most desired schools, all in the high 100s. Getting a spot in a G&T program is also a strong possibility since gentry children tend to perform well on these tests, but G&T is not a preference for most GPs, nor a guarantee, and GPs never want this to be their only plan.

It is at this point that the neighborhood circumstances force the consideration of a new school option. As long as GPs can still easily secure a spot at a school in their neighborhood that is already considered "good" by their peer group, it is very unlikely that a GP will consider a school *not yet* being talked about by other GPs. Only a very small handful of Innovator GPs framed their school-choice decision in a way that suggested they were committed to sending their child to the segregated neighborhood school, regardless of whether they got into a more established desirable option.

Characteristics of a Stage 0 School That Attract Innovator GPs

In addition to the desirable neighborhood schools reaching capacity, Innovator GPs will usually only consider a segregated school as a possible "new" option if the Stage 0 school itself has certain elements in place. *All of the Stage 0 schools referenced in this study were (1) considered decent schools, not failing by any standard other than being segregated; and (2) had some sort of enclave program within the school that served as an anchor for attracting gentry families.* Most also had some significant percentage of their students coming from outside the zone, a phenomenon one GP referred to as "drift." Each characteristic will be explored in detail below.

Not a Failing School

Most importantly, a Stage 0 school could not be considered "a failing school" and still have the potential to attract Wave 1 GPs.[1] This sentiment was expressed by Innovator GPs as a matter of fact. Karen was very firm in her statement: "If it was a failing school we wouldn't have gone. It isn't a failing school." Kevin was equally adamant, telling me, "It was always a perfectly fine school. It was not a failure in any way." Meredith was more specific: "The academics were very strong there. I think they got a B.[2]"

For a Stage 0 school to be considered as an option by Wave 1 GPs, the narrative on *insideschools.org* had to be positive. The school had to be described as having a strong leader who was providing a solid education. Leaders who are considered excellent when working with a fairly homogenous population may end up not being very strong when confronted with diversity, as will be explored in detail in chapter 5. But when their schools were at Stage 0 of integration, they were perceived by *insideschools.org* investigators to be good. The "word of mouth" within the GP community about a potential Stage 0 school would likely be nonexistent, not bad. There wouldn't yet be any GPs inside the school to say anything authoritatively one way or the other, though some might mention hearing it was a good school based on what they had read on *insideschools.org*. "Great" would never be used as a descriptor. GPs were not trying to fool themselves with inflated expectations. Jeremy, for example, was clearly trying to be realistic about the process of integrating his neighborhood school, explaining, "I am not trying to lead a revolution. I don't expect kindergarten to be great. Just fine."

Enclave Programs

In addition to being considered a decent school, Stage 0 schools that were able to attract Wave 1 GPs had some sort of enclave program within the school that allowed the few entering GPs to at least be sorted into the same classroom. Without an enclave program to harness a group together, Innovator GPs have a harder time networking with other GPs to solve the "collective action problem," an important process most Innovator GPs engaged in, and will be explored in detail in chapter 4. Without an enclave program, there is no guarantee of gentry children ending up together in the same classroom, even if they enroll in the same school. Most elementary schools have multiple sections of "general education classrooms" at each grade level, but usually have only one section of the special program. For GPs exploring their kindergarten options, the two enclave programs typically available to gentry children are G&T programs and Dual Language (DL) programs. An additional enclave possibility is the pre-K program, as there is also, typically, only one section of this special point of entry into a school. Each of these three types of enclave programs will be explored in detail below.

Nonwhite G&T Programs as GP Enclaves
As explored in detail in chapter 2, G&T programs are typically not appealing to GPs, in part because they are *not* considered diverse, and because they often exist within what are derogatorily referred to as apartheid schools. However, not all G&T programs in the city are white sanctuaries, and there are some schools where the G&T programs are utilized exclusively by nonwhite families. If the local school in a gentrifying neighborhood has a G&T program that is not currently being used by gentry families, it offers a potential tool for helping GPs solve the "collective action problem." Even if these programs are typically disdained by GPs, they still recognize the benefit of utilizing a G&T program for both keeping all gentry children together in the same class (assuming they all test in), and for effectively sorting the worst potential behavior and school-readiness problems out of their child's class, problems typically associated with poverty. The G&T screening mechanism usually allows gentry children through the gate, since the test primarily measures school readiness, something GPs are extremely good at instilling in their children, and usually keeps out the children who are most burdened by their poverty.

Thus, if a segregated neighborhood school has a G&T enclave where the gentry presence can be concentrated, GPs will usually try to concentrate their children there. Margaret, passionate in her stance against G&T, still utilized the program, calling it "a safe haven," because she knew her daughter would be with other kids "like her." This sheepish, but forthright, sentiment was shared by many GPs, such as Paula, who described the G&T program as a place where "the parents were more involved, they were more like me in some sense." The G&T choice by many GPs, despite it not being a preference, might be considered an affirmation of Wilson's (1975) theory of "safe diversity"—valuing difference only if it is harmless. GPs, in choosing G&T programs as an enclave entry point in a Stage 0 school, are specifically expressing a preference for the "safest" classroom. They may be one of the only white families in the G&T program, but at least they can find comfort in being part of a selective group. As Marjorie explained, "Teachers do an awful lot of teaching to the bottom third of the class, and that's less of an issue in G and T. The bottom third is pretty much the bottom third just because they were born later and are catching up. But it's not somebody who has major problems or something."

When expressing their preference for "safe diversity," gentry elitism was on display in its rawest form. The GPs weren't trying to hide their feelings of seeing their children and their families as different from their poorer neighbors in many ways that they didn't think needed to be explained. And in not hiding this sentiment, they were honestly trying to make clear why they resorted to G&T programs even though they thought they were wrong. As members of a social class with choices for their child, they didn't think there was an obvious moral choice. When choosing between polar extremes, *non*white G&T programs were, somehow, somewhere in the middle. These GPs *were* choosing to racially integrate, they weren't trying to isolate their children from nonwhite children and keep them in a white bubble. But they were choosing a situation that they thought would be less difficult for their child than entering a *non*-gifted classroom as the only white, middle-class child. They didn't seek out the most exclusive situation they could find; they didn't succumb to just utilizing the zone school. They found what they perceived to be a middle path.

DL Programs as GP Enclaves
DL programs are another popular enclave program capable of attracting GPs to a Stage 0 Segregated school. Anna used the DL enclave hook to try to organize GPs into her segregated school, explaining, "I was really trying to generate any kind of interest from like minded people through highlighting the French program. And I specifically wanted these people in my classroom." As Anna was clearly aware, DL programs offer the same benefits that G&T programs offer—allowing the GPs to concentrate their middle-class energy into one class. The ideal DL class composition is half-native language speakers and half nonnative. Gentry children can apply for spots in the nonnative half of the class, and also often apply for spots as native speakers. Many GPs are white foreigners, and they speak two or more languages at home. In New York City, it is also common for children to be raised by Spanish-speaking nannies or French-speaking

au pairs, creating bilingual children who are ideal candidates for these programs.

DL programs are also much more appealing to GPs who do not like G&T programs. They can self-segregate under the guise of being "cosmopolitan" and "open to ethnic diversity" as opposed to being "elitist." As Trista aptly surmised, "I think Dual Language is the new Gifted and Talented. Without the same kind of, you know, baggage." GPs choosing a DL program don't have to feel guilty about it the way they claim to feel guilty about G&T programs. These programs are not perceived as being "exclusive," but as "inclusive" of families from diverse language backgrounds who want to raise their children in a multicultural environment. Any stigma associated with DL is positive. Parents who choose DL programs feel proud that they are opening the world up for their children, as opposed to parents who choose G&T programs and fear that they are shielding their children from reality.

As outlined in chapter 2, reasons given by GPs for enrolling their children in G&T programs often included some aspect of the negative. Reasons given by GPs for enrolling their children in DL programs, however, were all effusively positive. Marjorie chose a DL program for her daughter because "languages in general are sort of an exercise for your mind. There are not many things it can replicate." Sharon agreed, and rooted her educational choice in language immersion because she wanted her daughter to "be as exposed, as close to an immersion style as possible to as many different languages as possible." She continued her effusive praise for DL: "Based on my own understanding of the value of different languages for kids, young kids, really young kids, what that does for them developmentally, not just for their future in terms of getting a job, but their future ability to think in complex ways. Because the world that my daughter will meet as an adult is extraordinarily complex, with so many different cultures, and issues and thoughts, and I want her mindful of that in as many ways as possible."

Monica put her DL support much more plainly, telling me that "China is going to be huge in their generation, you know, if you speak Chinese you'll probably get a great job," and thus a DL program in Chinese was "an amazing opportunity." Amanda, very aware that her Stage 0 school had many challenges, believed that "in the end, the advantages of the Dual Language program so far out-weighed those things." This sentiment is very important in understanding the allure of the DL enclave for prospective Innovator GPs in a Stage 0 school. GPs appear to be much more willing to put up with the discomfort of integrating a school if they feel like they are getting something out of the school that they simply can't get elsewhere.

Pre-K Programs as GP Enclaves

A third enclave program utilized by GPs is the pre-K program. In addition to serving as a concentrator of GP energies at the classroom level (many schools only have the funding or the room for one section of pre-K), GPs believe that pre-K isn't as consequential as kindergarten in terms of establishing their child's schooling path. If pre-K is a bad experience, they can try for something else the next year. Ivy, an Innovator GP who was actively trying to recruit more gentry families to her daughter's school, used pre-K as part of her hook, telling potential GPs, "It's an amazing school, send your child there. Look, it's pre-K, if it doesn't work out, you know for kindergarten send them somewhere else, but give the school a shot." Emily described pre-K as a "testing ground that gives you a sense of what the school is going to be," and provided insight into why GPs might view pre-K as an easier entry point than kindergarten: "So, we did love it for pre-K, but pre-K is such an intimate little thing, the way it is set up everywhere: two teachers for the classroom, 18 kids. I mean, so you're in this sweet little mandated play-based environment."

"Free-K", as one GP called it, was also a way to try out the school before committing to a kindergarten *and* save money that would have gone to private preschool. All GPs view early childhood development as important, so they all make sure their child has some sort of preschool experience whether it is public, private, or facilitated themselves through regular playgroups. Monica explained her decision to try her neighborhood public pre-K as pure economics: "Why spend a thousand dollars a month when you can spend zero?" Further, pre-Ks are more flexible in accepting non-zone families since not all elementary schools in the city have pre-Ks. This allows pre-K's to pull their student body from a more diverse lottery of district-wide applicants, often making a school's pre-K more racially and socioeconomically diverse than the rest of the school that is restricted by zone lines.

Enclave Programs No Silver Bullet

It is important to note that creating an enclave program in a Stage 0 school is not enough to attract GPs to that school. There are several segregated schools in gentrifying neighborhoods with pre-K programs, G&T programs, and DL programs that have failed to attract any gentry families. These enclaves seem to fail as a seed agent in schools that do not have the number one characteristic required to attract GPs: the school is a good school, and not considered to be a failing school by any measure other than being segregated. If the school housing the enclave program is not considered to be particularly strong, the enclave program won't make a difference. Karen, for example, did not enroll her son in a predominantly nonwhite G&T program because, as she explained, "It was a school that I knew was a failing school, except for G and T." Sam shunned the French DL program at a Stage 0 school, despite his passion for finding a French program for his son, because of the school's weak leadership. The principal "was failing," and, as Sam explained, "the tremendous challenges of running a dual language program require a strong principal who is on board."

Drift

Another interesting school characteristic found in most Stage 0 schools in this study was the phenomenon of "drift." When a neighborhood school is not being utilized by many of the children in the neighborhood, which often happens in gentrifying or gentrified neighborhoods as GPs seek out what they perceive to be better options, the seats in that school get filled by children from other neighborhoods, a phenomenon Lisbeth referred to as "drift." Parents of different social classes living within different spheres of influence all have a perception of what cohort of schools are acceptable for their children. While a typical GP doesn't include his segregated neighborhood school on his list, parents from other neighborhoods might consider that segregated school to be a much better option than their own neighborhood school.

So parents drift from their own neighborhoods to nearby neighborhoods seeking out the best option within their hierarchy of choice. Shawn described her Stage 0 school as being a place where "...something like half the kids were from other neighborhoods, because no one wanted to go there, from the neighborhood. And that was the thing, for a lot of people this school was a salvation." For a school to be "salvation" to one parent and "unacceptable" to another parent highlights the wide variety of preferences that come into play as parents choose schools. Parents are not making a choice based on some objective measure of "good" and "bad" that is viewed the same way by all who reference the data. Choice is a social process, not just for GPs but for *all* parents who consider themselves to have some kind of choice, and drift is one way this social process appears to play itself out.

Erich fittingly described drift as a form of "voting with your feet," and was unsettled by the number of children in the Stage 0 school he was trying to integrate who were coming from outside the zone, and what this meant in terms of parent involvement since no one was showing up for PTA meetings, as he explains: "So there was discussion among the cluster of more progressive parents, what really is going on here? And the parents were saying that a lot of the kids in the school don't even come from this neighborhood. So I said, ok, let's figure this out. I'm a consultant, I study numbers, so I'm very passionate about studying things objectively rather than subjectively. So I said maybe I'm the crazy one, maybe everyone here is really from the neighborhood. And I'm the loco person. So I filed a Freedom of Information Act request, and find out the percentage of kids at the school who come from the zone is 37 percent, or somewhere around there. So almost 2/3rds of the kids at P.S.____when my daughter was there came from outside of zone, which means they were coming from an even shittier school than P.S.____!!!! I thought that was really interesting. And to me, it became something like, if you're going to grade the schools, I know this city has a big problem grading schools, I know this system is so massive, but this should be a part of the equation, because the community is voting with their feet whether to go or not."

Drift also adds fuel to the debate that neighborhood gentrification unleashes about displacement. If GPs successfully start to integrate their Stage 0 neighborhood school, there are fewer seats available for non-GPs coming from other neighborhoods. Margaret was very sensitive to the potential anger displacement in a school could cause, and she explains why she and her GP friends chose P.S.____ as a place to send their children, "Partially, we chose P.S.____ because it was a school that had a lot of capacity, it really wasn't about pushing kids out, it was about there was plenty of room, it was listed on the DOE website at being at like 60% capacity, there was clearly a lot of room to grow, and that was the idea, to grow this school." Despite this understanding of the potential political problems, there was still supposedly anger from families in *other* neighborhoods who had planned to "drift" to P.S.____, anger that Margaret and other GPs were "taking their spots." Lisbeth, one of the targets of anger, grappled with whether she should feel guilty about this: "Are you really displacing them? It's not their neighborhood. But you are displacing somebody racially. So what makes a community? Is it a group of people who live next to one another? Is it a group of people who have the same basic philosophy? Is it a group of people who all have the same skin color? It makes you question so much about...like I said, my putting in at this school has just made me see this world and the city in such a different, in such a less idealistic way, a much more complex and nuanced way."

With regards to the integration process in a school, drift appears to have a positive impact. Drift's sorting mechanism stocks underenrolled Stage 0 schools with children whose parents may be poor, but who also have the social capital required to seek out a better school option for their child than the one that is given. These families clearly care enough about the education of their child to network with other families and find out what other options exist beyond the zone school. Accordingly, children who drift are likely to be better prepared for school and not as hampered by their poverty (Wells 1993), creating an educational environment that is much easier for teachers to manage, and thus more inviting to GPs who might be interested in enrolling their children in the school. If a GP's worst fears about a high-poverty school are not manifest due to the more self-selecting group of families who have drifted into the school, the integration process has a much better chance of successfully maturing.

Brie, an Innovator GP in her high-drift neighborhood school, specifically mentioned the optimism she felt knowing the poor, nonwhite kids at the school were being bused in: "But it's sort of interesting to look at that school... Somebody could look in that school and say, 'Oh, none of the people are white, none of the people are middle-class,' but in point of fact, the people that are getting, you know, quote-unquote bused in, are people who are spending a lot of time thinking about their children's education. Right, because actually, it's easier to stay where you are in your zone school that's farther north, than to bother to figure out that there's a district lottery that you can enter, and that there's this school that you could go to, and your kids could get bused to, which, okay, is difficult, but it's something. And so sort of, actually, I saw those parents as people who were, you know, they already had one check in their favor in terms of caring about their children's education."

Again, this raw display of elitism might seem condescending, but for a group of GPs who are members of the middle or upper middle class and who are doing something that none of their peers are doing—sending their kids to a segregated school—their attempt to explain to me why they were able to do it was painfully honest. I'm not sure how they could have explained the complexity of their situation without sounding elitist, other than to not say anything at all. They are elites living in nonelite neighborhoods, they are very aware of their privilege and their power, and they are very consciously trying to do what they think is right for both their own children and society, two ideas that are sometimes in tension with each other.

Characteristics of the Innovator GPs Entering a Stage 0 School

While neighborhood and school characteristics are important components of attracting Innovator GPs to segregated schools, the characteristics of the Wave 1 GPs themselves are probably the most important in sparking an integration process. As defined earlier, Innovator GPs are willing to be the first of their peer group to try something that peers consider risky—enrolling their child in a segregated school. These people are rare, and I have attempted to figure out what shared qualities they possess that distinguish them from their non-Innovator GP peers. From a wide range of backgrounds, all of the Innovator GPs in this study exhibited at least one of two traits: unique seeking and/or and a strong commitment to social justice. Each characteristic will be described in detail below.

Unique Seeking

"Unique seekers" are people who take pride in being different, people who *want* to be different, and many of the Innovator GPs in this study told stories in the course of our interview that suggested they fit within this niche. The unique seekers expressed their desire to be different in a variety of ways and contexts; but they all, at some point, honed in on this part of themselves.

Foreign GPs
All of the foreign GPs in this study easily fit the mold of unique seekers. Seeking a unique experience is part of their expat identity, part of the reason they left their country and came here to try on a new life. aAdditionally, as described in detail in chapter 2, foreign-born GPs simply see the world differently than American-born GPs, and thus are very different in their school-choice decision-making process, whether they are consciously wanting to be different or not. The foreign GPs in this study all comfortably wore their difference after years of practicing assimilation, and were the most fearless in starting the integration process in their local school, in part because they weren't thinking about the larger societal context of their decision. They were able to enroll their white children in a nonwhite school without fretting about what this said about them as people—be it good or bad. Astrid, a foreign GP, observed that at her school, "all of the parents who are integrating right now...well, 95% of the kids that came in that are white in the last two years are foreigners, or have at least one foreigner in the family."

Happy to Be Different
The nonforeign unique seekers in this study appeared to be in search of a unique status similar to the kind one looks for when going abroad, they just realized they could do it within New York City and never have to leave. Margaret, who grew up in Florida, put her desire to be unique front and center, as part of her identity. When asked why she moved to her

gentrifying neighborhood, she responded: "I mean the diversity, we liked, we were happy to be the minority of this kind of diverse neighborhood. I didn't like Neighborhood P,[3] I didn't want to be like, I didn't want to look like every other couple pushing a stroller, every other white couple pushing a stroller down the street. So for us we were just much more attracted to this neighborhood from the start." Margaret also thought growing up in a politically active household was partly why she felt driven to buck GP peer norms and try to integrate her neighborhood school, and she had the strong support of her mother (possibly also a unique seeker), who would regularly encourage Margaret with comments like, "That is so great, that's what I always wanted to do, and your father would never!!" This familial support was not mirrored by Margaret's husband's family, however, whom she described as looking at her like, "You are a freak!!!" whenever she talked about her daughter being the first white child in the neighborhood school and her integration efforts. As Margaret retells this story, it is obvious that she doesn't mind being called "a freak" by her in-laws. It is proof she has succeeded in not being like every other white woman in her peer group.

Avery, who was raised as a fundamentalist Christian, something rare in her native Chicago, also seemed to revel in being different, and she reflected on how her youthful involvement in a borderline religious cult might have shaped her view of herself: "And so I think that influenced me a lot in terms of... it's good to be different, it's good to be stubborn, I don't want to be one of those walk on the other side of the street parents. I deliberately go down the seediest blocks." Both women reference "the street" as the place they want to be viewed as distinctive, suggesting that their uniqueness must be visible to others for them to find fulfillment.

A Life of Interesting Projects
Jeremy, a Californian who was brought up by "leftist artists," revealed his unique-seeking qualities in talking about the various projects he has undertaken over the years, and how he likes to keep life interesting. Attempting to integrate his neighborhood school is simply one of these projects. As he explains: "I am engaged, now that I've started, I am engaged by this process [integration] as a project, and I'm a person who likes projects. I installed this floor on my own—local wood, from local mills—it was a project, I didn't know what I was doing, I still don't know how to do it, doesn't look very professional, but it was a project. And so for me, this is like a project that I'm engaged in, because it is fascinating, it's everything. It's politics, it's parents, it's humans, it's social. I find it very interesting to see how people react, to see what peoples' expectations are...and as someone with an arts background, that's how you

work. You start, you don't know what the end result will be. That's how I'm starting."

Ivy, a native New Yorker who did years of volunteer work in her Stage 0 neighborhood school before her son was a student there, appeared to share Jeremy's life approach of searching for interesting projects. She clearly took pride in being the unique person who dedicated herself to helping a school when she wasn't even a parent there. And, like Margaret and Avery, she seemed to want her uniqueness to be visible to others. She described her sidewalk interactions with nongentry community members who would say, "Who's this really nice lady who just did this? Wow, you're not even in the school and you're doing this!" She clearly felt validated by these encounters, and enrolling her son as one of the first white children in the school was also something she did with pride.

Unusual Childhoods
There were a couple of Innovator GPs who had the unusual experience of being white minorities in school when they were children. This experience seemed to make them unique as opposed to unique seeking. Like the foreign GPs in this study, they weren't consciously trying to be different in their school choice, they were just different. Timothy, for example, talked about his integration efforts at his segregated neighborhood school with a surprising nonchalance, telling me, "I went to an almost all black high-school in the South, so I wasn't super worried about it." Kate shared Timothy's casualness about enrolling her white children in an almost 100 percent black school, explaining how her own history of being part of legally orchestrated integration in upstate New York in the 1970s made her comfortable with her kids being minorities too. She was still able to remember the details of her city's busing for integration plan and the positive (for the most part) experience she had, as she describes: "The law was that you couldn't have a school that was more than 65 percent of any race. The entire time it was 65 percent black and 35 percent white. I started Kindergarten the year that the public schools were desegregated. So they got a shit load of federal money to start a bunch of magnet schools in bad neighborhoods. So I was actually bused 45 minutes each way for 13 years. We had a completely free magnet public Montessori school. The Montessori school around here is like $27,000 a year."

Shedding Privilege
Several unique seekers had completely opposite upbringings from Timothy and Kate, being raised instead in sheltered white enclaves, where they were the advantaged majority. For these GPs, unique seeking was manifest as an attempt to shed privilege. Maggie explained it as "not

wanting to be around all those parents, *even though I can kind of be like them, I don't want to be*. And I know them well, I went to prep school, I went to Harvard, and you know, I've been around very very type A people, but, and successful, and not to say that there is something wrong with it. I just don't want to be that." Sharon, a very well-heeled professional operating in the upper echelons of Wall Street who also attended elite private schools, expressed her rebellion against peer norms in terms of what she saw as the negative peer pressure that comes from being in the "in" group in a wealthy society: "I have many years in my life gone with the crowd and have suffered as a result, not so much that I went with the crowd, but more so that I didn't establish my *own* criteria, and stick to that." These antielite sentiments were echoed by Paula, a successful investment banker, as she explained why her family left a coveted citywide G&T school and instead tried to integrate the neighborhood school: "I felt extremely, I mean although I've been there for years and years, it's a very clicky kind of a thing. And although I'm in the click, I don't want to be in the click, I'd rather be independent."

Pioneer Neighborhood Gentrifiers
Paula also honed in on the possibility that one's entry into their neighborhood during the early stages of gentrification was a direct personality precursor to attempting to integrate their neighborhood school, a sign of their unique seeking. She moved to her neighborhood when it "was still 99% black," and did so because, "it was affordable. OK, I think that was the main reason. And, um, I don't know. You had a good vibe here. And I always go with my intuition. I mean, I didn't want to be in Bensonhurst, because my husband is Italian, and I could imagine my daughter with like big hair, long fingernails, and then I didn't want to be in Sunset Park with all the Chinese either. You know, so there was a level of comfort and coolness that I liked here." Lisbeth, another early white resident of her gentrifying neighborhood, self-analyzed her choices as stemming from "...a really poor sense of boundaries and limits." She continued, "I'm serious, it would be fascinating to do a complete psychological case study. It's like you move to a new neighborhood, I think on some level because you don't feel secure, you prefer to be the outsider. You're somehow more comfortable with that role. Maybe you don't want to compete. I've shrunk myself about it one hundred times over why we chose the things we chose. In some ways you want the adventure of it, you want to try something new, you want to be the first, you need to, you know, but it's really condescending, you're not the first person in the neighborhood who ever existed, who ever came along! But there is this kind of, I definitely think there is a real psychological aspect that goes along with gentrifiers, for lack of a better word."

Strong Commitment to Social Justice

In addition to unique seeking, or in lieu of unique seeking, Innovator GPs possessed a strong commitment to social justice. They believed that it was their civic responsibility to instigate change, *and* they believed they could make a difference through their own actions. Once the neighborhood circumstances forced the consideration of a new option, these Innovator GPs looked at the new option and made it a mission.

Shawn exemplifies the efficacious attitude of the typical Innovator GP. After describing herself as "a socially conscious do-gooder," who wanted to "make the subpar school better for everyone," she listed all of the ways she planned to effect change: "I'm going to be a class parent. I'm going to organize potlucks. I'm going to join the School Leadership Team. I'm going to join the PTA. I'm going to become president of the PTA. I'm going to join the president's council. I'm going to become president of the president's council of my district. I'm going to exhaust every possible option. I'm going to meet with the superintendant. I'm going to devote 20 hours of my week, every week, as an unpaid employee of the God damn school system, because my school sucks and no one will change it."

Ivy was similarly committed to the idea of utilizing one's own efficacy to improve a school, passionately preaching this idea: "Like I said, if parents stopped being so freakin' neurotic and started devoting a little time and energy in a school that shows promise, it doesn't have to take that much time. But if every parent donated one hour a month in a neighborhood, the effect that would have on a school, that would be huge! That's a huge moral boost for the school. That's a huge *actual* boost for the school!" Ivy continued with an argument for what GP involvement in schools could do for eradicating the racial tensions that accompany neighborhood gentrification: "It could potentially...it's great to raise your visibility in a neighborhood if you're talking about trying to assuage some of the tension between the people who come in and gentrify. What better way than to get involved in a school and for people in the neighborhood to see, 'Hey you're white, but you work in my school and I think that's great!'"

Margaret shared this devotion to changing society through her own actions, describing her "greatest heartache" as being "for these 500 kids who were getting completely shafted of a good public school education." She then added another child's face to her story of school choice, not her own child's, to illustrate why we should all consider it a moral imperative to do what she did and make the hard decision to integrate our schools. "My daughter's best friend lives in this building where like, I mean I don't know, that building is so scary! The lock is broken on the front door, the elevator smells like urine. And her best friend is so super smart, and they never would have left P.S.____, and it breaks my heart to think how this child, my daughter's best friend, would have been shorted an education if no one ever took the initiative to improve this school."

Brie, while also clearly committed to "the other 500 kids," took a less emotional approach to explaining her choice to enroll her child in a segregated school, rationalizing it as the only sane thing a person could do if they didn't want to be a "nasty" person. She very calmly articulated: "There was enough that was really great about the school that I didn't see the lack of socioeconomic and racial diversity as a problem. It just feels too nasty to say, 'Well, my child can't go there, because there are no light-skinned people there.' I mean, there's just a side of it that's nasty, and you want your kids to learn a lot of things, including reading and writing and math, and you also want them to learn about goodness and kindness and justice, and their own agency." While committed to social justice, she didn't want her own actions to be viewed as something heroic. Part of her commitment to what is "right" was reflected in her desire to normalize a decision to not take skin color into account. For Brie, true social justice is when these things don't matter.

Moving to Stage 1 Integration: A Catalyzed School or a Stagnant School?

For a Stage 0 school to move toward integration, the entry of the first wave of GPs is only the first step. The second wave of GPs, the Early Adopters, must then follow. Early Adopters are very similar to Innovator GPs in terms of who they are, and the neighborhood and school circumstances that inspire them to be part of their local school's nascent integration effort. Whether one is an Innovator or Early Adopter appears to be determined by the random timing of neighborhood births. A GP who sends her child to a school in Stage 1 of integration would also likely have sent her child to a school at Stage 0 of integration, if the school had been Stage 0 when her child reached pre-K or kindergarten age. A Stage 1 integrated school is not, fundamentally, much different from a Stage 0 school. Having only one white family, or even a few white families in the school, does not yet alter the school's basic culture. Some Wave 2 GPs are part of the gentry networking groups that I will describe in the next chapter. They just had younger children who, because of timing, enrolled in the second wave instead of the first. Indeed, some seemed to be jealous that they were not able to be "the first," because they, too, are unique seekers. Candice, a Wave 2 GP who joined her Innovator GP friend at a Stage 1 Catalyzed

School, spoke with admiration: "So, I mean, she was the first one to send her kids there, that's pretty cool." Another Wave 2 GP referenced the high status she perceived bestowed upon the school's first white mother: "And she was kind of a big deal with the principal, she had a really good relationship with the principal, because her son was like the first 'non,' he was like the first Caucasian kid to ever enter that school."

This early group of GPs—Innovators and Early Adopters—share a similar world view. The reasons why they stay in a school, or exit a school, are basically the same, and will be explored in detail in chapter 5. It also takes the work of both Waves 1 and 2 to attract the third Wave of GPs, a crucial step in the integration process, which will be explored in chapter 6. What is important to recognize at this stage in the process is the difference between a Stage 1 Catalyzed School and a Stage 1 Stagnant School. *Most* Stage 1 schools are catalyzed, because the type of GPs who enter as Innovators have personality traits that make them want to network with other GPs and bring in more GPs to the school. If they are entering the school with a social justice mission, the mission will not be achieved if they remain the only GP in the school. For a school to integrate, there must be additional GPs who come after them. Thus, while most Innovator GPs don't mind being the first, they do not want to remain alone. They network prior to their own entry and bring others into this network who will enroll their children in subsequent years. They catalyze the school through their activism in the PTA and their outreach to other GPs in the neighborhood. Meredith, a Wave 2 GP, describes how her friends with older children who had enrolled at her neighborhood school as part of the first Wave were "like booster booster booster. Bring your son to P.S.____, blah blah blah. They were really pushing it." She enrolled. Other Wave 1 GPs thought of themselves as "cheerleaders," or "representatives for the school."

However, in the course of this research, I came across a handful of Stage 1 schools that seemed stagnant. Despite a small GP presence, there was no movement toward further integration. The Wave 1 GPs in the school were not boosting the school. They were not networking to try and bring in more GPs to the school. They were GPs who were simply comfortable being the only white family, and they didn't feel the need to do anything to bring in more white families. Most of the foreign GPs I interviewed fell into this category of not caring about bringing in other white families, also evident in the fact that they didn't feel the need to network with other GPs to solve the collective action problem prior to entering the school. One foreign GP's son was the only white child in her neighborhood school for four years before the next white family enrolled. She was not a catalyzer, she simply didn't care to be. Another foreign GP

I interviewed not only didn't boost her school, but she also seemed put off by the idea that a new crop of GPs was networking to enter her school, because she found these people annoying. As someone who enrolled her child in this school from outside the zone, she thanked God "for racism," viewing this as the reason she found such a good school with open seats outside of her own terrible zone school.

It is not clear what impact Wave 1 GPs who simply create a Stage 1 Stagnant environment can have on the long-term prospects of that school integrating. It is possible that these few white faces can provide reassurance for other GPs considering entering the school. But if the GPs on the inside are not boosting the school and trying to bring in other GPs, it is likely that prospective GPs won't even notice that they are there. My research suggests that Innovator GPs must intentionally try to bring in other GPs for the school to eventually integrate, and will be explored further in chapter 6.

4

Solving the Collective Action Problem

While the characteristics of the neighborhood, school, and individual gentry parents (GPs) outlined in chapter 3 appear pivotal to whether a segregated school can attract GPs to start the integration process, there is an additional question that most of the Innovator and Early Adopter GPs in this study grappled with prior to entering their Stage 0 school: can we solve the collective action problem? The collective action problem is a situation in which everyone in a given group has a choice between two alternatives—A and B, and if everyone in the group chooses the alternative that is individualistically rational, choice A, the outcome will be worse for everyone involved than it would be if they were all to chose alternative B (Hardin 1982).

With regards to the specific challenge of school integration in a gentrifying neighborhood, the individualistically rational choice of the GP, choice A, is to keep their child out of the high-poverty, racially segregated public school, which appears to be the choice of most GPs. It is not rational for a person with means to put one's child in a situation where it seems highly possible that the situation will lead to a lower quality of school experience for that child than the one experienced by the parents, based on the available data about the average performance of segregated schools. However, if every GP in the neighborhood makes choice A, they are all arguably worse off because none of them use the neighborhood public school, and they all have to pay for private school, move to a different neighborhood, or transport their children to a less convenient neighborhood for public school if they can get a variance. Most importantly, from a proschool integration perspective, none of the nongentry children in the neighborhood school benefit from the neighborhood's socioeconomic and racial integration, further fostering a negative image of gentrification.

Arguably, if all of the neighborhood GPs choose alternative B, that is, all neighborhood GPs enroll their children in the high-poverty, racially segregated public school at the same time, this could produce the best outcome for everyone involved. GPs use the local public school, creating through their own collective actions an integrated school, and they save themselves travel time to a school outside of their neighborhood and possibly money if they feel like they have no other alternative than private school or moving. The majority of Innovator and Early Adopter GPs in this study believed that they had social and political capital that could help improve their neighborhood school, and that through their own individual actions they could make a difference if they could just figure out how to get others to act with them. They were searching for a way to choose alternative B, but there was little guidance from history as to how to go about this.

I found one major piece of research that tells the story of GPs successfully solving the collective action problem and sending their children to the neighborhood school en masse: J. Anthony Lukas's (1986) comprehensive journalistic account of school integration in Boston in the 1970s, *Common Ground*. The author followed the lives of three very different families, including Colin and Joan Diver, GPs who struggled with choosing a school for their two children in a time wrought with forced integration and busing wars. The Divers moved to their gentrifying neighborhood, the South End in Boston, wanting "diversity and integration" (162), but, "like so many of their class who had settled in the South End, the Divers had regarded the Boston public schools as the principal peril of their new environment. It was one thing to sacrifice themselves for what they believed in, quite another to sacrifice their children" (332).

Lukas describes the Divers as struggling over the question of what to do with their gentry children, weighing the moral complexity of what it means to "sacrifice" when a personal hardship could lead to a greater societal good. The description of their dilemma mapped much of what I heard from the GPs in this study almost 40 years later. The Divers were open to their neighborhood school if they could find a way to choose option B and make the decision that is not individualistically rational. They found a way through a group of two dozen or so GPs that held several neighborhood meetings to explore the possibility of founding their own private school. These discussions revealed the challenges of starting a school, and led to the decision that they could put the same organized energy into making their local public school "what we want" (Lukas 1986, 330). Subsequently, this GP group founded *Friends of the Mackey*, the Mackey School being their neighborhood school, which happened to have a new principal who seemed receptive to outside help.

Friends of the Mackey "quietly worked to transform the school, encouraging good teachers and supporting fresh ideas" (Lukas 1986, 330). They recruited neighborhood GPs to send their children to the Mackey School, while simultaneously convincing the principal to experiment with progressive education and "open classrooms," where teachers were facilitators and children pursued their own interests. This progressive teaching style—visionary and/or radical for that time—was the hook that convinced GPs like the Divers to give their neighborhood school a try. They were more willing to thrust themselves into a segregated school if they knew there was something unique and interesting about the schooling experience their children would receive, exactly what I have found in my interviews with the similar appeal of progressive schools and dual language programs. It also helped that there was a group of GPs who were doing it with them, organized via *Friends of the Mackey*, ensuring that their actions would be collective, and thus the school would no longer be segregated once they all entered together.

This type of formal organizing is just one of many ways the GPs I interviewed tried to unite their individual capital, and the stories I heard of trying to solve the collective action problem suggest that every method has a downside. Through my questioning of GPs about their school-choice process, I tried to determine how GPs go about networking with each other, how their relationships form and evolve, and the sequence of GP involvement, that is, what does it take to get one GP to follow the lead of another and to trust one another so that collective action can be taken.

Casual Playground Networking

The most informal style of networking undertaken by GPs in search of a solution to the collective action problem is talking with each other at the playground. I had many of my own playground conversations with other GPs about kindergarten, and also overheard many conversations between other GPs about kindergarten. These discussions were usually about what other people in the neighborhood had done for elementary school, and how the seats at the "good" schools were becoming increasingly hard to come by. Discussions of Stage 0 schools usually started and ended with the fact that none of the conversation participants knew anyone there.

Playground networking appears to help create momentum and buzz for a school at Stage 1 or 2 of integration, because there are GPs on the inside who can share firsthand information. Katrine, an Innovator GP in her Stage 1 school, recalls being bombarded on the playground by interested GPs. As she describes it: "And then this summer, and the previous summer, in the playground, I was just completely swamped, completely swamped with questions and conversations over and over again, with different women, the same women over and over again: 'Tell me about the school, we're thinking about this school, we're not sure, what do we do...'" But, if there is no Katrine to share firsthand knowledge, if the school is still in Stage 0 of integration, the informality of the playground setting appears to be largely ineffectual. Casually talking with GP strangers or acquaintances about the possibility of going to a segregated school together is unrealistic. There is no foundation of trust, nothing to illuminate whether the people conversing are serious.

Using Internet Technology to Network

A more formal and more effective style of networking utilized by GPs to solve the collective action problem is online networking. This type of networking, at least for the GPs in this study, was always combined with some type of face-to-face component. In one example, Jeremy parlayed the acquaintanceships developed in his apartment complex into a substantive effort to collectively attend his neighborhood Stage 0 school, simply by creating a virtual space where the interested parents could continue their casual conversations. Recognizing that spirited discussions started in the apartment building's adjacent playground were not enough to demonstrate whether the talk of entering the segregated school was serious, he demonstrated his own commitment by starting an online group dedicated solely to exploring the possibility of attending P.S.____, and recruited other acquaintances to join. His pitch to those willing to entertain his thought process, both online and off, was that "we can change the school to be whatever we want it to be." He argued that all of the great schools people get excited about were nothing special until parents got involved and "made them great." The internet conversations he facilitated were honest and explicit about intentions,[1] they were in writing, which gave them an air of permanence, and Jeremy's efforts brought a small handful of GPs into his Stage 0 school.

Another example of using the internet for networking purposes worked in reverse. The GP relationships started online, and then continued off-line. Maggie, a GP interested in enrolling her child in her neighborhood Stage 1 Stagnant school if she could entice others to join her, reached out on the neighborhood kids listserve, putting her consideration of this school in writing, looking for others who might be serious enough to respond to the discussion thread. Her posting, as she remembers it, read something like, "Anyone else considering sending their child to

P.S.____? Respond off-list to ____."[2] By their very nature, listserves are used by a more affluent class of people since they require computer access at home and some degree of internet sophistication. So, while Maggie's posting did not explicitly mention race or class, any response was likely to be from a person with a similar demographic background. Her posting eventually lead to a small gathering of GPs, providing the interested parties a chance to meet face-to-face. The meeting was described by one participant as gauging the interest level of other GPs about the school they were all considering, with GPs in attendance making comments like, "I'm really interested in it, we haven't heard from all these other schools, what are the pros and cons, and, if you guys are going to do it, I'm more interested."

In addition to exploring the interest level for the Stage 1 Stagnant school, the GPs at this meeting attempted to address their shared anxieties about the school's high-poverty level. Faye described how the GPs danced around this primary concern: "It was more talk about, they were more talking about, obviously the issue was poverty, because you know there was actually one woman who was black there…and she is considering, was…I don't know. So, you know, we all had, you've got to be smart with your words. It's not color, it's economics. It's poverty. Do you feel comfortable with sending your kid to a place where seven out ten kids are from an impoverished family? With poverty, we know what that means. You know what kind of household and language and television exposure and even toys and games, you know, so that's the issue. It was more about safety, and socio-economic comfort. I was the one spewing all the stats and information saying, 'It's going to be great, it's going to be great, blahhhh [says in a voice kind of mocking herself].'"

The statistics Faye is referring to are the awards the school had won for academic excellence, and the incredibly low class-size numbers, something she and other GPs recognize is a benefit of being a Title I school: more resources for impoverished children means more money to hire additional teachers. Intellectually, GPs like Faye are able to make the case for a Stage 1 Stagnant school. Emotionally, however, many of the GPs I talked to simply couldn't get past a gut feeling telling them not to enroll their child, unless there was absolutely no other option. In the end, only two GPs who attended this meeting enrolled their children.

Capitalizing on Existing Networks

While using the internet to strengthen acquaintance relationships or to locate like-minded GPs showed some limited success for the parents in this study, GPs networking with people they already know well, people who are legitimately their *friends* and not just acquaintances, appears to be the best way for them to solve the collective action problem. If GPs know each other, like each other, and trust each other, agreeing to enter the same segregated elementary school together does not appear to be an insurmountable mental leap, especially if there is a strong leader within the group taking the first step. In one example, preschool friendships formed the basis for this type of group transition.

Several GPs at the Sunshine Bear Academy,[3] a popular neighborhood preschool for gentry families, were good friends from the hours spent volunteering together at the school. When the time came to look for a kindergarten, these friends weighed their options together, agreeing informally to go somewhere as a unit. Bonnie described the camaraderie: "We had all started in the pre-school together and we decided we would all go to elementary school together so the kids would have a community around them. And as I always said, nothing gets integrated unless you go to it. It's like you can't wait for somebody else to do it, if people don't go, nothing changes. So I'm like OK, we'll go with a certain group of kids who already know each other, black and white, who are neighborhood kids, we'll have a support system as we work on change, you know just fundraising and stuff like that in the school."

Harnessing the kind of enthusiasm expressed by Bonnie was relatively easy under the charismatic leadership skills of a GP within the group, Timothy, who played a large role in determining where the group of friends would go, and was repeatedly referred to by other GPs as "a force of nature." With two nearby segregated neighborhood schools as possibilities, Timothy picked one over the other, and used his clout as a leader at the preschool to bring his friends with him. Since neither school was popular, yet, with neighborhood GPs, getting admitted as an out of zone family at either school was not a concern. There was space in both. His decision remains controversial in the neighborhood, as the school he did *not* choose was undergoing the beginnings of a demographic shift, and his leadership could have bolstered *that* effort instead of being funneled into a *new* effort. The story ends with the school he did choose reverting back to segregation, after he and his fellow GPs fled, and the school he didn't choose stuck in Stage 2 of integration, a possible indication that within a neighborhood, only one school can integrate at a time, and that gentry efforts that are too diffuse will result in no school fully integrating.

Regardless of the long-term impact of his decision, Timothy had legitimate concerns about the already integrating school, and he utilized his influence to push for his school of choice, demonstrating that a GP leader among friends can successfully manipulate a moment of collective action. He recalls his own power of persuasion: "And I told the other pre-school parents who were also all zoned for another school, that we're [him and his family] going to go to P.S.____. About P.S.____, I was like look, check it out, make your own decision. You know, this seems like a great school... And at that point I had a lot of influence, I understand that, over parents, because I was so involved in the pre- school, and at this point it was flourishing, and people, I was always at the park because my kids were young. And I had a reputation. So I knew that if I started to go to P.S.____, I could get some other parents to go there." His self-confidence was accurate. Under Timothy's leadership, half of the pre-K class at the school he chose was comprised of GPs.

The Potential for Backlash

Although networking with friends appears to be the most successful strategy for solving the collective action problem, there is no guarantee of success. Friends who overorganize risk stirring up racial politics in the neighborhood to a point where none of the originally gung ho GPs maintain their interest in enrolling their child in the segregated school. The most organized, mission-driven example of GPs attempting to harness their neighborhood's changing demographics to the benefit of the community school is illustrative of the dangers of overorganizing. In one gentrifying neighborhood, a group of GPs, who had been friends in the neighborhood for years, took their organizing efforts to a level that reached out beyond the friendship, and in the process appeared to overreach.

After many angst-ridden school conversations at dinner parties, these friends decided that they might be able to solve the collective action problem by forming an official group, "Our Neighborhood, Our School" (ONOS),[4] that would work to raise money for their local, Stage 0 school, and generate the necessary interest and buzz to bring in a critical mass of neighborhood GPs. Kevin, one of the group's founders, described ONOS as responding to the simple fact that "if parents [like him], who sort of had broadly kind of a middle class set of expectations for what a school should be, parents who were not happy with the neighborhood school opportunities but felt very connected to the neighborhood... if these parents who were finagling to get their kid into whatever magnet school or better public school option or sending their kids to catholic school instead sent them to P.S.____, that would be, that would be a really good school." The goal of ONOS was to figure out how to get these parents to make that choice, and was thus very similar to *Friends of the Mackey*. Like *Friends of the Mackey*, ONOS not only worked to recruit other GPs to send their children to the neighborhood school, but also tried to transform the school itself in small but significant ways. Most notably, ONOS raised money to upgrade various facilities in the school. However, ONOS was not able to alter the school's pedagogy, as *Friends of the Mackey* did with its persuasive efforts in favor of "open classrooms." This has made long-term integration efforts at this school more difficult, and will be explored in detail in chapter 7.

The efforts of ONOS were also complicated by fact that "racial harmony in the neighborhood is thin," as Margaret put it. While the organizing got GPs to seriously consider the school, the organizing also "set off alarm bells" within the mind of the school's black principal, despite the conscientious efforts of ONOS to avoid tension. The members of ONOS were self-aware enough to know that their efforts might be perceived as threatening, so, as Kevin explains, "we sort of tiptoed toward creating this ONOS thing as a way of saying look, we're not inside, we're not in the school yet, we're outside parents, but we have kids who are 2 and 3 and 4, and this is our neighborhood school, and how can we be helpful? And through helping, how can we help bring more resources to the school? And how can we help these parents with other options to get to know the school and instead pick that school? And then, once there is a bunch of those types of parents in the school, then we'll just join the PTA and be part of the school, and there will no longer be an ONOS, then that's how we'll go forward. And that was the notion, it was a very sort of intentional strategy of let's do this in a way that is minding of the community, and minding of the parents. Let's really try not to use coded racial language. Let's not set off people's alarm bells that we're all racist."

Despite these earnest intentions to be respectful of the existing school community, "alarm bells" went off, and the principal, Dr. Caraway, described by many as "paranoid," unleashed a fury. None of the GPs from ONOS that I spoke to could pinpoint exactly what her grievances were with the group—race? class? attitudes? tactics?—they just perceived that she was not open to a new demographic shaking things up in her school. Kevin didn't even end up sending his own child to the school, vaguely explaining; "I had a particularly poisonous series of interactions with her, and she made clear her personal vitriol. And I really didn't trust her to not, not have that reflect on my kid. And so, I think we had to make the decision to send him somewhere else." He was one of at least four ONOS members who were turned off by Dr. Caraway's animosity to the point of turning away from the school, despite hours of volunteering for the school and large financial contributions. Helen provided the most vivid description of the principal's backlash and her decision not to enroll her child, despite her involvement with ONOS: "It was really negative. The principal was really awful. She did not want anyone in the school, not at all. And it was going to be a fight to get in there and to be successful. And I went on a tour, and she made these sweeping statements about how white people were coming in and threatening her Title I status...it was ridiculous." Thus, despite the substantive work done by ONOS, only one gentry family in the group ended up enrolling their daughter that first year.

Word of Dr. Caraway's animosity spread beyond ONOS members to other GPs in the neighborhood, impacting their school-choice process as well. Meredith, who wasn't involved with ONOS, didn't even give P.S.____ a chance, explaining, "There had been a lot of problems with the principal there, who was, it just seems like, a tyrant—this horrible woman who was really divisive. Parents would come in and say, 'We want to write a grant for blah blah blah,' and she would say, 'No, I don't want you to.' So, really discouraging. And as happens often, she was encouraging division between parents, and was saying, 'I'm a black woman, blah blah blah,' even though half of the parents who were trying to make change in the school were themselves African American." Amber, a GP who had sent her child to an all-black nursery school and clearly would have been open to trying the school, heard that "the principal was atrocious and it was filtering down to the level of the student's experience, the student and family experience wasn't great, it got very just...ugly." Connie's critique was probably the harshest result of the rumor mill, stating that she had heard "...this woman was mis-educating an entire generation of kids."

GP Visibility Complicates Politics for the Principal

Dr. Caraway's reported resistance to change was on display in part because she knew a group of GPs was planning to enroll in the school. Had she not known ahead of time about the intentions of the GPs through the well-publicized work of ONOS, perhaps there could have been a more conventional assumption of school leadership by these GPs within the PTA, a less threatening venue. A principal in a gentrifying neighborhood facing "new" parents knocking on the door is in a difficult political situation. It understandably feels threatening when a group *with zero children enrolled in the school* is already making demands, even if the demands are veiled under the premise of "volunteering to improve the school." The changing neighborhood is already causing tension within the larger community, and all constituencies are navigating the boundaries of what the neighborhood might or might not become. The "old" parents are not necessarily going to embrace the "new" parents coming into the school (despite research on the benefits of school integration), especially if the "new" parents have a different vision for how the school should be, and are asserting that vision before they are even members of the school community. Dr. Caraway seems to have felt forced into a position where she had to publicly defend her turf to prove her loyalty to those families already in the school.

The experience of ONOS stands in sharp contrast to the experience of *Friends of the Mackey*, suggesting that the school-leadership variable is a key component of whether GPs are able to successfully organize themselves for the purpose of integrating a school. The Mackey School principal is described as "being receptive to outside help." Dr. Caraway, as perceived by the GPs, was not receptive, rendering much of the work of ONOS obsolete since their goal was a collective enrollment of gentry children, and only one gentry child went, at least that first year. This leadership variable appears to become even more important in determining whether GPs who enter a Stage 0 school keep their children enrolled, and will be discussed in great detail in the next chapter.

Long-Term Benefits of Organizing, Despite the Backlash

Despite the backlash, ONOS did have some long-term benefits in terms of solidifying the loyalty of *some* neighborhood GPs to the school. Once a new principal was firmly in place (the resistant principal, Dr. Caraway, was "ousted" or "retired," depending on who is telling the story), GPs who had younger kids and had been involved with ONOS before it was disbanded cited this as their reason for giving the school a chance. Mary, a GP who had the option of sending her child to private school, tied her decision to try P.S.____ directly to ONOS, explaining, "I went to that ONOS meeting, that initial meeting, my kid was probably 9 months old, so I felt vested with them, because I had donated to ONOS, done bake sales for ONOS, raised money for ONOS, I just felt more of a psychic connection with P.S.____ because of that involvement. I didn't really look at anything else. I did look very heavily at private schools. But if I was going to do public, I was going to stay at P.S.____. That was my feeling about it. I knew the people."

Lisbe listserve th shared Mary's sense of loyalty, and also cited an event that had been organized by ONOS that had a long-term impact on her thinking about the school and her decision to enroll her children: "What convinced me to do it, honestly, is they organized a meet the teacher night, ONOS organized it, and, well they suggested it to the principal and the principal went through with it, and there was a lot of this on the listserve, this was the big thing, the neighborhood listserve, and so there was a lot of talk on the listserve, and it was like, 'Oh, I can be part of something. I'm a person who is going to make a difference in my neighborhood.' And a lot of people with interest were wary, and when the teachers stood up to talk, I was like, 'These are really intelligent women,' they were, the lower grades especially, they had a really interesting pedagogy, they were excited, they were upbeat, and I'm like, 'This is not so bad, this is much more people making assumptions about what this school is, than what the school actually is. It's not a sit down, shut up school.' You know, I went to one of those schools that was still using corporal punishment in the 70s! So it's like, it wasn't that kind of place. So I was like, 'OK, I can do this.'"

Co-opting the School Leadership in Organizing Efforts

The "meet the teacher" night organized by ONOS, described above, was a strategy employed in another neighborhood by a single GP, Sharon, who simply focused her GP networking efforts on meeting not with each other, but with the school's leader. She never thought the collective action problem GPs faced would be solved through self-contained conversations about whether they were willing to take a chance on a segregated school together. After meeting the principal of her Stage 0 neighborhood school, Dr. Boxer, whom she found very impressive, capable, and assuring, Sharon thought the collective action problem could simply be solved through other GPs meeting the principal and having the same positive experience. So, as Sharon explains, "I simply went to her and said 'Look, if I get you some more parents, will you do a special evening?' and she said 'Yes.' I said 'Where you are basically talking about the school?' and that's what we did. I just used my own resources, and we got about 60 parents in the catchment to come and talk and listen."

Sharon's "own resources" were far more old fashioned than the listserve or other types of internet networking described earlier in this chapter. She simply made a flyer describing the evening information session, and then sent it to all of the preschools, churches, and community centers in the area, and also asked the doormen at every building in the zone to hang it up and share the information with young families. The families that listened to Dr. Boxer's presentation were similarly impressed, and Sharon's efforts brought in a few gentry families the year she enrolled her own son in kindergarten, setting the stage for an explosion of demographic change.

No Pacts

None of the organizing efforts described above—neither the informal nor formal—tried to utilize pacts: promises by GPs to enroll their children.

Jeremy rightly labeled pacts as "an unrealistic expectation." He knows that "everybody is agreed that there are preferred options out there, and everybody has a subjective thing of what that is." If the preferred option materializes, he wouldn't want others "not to do that" if that is what they really want, because of course, given the chance, he would pick his preferred option too, which is *not* the Stage 0 school.

The school-choice process in New York City involves many waitlists, making the process quite open-ended through the first couple of months of school (recall Shawn in chapter 2 assuring me I could get any school I wanted if I was willing to wait until October). It is difficult, then, for GPs to "take a leap" and enroll their children in a Stage 0 school based on faith in the intentions of other GPs in their network, knowing that all it would take to back out of a commitment to enrolling in the Stage 0 school would be getting off of the wait-list at a popular, already diverse school. Faye explained how everybody at her GP meeting gave the caveat that "they were going to go to _____ [the Stage 0 school], *unless* their kid got into_____ [most desired neighborhood school]," and they all said this with an assumption that they wouldn't get in.

However, some people get lucky, and group resolve can quickly disintegrate, severely complicating the collective action problem. GPs trying to solve this problem want to hear others commit, even though they are usually not willing to commit themselves, making some sort of formal pact completely unfeasible, and the informal intentions of others all a GP can look to when making an individual decision. Even members of ONOS, which came closer to being a pact type situation than any of the other GP organizing efforts, made it clear to each other that one's child would always come first. As Kevin recalls: "But we said from the beginning to everybody, this is not a moral question. No one is going to be judged whether you send your kid here or you don't. This is not a...moral question, you have to do what is right for you kid in the end."

The complication of relying on informal intentions sometimes causes those GPs who do enroll their children in a Stage 0 school to be taken aback at how few of them show up on the first day of school. Maggie and Candice both expressed "surprise" that they were the only two GPs who enrolled their children, based upon their impressions of how their GP networking meeting unfolded, and the positive feelings they witnessed. Maggie reminisced about losing a supposed ally, and how it was really impossible to connect anyone's decision-making process with their final decision. She recounts how Faye "was like super gung ho, super interested in scoping out the joint all year, and she had the numbers, and her husband is an economist or a banker or something, and they had done these massive spreadsheets. I mean I'd seen some of it, but I hadn't really gotten that elaborate. You know the funding per child was higher than P.S.____, and this is this, and everything is great about this school. And then in the end, it killed me, because she was the most into it, and then she sent her kid to a GT program. I was like we lost her, we lost Faye!"

Lisbeth was similarly stung by the loss of supposed allies, after years of working with ONOS, and remembered the process as "ugly." She tried to find a way to explain why some of her friendships ended over the "ugliness" of people not following through on what she thought were genuine commitments to sending their children to school with her children: "When your children are very young, and before you have to start making hard choices, there are so many things that people agree on, let's give them organic milk, and stuff like that, and so you get the sense that people have the same basic belief system. My back yard neighbor calls it a 'constellation of prejudices,' we all kind of believe the same thing, until really, you're forced to make a larger societal choice. And my feeling was, you kind of have to walk the walk. It's very easy to say, 'Yes, I believe in a good education for everybody,' but most people won't do anything about it. They won't do anything meaningful about it, or they'll write a check, or they'll sponsor a kid in a read-a-thon, and that's fine, but society doesn't change that way."

These examples illustrate the difficulty of solving the collective action problem by organizing neighborhood GPs into a group willing to enter a Stage 0 school together. Each gentrifying or gentrified neighborhood in this study was different in the way friendships and acquaintances developed and played themselves out. As the above stories demonstrate, relationships must be delicately cultivated, and loyalty must somehow be nurtured without pacts. The emotions of caring for one's child can never truly be separated from what GPs would like to be a very rational school-choice process. And the pressure of making the "right" decision for a child can lead to a sense of betrayal among friends. These complicated feelings start prior to entering a school, and often continue once the gentry children are enrolled, affecting whether GPs decide to stay or go.

5

Retaining the Innovators and Early Adopters

For a segregated school to integrate, attracting the first two waves of gentry parents (GPs) and getting them to enroll their children in the school is a solid beginning. However, to continue this demographic shift, not only must these two waves of GPs subsequently attract Wave 3 GPs, the Early Majority, they must also keep their own children enrolled in the school. Retaining Innovator and Early Adopter GPs is not a given. Despite having solved, in most instances, the collective action problem, and having an accordant close group of GP friends in the school, being a super minority can quickly become untenable for many Innovator and Early Adopter GPs, and exit can be rapid. In one school, the Innovator GP exodus happened after a couple of weeks, too brief for the school to even be considered Stage 1 Catalyzed. In another, the school lost all of its Innovators after a year, but got most of them back after a new principal was installed, an unusual double bump of catalyzing in a short period of time that emphasizes the importance of school leadership in integrating a school. A third school was catalyzed for a year by a particularly energetic group of Innovator GPs, *and* it attracted the second wave of GPs, only to have almost all of them—Waves 1 and 2—leave at the end of that second year, preventing the school from ever reaching the second stage of integration. For a school to be considered Stage 2 Integration: A Changing School, the Innovator and Early Adopter GPs must stay in the school long enough to attract the third wave of GPs. If Waves 1 and 2 exit, the integration process halts.

After Innovator and Early Adopter GPs have made the decision to enroll their child in a Stage 0 or Stage 1 school, the familial strain must be exceptionally rough for these GPs to give up on integrating their local school. As explored in chapter 3, Innovators and Early Adopter GPs are either unique seekers, extremely committed to social justice, or both, and the way they describe their decision to enroll their child in a segregated school suggests that, for most, this decision has become part of their identity, or part of a mission. They take pride in being the kind of person who would make this decision, and backing out would remove a part of themselves. Most of the schools in this study that were catalyzed sometime within the past ten years made it to Stage 2 of integration, suggesting the early waves of GPs that enter a school *will* stick it out if minimal conditions are met. They are not looking for reasons to leave, only for reasons to stay.

Innovator and Early Adopter GPs who persisted usually cited their close friendships with other GPs in the school, a belief that their child is getting a good education, and strong support for the school principal. Alternatively, Innovator and Early Adopter GPs who exited the school had negative relationships with their school's principal, ranging from zero faith in the school leader's competence to outright hostile interactions. Even if they thought their child was getting a good education, and even if they had a strong support network of other GPs, the perception of extremely poor school leadership is what drove them out. Because most GPs entering Stage 0 and Stage 1 Integrated schools had concerns about the "gentry/nongentry culture gap," which will be explored in detail in the next section, they needed a school leader who could acknowledge and try to bridge this gap. In the schools that failed make it to Stage 2 of integration, the principals were described by GPs as being resistant to the new gentry demographic, and as incapable of doing anything to accommodate a group with different expectations and needs. These principals were perceived by GPs as not having the skills necessary to handle a new type of diversity, and were blamed for exacerbating the significant gap that exists between what gentry and nongentry families expect from their school.

The Gentry/Nongentry Culture Gap

The "gentry/nongentry culture gap" (G/NG Gap) is the perceived difference in attitudes, opinions, and priorities about parenting and schooling that often exists between GPs and their neighborhood counterparts, the non-GPs. Both race and class appear to contribute to this gap. In New York City, where race and class are often inextricably linked, it is not easy to determine. In a school system where approximately 75 percent of the students receive free or reduced lunch, poverty is likely the biggest contributor; but the G/NG Gap described by GPs in this study appears to be more prevalent and challenging in the segregated schools that are predominantly African American, as opposed to schools where the nonwhite population is more racially diverse with a black and Hispanic mix. The G/NG Gap can most easily, but inadequately, be summarized as gentry families preferring a more "progressive" style of interaction with their children, both at home and in school, and nongentry families preferring a more "traditional" or "authoritarian" style of interaction with their children in these same venues.

Different Parenting Styles

Kohn (1963), in "Social Class and Parent Child Relationships," attempts to discern the different values of middle versus working-class parents, categories that do not perfectly correspond with gentry versus nongentry parents, but come close in terms of education level and income. Succinctly, his findings reveal that while both groups value honesty, decency, and respect for others, there are real differences in their approach to parenting. Working-class parents "...put far greater stress on obedience to parental commands than do middle-class parents," and also on "neatness" and "cleanliness," believing that children must conform to "external proscriptions." Alternatively, middle-class parents derive their values from the ideal of "self-direction," and they stress the importance of "curiosity, happiness, consideration, and—most importantly—self-control." Kohn explores the possible causes of these different orientations toward parenting, honing in on occupational differences, and what is expected of workers in different types of jobs. He concludes that "middle-class occupations require a greater degree of self-direction; working-class occupations, in larger measure, require that one follow explicit rules set down by someone in authority." Accordingly, these expectations translate into what parents expect from their children (475–476).

Lareau (2003), in her more recent exploration of different parenting styles, finds disparities similar to those described by Kohn, and she further develops a theory of how parenting styles play out over a lifetime, with "unequal childhoods" leading to the "...transmission of differential advantages to children." Middle-class parents approach their parental duties with "concerted cultivation," working consciously to "...stimulate their children's development and foster their cognitive and social skills" by talking with them, playing with them, reasoning with them, teaching them to solve problems through negotiation rather than physical force, and developing their interests. They follow the guidelines of professional child development experts who generally recommend these practices, and whose recommendations have become increasingly progressive over the decades. Poor families, who are often challenged to simply provide the basic necessities for their children, view "sustaining children's natural growth" as an "accomplishment," and do not typically engage in the same intensive parenting techniques of discussing everything with their children and involving themselves in everything their children do. Instead, these parents provide a space for kids to just enjoy being kids, but send a clear message that children must do what they are being told when in the adult realm. There is little room for negotiation in these households (5).

Another point of difference is the kind of relationship each type of parent has with authority, and how this is passed down to the child. The relationship between lower-class families and authority tends to be more strained than it is for the middle class, and lower-class parents model for their children a "sense of constraint" and powerlessness when facing hardship and negotiating with those in power. They tend to acquiesce to those in charge, and pass this way of interacting down to their children, expecting them to also comply with those in charge. Conversely, middle-class children develop a "sense of entitlement" to pursue their own interests and goals. When they encounter authority, it is "...common practice among middle class children to shift interactions to suit *their* preferences."(Lareau 2003, 6) They do this with their own parents as well, often leading to drawn out whining and negotiating sessions, something that decidedly does not happen in a low-income household. These skills, though sometimes annoying, are advantageous in American culture, and the fact that they are commonly expected of children and exhibited by the parents in middle-class families, but not expected or modeled in poorer households, matters. It matters not just in terms of how the children develop, but also in terms of how parents interact with schools and what they demand from schools.

Lareau describes the way middle-class parents involve themselves in their children's schools as volunteers and advocates for their children, contrasting this with the way poor and working-class parents understand their role in their children's education "as involving a different set of responsibilities from those perceived by middle-class" parents. These responsibilities are limited to ensuring their kids do what they need to do at home. They expect that "teachers will teach" and their children "will learn" and if problems arise, the school will get in touch (214).

This difference in attitude toward school was specifically noted by several of my GP interviewees, who described the lack of participation by nongentry parents in their Stage 1 schools as problematic, a reason why the schools were not as good as they could be. Paula, working extremely hard not to sound racist, since her observations, though identical to

Lareau's, were not backed up by systematic research, explained to me how she and her fellow GPs tried to teach the nongentry parents to get involved in their school, and that "mediocrity is not acceptable, because our children are there, and we have a responsibility as tax payers, and as parents, to hold the schools to a higher standard." She was trying to instill her middle-class beliefs about what parents should do in schools on the nongentry parents, who didn't seem to share this belief. Knowing that I am steeped in the research, she felt free to say to me, "And I'm sure that you know, Jennifer, that, um... African Americans [in her school the low-income population was almost 100 percent African American], they do not volunteer, because it's not in their mindset, so it's something that has to be taught." Thinking of Lareau, I agreed and said, "Some parents do not view school as their job, they think it is inappropriate to involve themselves too heavily." I didn't comment on whether it was appropriate to try and teach a group to be different, and simply listened to how this perception of difference affected how GPs feel about their schools. Almost every GP I interviewed described a "lack of parental involvement" as a reason why some schools were not on their list of options, so it is clear that this difference in attitude toward who is responsible for school is affecting the integration process.

Anyon (1980) builds on the idea of how class differences impact schools in her article, *Social Class and the Hidden Curriculum of Work*, arguing that teachers also have different expectations for children from different social classes. She found that progressive education—with lots of opportunity for students to engage in their own decision making—was more likely to be implemented in high- but not in low-income schools, and that working-class students were more likely to be assigned mechanical tasks that involved rote learning. Most importantly, she found that conservative pedagogy *was* dominant in the schools with lower-class students, affirming a perception held by GPs about their neighborhood school. Anyon views this type of schooling dichotomy as part of a larger subversive goal to disempower the lower class and reproduce society's prevailing power structure. Alternatively, one might interpret Kohn's and Lareau's research on parenting differences and argue that schools are simply meeting the expectations of the parents who utilize these schools. It isn't clear who is right about *why* predominantly low-income schools tend to be more pedagogically conservative—the causal direction—but most of the GPs in my study affirmed Anyon's assessment that the lower-class schools in their neighborhoods were too conservative, too focused on skill and drill, and not progressive enough. And these attributes were a major reason for avoiding them.

Unable to Debate Progressive versus Traditional Pedagogy

The existing literature, while helpful in explaining possible origins of the G/NG Gap, fails to fully capture the divide and what it actually *looks* like when these competing parenting ideals—complicated by gentrification's race and class divide—are on display in the same space. Anyon and Lareau compare and contrast different schools, not parents within the same school. Because our neighborhoods and schools are typically segregated by race and class, the G/NG Gap is rarely made real with an actual public clash. When the "progressive" versus "traditional" debate plays out in parenting and school reform circles across the country, it is usually among people of the same race and class who are debating on a nuanced continuum: How progressive is progressive enough? Does the whole language approach go too far? How traditional is too traditional? Does memorizing multiplication tables and regular quizzing help kids or hurt them? Within newly integrating school communities, these debates are much more delicate and fraught. Because of this country's racial history, questions about intent and outcome appear to become much more personal, especially in gentrifying neighborhoods where the sense of "the haves" versus "the have nots" is particularly stark. Thus, what might be a simple discussion in a Westchester County suburban school board meeting —whether too much homework at a young age is appropriate, for example—potentially becomes a race/class battle in these gentrifying neighborhood schools. Even though low-income families do not tend to be as vocal and involved in their schools as middle-class parents, evidence from this study suggests that they will speak up if they feel threatened, and that principals will also serve as their mouthpiece to defend the status quo.

Shawn, an Innovator GP who found herself engaged in many school-culture arguments with the principal during her time in a Stage 1 school, bluntly described the difficulty of talking about change in this environment, and how "the problem is there is this sick little switch in the system where if you go in, and even if you positively critique or show people possibilities, they're like 'What, what's wrong with my thing?' And people get really defensive, they defend their shitty thing, because it's theirs." Avery also referenced the non-GPs' "happiness with the status quo," their perception that "you're judging what we have as inadequate," and her impression that they were "watching the gentrified come in and do their song and dance, waiting for the explosion," sending the silent message to the GPs that "we don't need you." Timothy was completely bogged down by this defensiveness and seeming inability to discuss changing anything. He was willing to accept that the school's program was traditional, but wanted to be able to discuss the boundaries of what was an acceptable amount of strictness. As he explains: "I thought it was really punitive, the kids often got recess taken away from them. And those things really bothered me at my core. I hated waiting in the auditorium in the morning for my kid to be dismissed, and watching the guidance counselors yell in the bull horn in their faces and stuff like that. But I seemed to be one of very few who was bothered by it. So, there were certain things I was willing to kind of let go of, because I felt like well, I can't change everything just because of me, and they were feeling like that was the right thing to do, *but what bothered me was that there was no room to discuss it.*"

Cultural Misunderstandings That Defy Conventional Labels

The G/NG Gap goes beyond a simple progressive versus authoritarian dichotomy in more ways than being difficult to discuss within the integrating community. It can embody larger cultural misunderstandings that don't necessarily fall into these neat categories, and are hard for GPs to define with conventional labels. Sharon's attempt to describe some of the non-GPs at her Stage 1 school is a good example of language failing: "It's really tough, some tough parents in there. We just would not mess with like...I wasn't going to walk up to someone who weighs three times as much as I do while she is screaming epithets as she is dropping her son off. *I don't know what that is*, but it's a very different way of... *everything*. And um...you know, like gang member type parents. And that is not color, that's something else. That is class, that is...[long pause] culture."

Shawn offered the term "thug" to describe this "...[long pause] culture," reminiscing that "...by the end, after all I'd been through, I was like, I'm not from around here, I'm not from ____[her gentrifying neighborhood],____ is a totally different place, everyone is a thug—from the guy on the corner to the superintendant of schools. These people are crazy." Lisbeth suggested "ghetto families, for lack of a better word," describing them as "...living in projects, on cell phones in nail salons, selling drugs," and gave an example of how she has seen these life circumstances impact the children in her school: "There was a girl in my daughter's class in first grade, who came to school in first grade and was simulating fellatio on boys in first grade! You know, it's first grade, you can only imagine what that little girl has been exposed to." The GPs who offered these harsh descriptions of the nongentry made it clear they didn't see all nongentry as exhibiting these characteristics, just a small subset. But this subset created moments in their schools where they were truly taken aback by what was going on. These were moments of genuine culture shock that stuck with them.

Incidents That Cause Confusion and Dismay

The G/NG Gap is exacerbated by these small moments of culture shock, as they can add up over time and leave both sides undoubtedly confused, and often dismayed. This was the case at one Stage 1 Catalyzed school, where the GPs were trying to organize volunteers to come in to the cafeteria at lunchtime to help manage the chaos, only to be kept out by fear of child molestation. As Meredith recounts with both humor and horror, some non-GPs in the school responded to the proposal with, "How do we know who is coming into the school? We need to protect our children! How do we know these people aren't going to molest our children?" To which Meredith sarcastically replied (in her mind only, of course), "Yeah, right, *that* is something we really need to be afraid of!" Avery, another GP in the school at the time, explained how the non-GPs wanted these lunchroom parent volunteers to go through a program called Learning Leaders before they could come in and open milk cartons, and she was equally baffled by the resistance to something that seemed so innocent and helpful. The G/NG Gap is evident in her recollection: "You know, it was basically bringing hands and ideas. It was not trying to change curriculum, nothing dramatic. It was simply, 'Let's ease the hardest part of the day, when you have no teachers and few adult hands in the lunchroom.' We were literally going in and opening up milk cartons and handing out sewing cards. And yet, somewhere along the line, there was an ego that got trip-wired. I don't know what it was. But all of a sudden, it was 'Oh, you have to go through the Learning Leaders program before you can even volunteer in the lunchroom! No, you cannot touch the students at all!' I heard yelling at a meeting, from another parent, 'I don't want you in the lunchroom opening my kid's milk unless you've gone through Learning Leaders! I don't want you touching my kid!' Like heaven forbid you put your arm around a kid's shoulder!"

Since this study focuses on the perceptions of GPs, I don't know why there was such great concern by non-GPs about child molestation at this school. But, the GPs who were at the school at the time didn't know either, and in the course of debating this parent-lunchroom-volunteer proposal, they never found out. It was as if they couldn't have a conversation about it, because each side was so taken aback by the other side's sensibilities that there was no room for discussion.

Another example of the G/NG Gap that was on display at a Stage 1 school happened during a kindergarten graduation ceremony. The principal, after watching the five- and six-year olds walk across the stage to get their kindergarten diplomas, got up to offer remarks. As Shawn recounts, his speech played completely differently with his two audiences:

"He gets up and he says, 'I didn't really prepare remarks, I just want to talk to everyone, I'm so happy to see you all here. I just want to say one thing, I said the same thing at the 5th grade graduation, look at these boys, they're looking sharp, I never saw so many nice suits. And girls, just 'cause it's in the store, doesn't mean you have to buy it. Kids today with their inappropriate clothing!' And I was like, 'What? Are you kidding me? All of the girls are wearing white dresses and fold down ankle socks!' But he is making these strange comments, and the black parents were giving him the, 'Uh huh, uh huh, yeah, that's right, look at the girls today in their outfits,' like you hear in church, and I'm like, 'What? Are you looking at what I'm seeing? What did he just say?' And there is clearly this divide. There are people in the audience who are like, 'Oh My God!' And people who are like, 'That's right!'"

The Unbearable School Norm of "Yelling" Adults

If the G/NG Gap were only manifest during infrequent events, like a graduation or a PTA meeting, it might not drive GPs from a school. But when the G/NG Gap is evident in day to day school norms, the GPs in this study clearly found it intolerable. The most unbearable school norm described by GPs, which was prevalent in schools in the early stages of integration and kept coming up over and over again as contributing to the exit of Innovator and Early Adopter GPs, was the perceived common practice of adults "yelling" at young children. The GPs viewed "yelling" at these schools to be an accepted way of adults interacting with children, and in the schools where the GPs left in droves, they saw "yelling" coming from principals, teachers, school aides, and non-GPs when they were picking up and dropping off their kids.

No GPs I interviewed were comfortable with this perceived norm, though the foreign GPs tended to be more understanding. And many were truly surprised to find that not only is the authoritarian end of the schooling spectrum alive, which would be tolerable for most of these Innovator and Early Adopter GPs, but it is also flush with what GPs perceive to be extreme and outdated manifestations of a more traditional school environment—strict discipline with yelling adults. Avery, clearly resigned to the stickiness of the norm at her Stage 1 school, explained that she was leaving "primarily because of the discipline issues. I figured the older, the higher up you got, the more effect there would be on him. I didn't know enough about the upper grade teachers to automatically be comfortable, because I know there were some yellers in the bunch. And I didn't want him to get a yeller. It's a crap shoot every year who you're going to get." Amber was "appalled" by what she "saw in the hallways and in the cafeteria with the way some of the teachers would speak to students." She remembers many teachers "screaming at the students," and quickly concluded that "the pre-K was fine, but there was no way she was going to see the Kindergarten year of that school." Erich used the word "insanity" to express his disdain for the yelling and strictness norm, which he attributed primarily to the administration: "There was just a lot of yelling in the halls, a lot of screaming at the kids, if the kids were acting up they would be punished by not allowing them to go to recess. It was like, you need to give them more recess time if they are acting up! Punishing the whole class if one kid is acting up is insanity to me!" Cindy's son "hated" school, and she attributed it to a classroom that "was kind of disorganized and there was a lot of yelling and there was no standard of discipline in place." Clearly trained in diplomatic speak, Cindy expanded on how the yelling drove her out of the school, explaining, "I do think it is a little strange when you're walking down the halls of the school and you hear teachers shouting and screaming shut up at the kids, that is not a good thing. You know, it is one thing if, our kids get yelled at enough at home, but to have to go to school and get yelled at too, it is not a good thing. So, I just wanted out of the school at that point."

Meredith was not just concerned about "the policing of kids" and the impact this was having on her own children, she was especially aggrieved by the way the yelling seemed to target the young black boys in the school. She described a scene where the black boys were "...being treated like prisoners, lined up against the wall, like they're being incarcerated already!" She was clearly pained recalling this story: "It was so tragic, so so tragic. You know I was so aware of my own privilege in the situation, knowing I could pull my kids out at any time. And there are some parents for whom this is their chance!" Lisbeth was equally horrified by the way the school aides' yelling always seemed to hone in on the black boys, and she told her principal, "They would never dare speak that way to my children. They speak that way to the black boys. So not only is it horrible for everybody, but they're reinforcing a stereotype that black boys can be spoken to in a way that white boys and white girls are not spoken to."

Yelling versus Telling?

In *Other People's Children*, Delpit (1995) explores the different styles of communication exhibited by people from different racial and class backgrounds, and how these differences might negatively impact learning. For example, Delpit sees a problem when a typical white, middle-class teacher uses a passive communication style with her low-income black students, such as *asking* them to take their seats instead of *telling* them to take their seats. She argues that this passive communication style is confusing because of a low-income black child's expectations of how authority figures should act, and this mismatch hinders their academic progress. She asserts that white, liberal educators who value student-centered pedagogy and soft, conversant, negotiated power end up alienating and confusing children who are used to explicit instructions and assertive, strong authority figures, a parenting style more common in the black community (33–35). My research suggests that this cultural mismatch also appears to be working the other way. The teachers in predominantly poor, minority schools, who are reportedly mostly black and have adopted the more teacher-centered, authoritarian style of instruction that they view as appropriate for their students, are turning off GPs who want school climates similar to their own progressive, child-centered homes. The "yelling" described by GPs *could* simply be a misperception of Delpit's described assertiveness. What GPs think of as "yelling" might just be a firmness and directness that these GPs are not used to, that is not part of their culture. Regardless, it contributes to the G/NG Gap in a powerful way, because GPs do not want their children spoken to in *that* way, whatever its label.

Physical Discipline

In addition to the different cultural norms around "yelling" and how children should be spoken to, there are also different cultural norms around physical force, and when it is appropriate to gain compliance from a child. In schools, corporal punishment has been on the decline across America for decades. It is illegal in a majority of states, including New York, and is rarely used in those states where it is still statutorily within bounds. At home, however, there is wide disagreement over what is appropriate when it comes to physical discipline, with lower-class families still gravitating toward picking up a belt, and higher-class families instead resorting to verbal lashings and ad nauseam reasoning with their children. Problematic for lower-class families, their discipline strategies are not in line with middle-class parents *or* with child-rearing experts, and this causes them to fear their child's school, as they worry about being turned in to child-protection agencies for something they do not agree is child abuse. The relationship between the lower class and their schools thus can become adversarial, and not the partnership middle-class families take for granted. This fear appears to be another reason why lower-class families do not volunteer their time at the same levels as the middle class (Lareau 2003, 228–232).

This different attitude toward physical punishment doesn't affect the relationship between the gentry and the nongentry in quite the same way the controversial norm of "yelling" does. The illegality of physical abuse is absolute, whereas verbal abuse continues to live in a gray area. There was never an incident of physical abuse shared with me during my interviews; it was just verbal abuse that GPs found troubling. However, I did hear one story from several sources that portrayed the principal in a Stage 1 Catalyzed School as creating the same kind of adversarial environment with the school's GPs around the issue of "child abuse" that Lareau describes as commonplace for non-GPs, and it poisoned the integration efforts.

Timothy, who had been working hard to get parents more involved in his Stage 1 school, was on the principal's radar as someone agitating for change. He advocated letting parents walk their children to the classroom, he advocated for more fundraisers to pay for extracurriculars, he worked with other GPs to try and take action on these issues. When the principal, who is described as becoming increasingly cold to the GPs after a fairly warm start to the school year, called Timothy to tell him that his daughter "had been visiting the nurse a lot lately," Timothy was extremely alarmed. He works in low-income schools as a social worker, and he took this comment to be a veiled threat from the principal: child protective services would be called if he didn't back off. It is possible Timothy was just being paranoid, and the principal was completely misunderstood. But even if it was just paranoia, for Timothy it was a taste of being on the other side of the class divide, the side where the parents are paranoid about such threats. Timothy imagined sliding across class lines into a space where he was no longer the one in charge, he was the one fearing authority. He had intellectually understood this power dynamic, but never felt what it is to be on the wrong side of power with little recourse. As a parent with choices, he fled this situation. The G/NG Gap was one thing when he still believed he had choices and was in control. It was quite another when it felt like the gap was being erased by the principal and he was being conflated with a less powerful group. Instead of his resources lifting all boats, he felt their lack of resources pulling him down. It terrified him. And other GPs, the ones who had heard this story and that of another GP who also unexpectedly left the school, were scared too.

Final Straws

The G/NG Gap is not always as overt as the "yelling," the lunchroom battles, the playground tensions, or Timothy's disturbing brush with the dark side of authority. It sometimes appears in very subtle ways that would never be enough to drive out an Innovator GP if it were the only thing. But when a subtle thing is combined with the overt discomfort and a seemingly subpar education, it can be the last straw. Anna, whose integration efforts were also hampered by the extremely small number of Innovator GPs who entered her segregated neighborhood school with her, describes the classroom scene that convinced her that she had to go: "So I would be in the hallway looking through the window. It was heartbreaking for me because I'd put so much into making it a success and to see it fail was heartbreaking. But also coming face to face with my own classism and racism. Most of the children were from poor black families, parents brought their kids to the door, didn't even take them to the classroom, kids made their way into the building by themselves. And what really drove it home for me, I'll never forget, is institutional school lunch being delivered to more than 90% of the class, their little aluminum trays with soggy green beans, and my daughter would take out her little Care Bears lunchbox with an apple, and I just thought, 'She is so different, she is so clearly different.' And it wasn't about her being the only white kid necessarily, she was a different class, she brought different food every day than everyone else around her. And that really hit home for me, the food."

The Conflict between Principals and GPs

The G/NG Gap, despite the very complicated emotions it generates, doesn't automatically drive Innovator and Early Adopter GPs away from a school. They *want* to stay, and they *will* stay if the G/NG Gap is perceived to be effectively managed by the school's leader. In the schools in this study where the Innovator and Early Adopter GPs left before the school was able to reach Stage 2 of integration, the principals were described by the GPs as ineffective. The theme of weak leadership came up repeatedly as a reason for GP exit during the fragile early stages of tipping in, which was generally surprising to the GPs considering the fact that all of these leaders were either described positively on *insideschools.org* by the school reviewers, or, if they were new principals who had yet to be reviewed, they had made a notably strong first impression on the GPs. Seemingly excellent leadership was, in part, why these schools were chosen. But decent reviews and encouraging first impressions were not adequate predictors of a good leadership fit for newly integrating communities. What it means to be a strong school leader depends on the context; and the eventual GP disenchantment with many principals highlights the reality that different criteria are used by different groups of school consumers to make decisions about what a high-quality education should look like.

Different cohorts of parents not only have a different list of school attributes that they find important and seek out—causing certain schools to be viewed by some groups as unacceptable whereas the same schools are viewed as top choices by other groups, the hierarchy of choice explored in chapter 2—but they also seem to have different attitudes toward school leadership and what is expected from the head of a school. As described earlier in this chapter, parents of different social classes have different ways of interacting with schools, and different ideas about how involved parents should be in a school. For a leader who has been successful with one type of parent and student body, new demands by new parents are not simply going to be accepted as best for the school community. Principals and GPs often ended up on different sides of various debates over what should or should not be allowed in the school, with principals sticking with what had been working for them and their families prior to the arrival of the GPs. The resulting negative perceptions of principals shared with me by Innovator and Early Adopter GPs, and their explanations of why they left schools before integration had a chance to securely take root, will be described below.

GPs Demand Good Services

GPs repeatedly attributed their exit from Stage 1 schools to the perceived failure of the principal to listen to their concerns, which were admittedly different concerns than principals were accustomed to hearing. In Anna's school, where her daughter ate quietly with the lone Care Bears lunchbox, the principal, Dr. Carson, is described by Anna as simply "failing" to do anything to meet the different expectations of the incoming GPs. She staffed her new French kindergarten program with "extremely weak," last minute hires "from hiring halls," despite what Anna described as her voracious efforts to help Dr. Carson find good teachers through her own education network.[1] Anna was a teacher and had spent many years at a prestigious education graduate school. She had connections and resources that Dr. Carson reportedly never tapped into, despite Anna's repeated offers. Anna remembers her as "totally inept when it came to taking charge of quality. She just seemed totally unable to help herself to make it a better school. Here is someone, she didn't know how to accept help or use help." When Anna tried to discuss her daughter's "completely unorganized" kindergarten classroom, where "the cubbies were not even assigned," Dr. Carson gave her "some lame answer, the run around," appearing completely uninterested in working with these allegedly weak teachers to improve her daughter's situation. Anna left the school after two weeks. The other two Innovator GPs in the school pulled their kids out the first week. Anna would have stuck it out longer, but for her husband, also an educator, who was "completely devastated and appalled" and said, "We have to go *now*, we'll home school if we have to."

GPs demand that their school leaders be responsive, this is part of their ethos, this is why education researchers think the very presence of middle-class families in a school can make a difference in the lives of poor children. As Kevin, a GP particularly sensitive to what his own gentrifying actions might do to others, put it, "There is one thing that gentrification could do that's positive—make stronger institutions. Because if there is one thing that middle class parents are really good at, it's demanding good public institutions. Right, that's what the middle class knows, we know how to operate bureaucracy and demand good services, especially for our kids." When Anna tried to take her privilege and help all of the children in the kindergarten class by demanding a better service, she was ignored. At a minimum, GPs will not be ignored. They have choices; they will leave and go to a school where they think their voice is respected. Even if a principal can't actually *do* anything, she must at least demonstrate in some way that she is hearing the complaints of her parents and appreciates their commitment to improving the school. Timothy made this point when he told me that he would have kept his child enrolled, despite the many challenges, if, as he put it, "I had at least felt like my work was appreciated."

School Leadership Exacerbates Problems

In another school that experienced mass GP exit before reaching Stage 2 of integration, the teachers were generally described by GPs as "very good," "great," "excellent," so the principal, Dr. Fox, had a solid starting point for retaining his GPs. But, Dr. Fox is described as exacerbating the tension caused by the G/NG Gap—complaints from GPs were mostly about lunch and recess—with his "race baiting" and "bad mouthing some parents in the neighborhood to other parents, saying things like, 'Oh these nouveau-riche parents want to come in and take over, remember how our neighborhood used to be before all these nouveau riche-people showed up?'" One GP described him as "acting like Al Sharpton." Another said he fostered an "us against them environment," and he allegedly sent "horrible, stupid, hostile, mean, petty, threatening" emails to two of the GPs at the school, accusing them of "trying to bring down a strong black man."

Dr. Fox is portrayed as parlaying the G/NG Gap into extremely negative racial politics, and trying to turn any criticism about the school into a racial issue. Shawn described him as "thwarting every attack by saying, 'It's these white people, they're racist, they want private school, they want this, they want that, they want to make this school into a cooperative,' things that make no sense at all." But his tactics were effective if his goal was to drive away the GPs, as Shawn concludes, "If you say enough of it, and people want to believe you, they'll believe you. So, eventually we all just sort of left, in fear and in shame." Her choice was not easy, despite the difficult situation she described, because, as she explained, "I'm not a racist, there is nothing wrong with these kids. And having to take my daughter out of the school, it hugely undermines what I'm trying to teach her about race relations. It's really weird, it's a weird situation."

Weirdness and Rejection

Weirdness is a common theme among the many descriptions of these school leaders who are remembered as being both unwelcoming and unaccommodating. Cindy explained how her son got in trouble in his kindergarten class for raising his hand during a lesson, "because apparently you can't do that." He now lived in fear of getting in trouble and having to sit under the big T for Time Out. Cindy found this disciplining for hand raising *so* "bizarre" that she took her concerns to the principal, Dr. Caraway, who didn't think it was strange at all, and who did nothing to help mediate the classroom-culture disagreement between one of her teachers and one of her parents.

Kate was driven to tears within the first week of school by Dr. Caraway, because she unknowingly violated some vague flier protocol by inviting fellow pre-K families to a pizza party without first getting Dr. Caraway's approval to distribute the invitation. It was Dr. Caraway's weirdness about the situation that Kate found so maddening, as she describes, "We were at a meeting with parents about procedures and things, and the principal was talking about how, I mean the way she was talking you would think that somebody had distributed some kind of communist propaganda, and she is talking about how somebody had the audacity to distribute something without it going through her office! And I'm thinking 'Oh my gosh, how horrible, what did this person do?' And I had no idea that she was talking about my pizza party invitation. And then once it finally dawned on me, I don't know how I made the connection that she was talking about me inviting my child's classmates to pizza, on a Saturday in the park, but I went up to her and tried to talk to her calmly about it.

And she was just so defensive, trying to hold on so tight to whatever little power she had left. And she just made me feel like I had done something awful. I invited the kids to pizza! I just don't get it!"

Paula described an even stranger interaction with this same principal when she and a few other active GPs in the school organized getting Barnes and Noble to give $4000 worth of book cards so all the teachers would have a $100 gift card for books. According to Paula, Dr. Caraway thought they were "trying to bribe the teachers and turn them against her," so she left a message on Paula's answering machine telling her, "Oh you can't do this, the DOE, it's against the rules," and then, thinking she had hung up, continued to say on the machine, "Just wait until Ms. ____ and Ms. ____ [referring to Paula and her friend] hear that! Ha ha ha ha ha [cackling like a witch]." Paula concludes, "It was so bad, it was straight out of the movies."

Bad Leaders or Bad GP Tactics?

Whatever was driving these principals to seemingly reject the GPs and their attempts to bring resources to their schools is not clear. Some GPs thought these school leaders felt threatened and were trying to hold onto their power base; some simply thought the various principals were "not the brightest bulb in the box," "insane," "crazy," "incompetent." A few GPs blamed themselves, and thought, perhaps, their tactics were insensitive to the existing school culture and off-putting to the nongentry. And, due to the G/NG Gap, they simply couldn't find the right way to enter the school and offer what they had without inciting tension, despite their earnest intentions to do good. Paula thought *successfully* integrating GPs "showed the proper respect to teachers and parents," whereas those who were not successful "felt like they were a little better than everybody, they didn't mesh with the old parents, they didn't know how the dynamics of the school really worked." These dynamics were the "school is your job, home is my job" dichotomy common among lower-class parents, and it was truly confusing to the GPs who had never really interacted with families with this attitude about school.

Avery offered a similar critique of herself and her GP peers for possibly failing to have the proper "cultural sensitivity" in their integration efforts. Her reflection on what happened is an attempt to take some of the blame off of the school leader: "There wasn't enough, honestly, ego-stroking or catering, there was not enough acknowledgement. It came across as, 'You're broken and you need fixing,' rather than, 'We've got extra hands, we've got extra energy, let's build up what you already have.'

The perception, for whatever reason, was 'You're judging what we have as inadequate.' I think that there needed to be a bit more weaving of the parents together. Before saying, 'We're doing this,' there needed to be more weaving. The pack mentality was so strong in our group, we knew each other so well, and it's far easier to stand on the playground and talk to those people you've known for four years than to introduce yourself to someone new...So I think that's where some of the breakdown happened. It was, 'You guys stick to your own kind.' Even though we weren't all white, but there was still that feeling of gentrified, and a pack."

School Leadership Successfully Bridges the G/NG Gap

Standing in sharp contrast to the perceptions of school leadership described above, the schools that successfully retained the Innovator and Early Adopter GPs had principals who were highly respected by the GPs, who were viewed as willing to listen to GP concerns, and who were described as at least *attempting* to meet the different expectations of their competing constituencies. These successful school leaders faced the same conundrum of how to bridge the G/NG Gap, but they are portrayed as taking on the challenge and showing a high level of respect to GPs to get them to stay. Different neighborhood and school circumstances made this political balancing act much easier for some than for others.

Circumstances That Make Managing Tipping In Easier

Two factors seemed to make it easier for principals to bridge the G/NG Gap. First, a school with a diverse *non*gentry composition appears to be more welcoming of gentry families, as there is no one dominant culture that already exists in the school beyond the school culture. The principal is already skilled in managing a diverse constituency, and adding GPs to the mix is not jarring in the way it is when a school is primarily comprised of one ethnic/racial group. Schools considered "diverse" and thus desirable by GPs also tend to have a healthy racial mix of the nonwhite student population, which will be explored in more detail in chapter 8.

Second, a school that is in a neighborhood much further along in the gentrification process has a surrounding community much more accepting of school change, which gives the principal political room to adjust the school's culture to better match the preferences of the GPs. In neighborhoods in the early stages of gentrification, the battle over who the *neighborhood* belongs too is still being fought, which seems to make principals feel pressure to side with the non-GPs if there is disagreement over school culture. In neighborhoods further along in the gentrification process, principals also benefitted from the large number of *non*gentry students who drift to underenrolled schools in gentrifying neighborhoods from other neighborhoods, a phenomenon described in detail in chapter 3. Parents not of the immediate neighborhood have a harder time finding the time to engage in the PTA and fight change, making the adoption of GP ideas much easier for a principal. Additionally, principals with a large number of Innovators who are foreign GPs seem to face far fewer suggestions for change, a circumstance that appeared to make managing the G/NG Gap easier, but also often lead to stagnation, since foreign GPs do not typically engage in boosting. But, regardless of neighborhood or school circumstances, all principals who successfully retained their Innovator and Early Adopter GPs were described as being open to their new demographic, and willing to listen to their concerns.

School Leaders Must Appear Open to Their New Demographic

Sharon, who was a GP leader in the efforts to bring more GPs into her Stage 0 school in a fully gentrified neighborhood, attributed her school choice primarily to the principal, Dr. Boxer, whom she viewed as being "so open." Sharon school shopped more than most GPs, because she actually *could* afford private school and was not constrained by family finances in her schooling options, and she described the superiority of Dr. Boxer to the others she saw: "I've been to many schools, and I've sat through tours, and I was so turned off by the principals. They were contemptuous, condescending, stupid, in the sense that they don't recognize the value of parents and just take advantage of everything that comes their way. Dr. Boxer knows, because of how bad the budgets are, she will look at anything. She embraces the help from the parents." Sam, an Early Adopter GP in the school, shared Sharon's assessment of Dr. Boxer's openness, recalling that when he "said to Dr. Boxer, 'When can I come see you?' She said, 'Make an appointment and I'm there to listen to you.'" He continued, "She's not hiding. She probably knows I'm going to come in and not be that happy, but she's willing to listen, that's her job to deal with that. And I think she respects that our kids are there and we're concerned about them and we're active in their lives." Melanie, another Early Adopter GP, also spoke of Dr. Boxer's openness as a key reason she enrolled her child in the school. She recalls "meeting the principal and seeing the school and saying, 'Wow! The principal is so amazing and her door is open and she definitely has that policy where if you have an issue, if you have a problem, whatever, you can come to her.'"

Dr. Jones, whose neighborhood was far less advanced in the gentrification process, also used openness and inclusiveness as her primary political strategy for retaining GPs, and was aided by the fact that her predecessor was considered ineffective and *un*inclusive. Since the previous principal is described as driving out the first group of Innovator GPs at the school, Dr. Jones had a very clear example of what *not* to do if she wanted a more diverse school, if she wanted to retain this second group of Innovators, many of whom were also part of the first group that left the school, but who came back to give her a chance. She succeeded in appearing open to change, and was described by all of the GPs in this study as "wanting to be inclusive," and "wanting everybody to get along and feel like they are welcome." Margaret was particularly effusive in her praise, perhaps because she was one of the Innovator GPs who helped push out the previous principal. She enthusiastically explained why she stayed: "Listen, the big difference is that the new principal has really opened the doors wide open, welcomed increased parent engagement across the board, so you have many more involved parents than you did before... One of the greatest lessons of this school is the power of the principal. I mean you can just see how the new principal just raised the standards across the board, and improved the school in just a myriad of ways *and made it so much more comfortable for so many parents.*" Mary, another GP who returned to give the new leadership a chance, called Dr. Jones "a breath of fresh air, because she has at least made parents feel welcome. And the more parents feel welcome, the more they will contribute, and that is across the line, socio-economic or whatever, she is able to reach out to parents who fit my demographic, she is able to reach out to parents who are low-income, middle-income, black parents, white parents."

Dr. Jones has had to mediate battles between her diverse constituents, most memorably a battle over how cold is too cold to send children outdoors to play, a drama particularly important to Early Majority GPs that will be further described in chapter 7. The integration has not been easy. But her simple willingness to open up the door to dialogue is what has made the beginning of the integration process at this school possible. GPs in the neighborhood know her as a principal who "cares about parent's concerns."

At another school in a neighborhood even less gentrified than the one where Dr. Jones has been working to build bridges, Dr. Smith wears his openness to the GPs much more quietly, and instead preempts GP concerns with supreme confidence in his school's program. He has won awards for turning his school around and has a reputation among GPs in the neighborhood as "a mover and a shaker," and is considered a "big deal" because "he took this school from crap and he made it into a big deal." The majority of Innovators and Early Adopters in his school are foreign GPs, a group less concerned with the G/NG Gap than nonforeign GPs, and he has benefitted from being able to welcome these foreign GPs without having to worry about them clamoring for change. In the rare instance when a GP approaches him about change, however, he has appeared open to their suggestions and given them what they want. For example, Ivy, one of the few nonforeign Innovators at the school, recalls a meeting with Dr. Smith where she expressed concern that the school required mandatory Saturday school, something she didn't think her son would need, to which he responded, "Well, it's not really *that* mandatory... it's not that mandatory, but if your kid isn't doing well, I don't want to hear anything." This answer satisfied her, and she doesn't send her son to the Saturday program.

Dr. Smith also seems to skillfully handle the school's new diversity by being able to talk to his different constituents in different ways, just like a successful politician, highlighting the things he thinks they will care about, thus appearing open and approachable to everyone. In our interview, Ivy mentioned the school's "Renzulli"[2] method, something not referenced by any of the other neighborhood GPs I interviewed, neither those who chose to enroll their children in Dr. Smith's school nor those who didn't. Ivy bragged to me about how Dr. Smith refused to become a G&T school, "because he believes every child is gifted," and how "he uses the Renzulli method, going above the G and T model." He seemed to know Ivy would be impressed with "Renzulli," and made sure this was a part of their conversation. Robert's portrayal of Dr. Smith provided further evidence that he is able to morph into being open to whomever he is talking to. Robert described him as one of those "guys guys" who will "pull you aside" to talk about sports, "that kind of thing." Robert also acknowledged Dr. Smith's self-assurance, and how "he is very big on maintaining control of the school, he wants to do things his way, he doesn't want any of that to be changed or to be challenged." But, despite this assertion of control by Dr. Smith, Robert also viewed him as "realistic, he can see what people can bring to the school, and I think he is enjoying that, he is definitely appreciating us being there." This feeling of being appreciated is affirmation that a school leader is open to the arrival of GPs, and a large part of what GPs need to stay in a Stage 0 or Stage 1 school.

Tolerance for the Difficult Process of Integration

Skillful school leadership is crucial to a school's chances of making it through the early stages of integration, as Innovator and Early Adopter

GPs must have confidence in the principal's ability to manage the G/NG Gap and feel appreciated by the principal to stay in the school. Additionally, the GPs who stay have an unusual ability to tolerate an imperfect situation, even when they realize they could choose something else. This trait is part of the social-justice orientation exhibited by most Innovator and Early Adopter GPs. They realize that part of caring about their community and believing in social justice is a demand *on them* that they will not get everything they want. As minorities, they can fight to have their voices heard, but because of their small numbers, they will not always prevail. Astute principals can listen to GPs and assure GPs that they are all working toward the same goal, but astute principals also have to manage their relationships with the non-GPs in the school, and choose their battles wisely. Thus, Innovator and Early Adopter GPs who enter their segregated schools *and stay* in their now less segregated schools, seem to be able to handle not winning every battle, and are able to deal with not having an "ideal" educational situation for their child.

No School Is Ideal, Not Even Private School

In some cases, the GPs are able to rationalize their way out of even thinking there is such a thing as an "ideal." Lisbeth was particularly good at this, explaining that because she had three kids, she would have to find a school that was ideal for each child's unique needs, transport them around to three different schools, and that was "crazy." She went on to argue that "when parents chase around after the perfect school, they're basically sending their child the message, 'You're helpless, you must be taken care of in a certain way,' instead of teaching them to figure things out." Kate managed to turn her ideal *into* the local school, arguing that "there is nothing better than knowing that the kids my children are going to be hanging out with for the next 15 years have a good education. Those are my kids' friends, whether they end up going out of the neighborhood and going to a private school or not, they are still going to be on the playground with those kids. So I want those kids to do well, so they're not trying to get my kids to do bad things."

Kate also made the case that too much privilege was scarier than deprivation. She argued that "you want what is best for your child, but it's hard to always know what that best thing is. A lot of people think the best thing for their child is to spend $25,000 a year on their education. But if you look at those kids 10 years later, who has had the drunk driving conviction? Who is doing blow jobs in the bathroom? That kind of exclusivity at those schools, it scares me more than somebody bringing a gun to my kids' school. It's much more likely that my kid would get in trouble with a bunch of rich kids than with kids from the neighborhood." Loren had similar misgivings about private school, even though he ended up enrolling his biracial son in private school when he was offered a full scholarship. Reflecting on this decision, he concluded that "private schools bring a whole different set of problems. Instead of having to deal with less educated, lower-income people, we're having to deal with such high income people that they are living in a different reality. It's certainly a weird existence now, we go back and forth between my son coming back from school saying, 'Can we get a country house for the summer?' to kids on our block saying that we 'live in a mansion,' because we live on all of the floors in our house. So every time my kids say something outlandish like, 'Money is no object,' I have to refer them back to the block that we live on and get some perspective through the community we live in."

Astrid went on an antiprivate school tirade as justification for choosing her local school, exclaiming that she didn't want her child to come home and say, "Why don't I have a Gucci bag? I want to have this hairdresser and not that hairdresser." Astrid's husband, who tutors private school students, has described his students as "coming in and crying because they have last year's Gucci bag and not this year's Gucci bag. And it's a disaster to them!" So, as a couple, they decided they were "not going to subject ourselves to that kind of thinking." Patricia could see the value of private school if her children "develop some special talent that only this one private school has," but for kindergarten, with twins, it would simply be "$60,000 for them to draw pictures," or as Faye put it, "$30,000 so your kid can learn the difference between citron green and lime green." Patricia also didn't want her children to get that sense of entitlement Loren was experiencing, where they "think it's normal to have a house in the Hamptons." Brie, who herself attended private school for 13 years, could find value in private school, because, as she humorously put it, "there are clearly some benefits that accrue for a child who is in a class of kids, a disproportionate number of whose parents think that it's really fun to kick back and read a book by Henry Gates, because that's just their idea of a good time." But, she argued that the greater upside comes in public school, where kids learn to be "in the real world, and learn about being with people who are not as rich as you are."

Sympathy for the Principal's Competing Demands

In addition to being incredibly good at rationalizing their decision-making process, GPs are also a very self-aware demographic, and several expressed their understanding that despite the resources they can bring to the table, they pose a challenge to their principals. They sympathize with the difficulty school leaders face in trying to please all of their constituents, including themselves. Amanda assumed that her principal was not "adverse" to trying something new, she just "hasn't had a lot of parents coming in and saying let's try something different out." She understands that it can take "years of pressure" to change a school's priorities and norms. Lisbeth also expressed tolerance for the time it would take to figure this integration thing out, explaining: "We are the minority, we have to play by other people's rules. We don't get to just come in and start pushing people around, pushing our agenda. Some families want more homework, no recess, more of a pull yourself up by your bootstraps sort of thing, and then you've got the white and middle-class black families who want this more Renzulli, progressive approach, and everybody is at each other's throats, and the poor principal is like Obama. Nobody is happy."

The Children Are Happy

Lisbeth's children *were* happy in the school, as were all of the Wave 1 and Wave 2 gentry children who stayed enrolled (in the minds of their parents at least), so "nobody is happy" referred to the adults struggling with the parameters of good schooling and wading through uncomfortable race/class politics. GPs who didn't exit always assured me that their children were happy. They didn't want me to think they were negligently sacrificing their children as guinea pigs for a greater good. But, they also didn't want me to think that they were unaware of the trade-offs they were making in choosing to integrate their neighborhood school. Maggie, for instance, while not thrilled with her son being given homework in kindergarten, rationalized it in terms of how she thought might benefit the whole community, "The whole idea of homework in Kindergarten for some people is like, 'Whoa! What is this!' But you know for me, I am not loving it, but I realize what it's for. I mean it's for your kid, but a great deal of it is for the family. And I think it is really like this way of putting expectations on families that they may not have had before for their child's education. I mean you have to sit down and do these things. We have a reading log where you are supposed to write down the books you are reading each week, and the kid is supposed to color in the chart if they liked the book. And it seems very basic to me, of course you would read every night to your child. But I think the idea is, hopefully, that it is going to be basic for everyone." Amanda, a GP in a different neighborhood in a different Stage 1 school, had an almost identical response as Maggie to the homework, "I mean, the other thing is the homework, which I just think is excessive. It's so unnecessary. I mean, she could do a little bit. I think a little bit of training is good. But frankly, you know, in the school the reason they have it is that they're dealing with parents who may have never had a tradition of sitting down with their kids. They feel if they don't get parents involved when it's easy, you know, they're never gonna get them involved, and I see that that's partially necessary."

Too much homework wasn't the only nuisance GPs thought they were tolerating. Candice, a foreign GP whose second language is English, was bothered by "that language that African Americans often use, that wrong grammar," (I gave her a quick history of the Ebonics debate and how "wrong" grammar is considered by many prominent linguists to be a different dialect) but she knew that her own child would "grow up to learn proper English," so it was tolerable. Sharon had to endure her son's coinage of the term "yo people," and be prepared to engage in regular discussions about these people who are "always saying 'Yo,'" and how it isn't about race, because there are white kids in his class who say, "yo yo," all the time, and there are black and Hispanic students who don't. Sharon had to discern, with her son, what it means to talk this way, and why it is appropriate sometimes and not at other times, a verbal journey for mother and son likely unique to gentry families immersed in the challenges of the G/NG Gap.

Tight-Knit Communities

Aware of the trade-offs of their school-choice decision and in a heightened stress situation as the school's minority group, Innovator and Early Adopter GPs sought each other out, if they weren't already friends prior to enrolling their children in the school, and they formed "tight-knit" communities within these schools. The strength of these relationships also helped keep them from exiting their schools. Astrid referred to her community as "almost like a family." When she had to take her daughter to the doctor at the last minute, she said, "Who wants my son?" and within seconds, two or three GP friends volunteered. She expressed to me, with genuine warmth, "It's so nice to have that kind of community." Candice, not used to being part of such a close group of people, expressed "surprise" at how much she liked hanging out at the playground after school because she "really liked the parents." Margaret talked about how she and her fellow Innovator GPs "cried together" as they struggled to find their place in the school, a powerful bonding experience. And Paula called herself "very, very lucky to find such a nice group of people to work with."

In this supposed age of *Bowling Alone*,³ the word "community" was used repeatedly by the Innovator and Early Adopter GPs who persisted in their schools to express why they felt comfortable doing what they were doing. In each other, they found the support they needed for making what they perceived as a difficult choice.

A handful of GPs also finally found acceptance from their non-GP neighbors in these schools, and were able to shed a bit of their outsider status, something they valued as "unique seekers." Now, not only did they get recognition from their own peers for the uniqueness of their attempt to integrate a school, but also, they found some recognition of their uniqueness from non-GPs. Avery describes her acceptance by non-GPs in her school as "gradual," claiming that she "honestly didn't feel fully accepted as a parent by the rest of the parents [referring to the non-GPs] in the class until this year." She "didn't feel dissed," but she felt like many of the non-GPs were simply "waiting to see what I would do." And because she stayed, after four years she thinks she has finally "earned their respect." She expressed this with a glimmer of unique-seeking pride, prompting me to remember a similar feeling of pride in finally being accepted by my students when I started my third year in the same urban high school. They expressed such surprise that I had returned, again, and that was finally enough to *earn* their respect. Actions were the only thing that had meaning. GPs who persist in their integration efforts *show* they are serious about being true neighbors. Bridging the chasm of the G/NG Gap takes time, and GPs must have the patience and tolerance for an imperfect schooling situation to persist, because they are the ones who can easily choose to leave and do something else. This is what their privilege affords. This is why *their* choice is key to integration.

Those Who Exit

The GPs who took their children and left the Stage 1 schools they judged as inadequate usually did so at the end of the school year, seeking a spot at a different school for the next school year—in first grade if they had done kindergarten, or kindergarten if they had done pre-K. This allowed them to start the search process over and take new tactics, which included trying for a spot at public schools they hadn't considered the first time around (usually schools located further from where they lived), or trying again for spots in popular public schools that had previously not had room. First grade is less competitive, as most families have settled into a school in kindergarten and are not searching for something new. When families move away, as they periodically do, spots open up in the older grades. A handful of my interviewees expanded their school search to include private schools, seeking financial help from their parents or cutting corners elsewhere in their spending. And a few had friends who had left for the suburbs, abandoning the urban living experience entirely.

I had two interviewees whose integrating experiences were so bad that they left early in the school year, not wanting to wait an entire year before getting their child out. Both of these parents were able to work their existing relationships within the New York City Department of Education (NYCDOE) to find an alternative. Timothy, the social worker, worked in a different school district than the one where he resided, and he was able to find a spot in the first grade at a popular progressive public choice school in the district where he worked. It was during October, that magical month where I was assured by another GP that I could find a spot anywhere if I just waited for schools to figure out how to maximize their enrollment numbers for funding purposes. The other GP had already been working with someone in the Office of Enrollment when she first discovered that the district lines had recently been redrawn and she was unexpectedly living in a different district than the one where she had been researching her school possibilities. This enrollment specialist had encouraged her to send her child to the school she wanted to leave, telling her she had the power to make a difference, especially with her experience as a former teacher. He was sympathetic when she *did* try and things weren't working out, and he managed to find her a spot in a dual language program in a different school in a different district. Again, it was October, that enchanting month when spots open up. This mother was, however, prepared to home school if no other options were available, and then try again for first grade somewhere else. She would find another option, as the gentry always manage to do.

6

Attracting the Early Majority

For the purposes of this study, a school reaches Stage 2 of integration when it successfully retains its Innovator and Early Adopter gentry parents (GPs), and is now called a Changing School, in reference to the way GPs talk about a school at this stage of the integration process. The number of GPs needed in a school for it to be called "changing" varies slightly. Table 6.1 provides a demographic breakdown of the schools in this study that GPs referred to as "changing."

The three schools in this study referred to by GPs as "changing" had a 5 percent or less[2] white population. Most of the demographic change in a newly integrating school is concentrated in the lower grades, so the overall school percent of white families can be tremendously low and the school can still be considered changing. Emily best summed up this type of GP interpretation of what change can mean, explaining that "what had been happening, parents had been sort of working from the bottom up, pre-K, K, 1st grade, 2nd grade, but the upper grades still were lackluster, traditional, sort of chalk and talk, and quite honestly the look of the population was very different. The younger grades were much more

Table 6.1 A demographic breakdown of schools gentry parents consider "Changing Schools"[1]

	P.S. 1000	P.S. 1001	P.S. 1002
% White	4	5	2
% Black	87	33	73
% Hispanic	6	60	23
% Asian	2	2	1
% Free and reduced lunch	70	79	93

diverse, um, from the lower grades as it was for the upper grades, because the upper grades still sort of resulted from the older influences of the neighborhood."

The phrase, "It's changing," was used in reference to all of these Stage 2 schools, often by Innovator and Early Adopter GPs already in these schools who were trying to encourage more GPs to join them. Rhonda's introduction to her Stage 2 neighborhood school was common for Wave 3 GPs, the Early Majority. She heard about the school from a GP friend with a child already enrolled there, who told her, "It's such a wonderful place, and there are such good parents, and, you know, it's changing, and all that kind of stuff." Jeremy, an Innovator GP, considered one Stage 2 neighborhood school before deciding to pioneer another because he had heard it was "changing," specifically being told, "Try P.S.____, there are white people there!" The phrase is usually said with hope, but sometimes said with trepidation. A couple of potential Wave 3 GPs I informally interviewed at the playground, who were considering a neighborhood Stage 2 school but hadn't yet decided what to do, talked about how the school was "changing," but it was clear they weren't sure if it had changed *enough* for them to consider it a viable option for their children.

For Changing Schools to transition to Stage 3 of integration and become Diverse Schools, completing a successful bout of tipping in, they must attract this skeptical third wave of GPs to their school through effective salesmanship. At this point in the integration process, neighborhood circumstances are very similar to those described in chapter 5 when the school was at Stage 0, except the neighborhood is a bit further along in the gentrification process, making the scarcity of spots in desirable neighborhood schools even more of a problem. The neighborhood GP network is slightly larger, but it is no longer needed to overcome the collective action problem, since the neighborhood school now has a core group of GPs—the Innovators and Early Adopters—already on the inside. The GP network is now simply a source for buzz about a school, and GPs inside the school have to effectively use this network to sell the school to their GP peers in the Early Majority who are not yet on the inside. Wave 3 GPs may be peers in neighborhood choice, but not in unique-seeking or social-justice sensibilities, and the integration process at this stage takes on a completely different dynamic than it had in Stages 0 and 1.

Characteristics of Early Majority Gentry Parents

Early Majority GPs are not risk takers, and will only try a school once others have proven its viability. To explain how a school is sold to Early

Majority GPs, it is important to understand in greater detail how Early Majority GPs differ from Innovator and Early Adopter GPs. Gladwell's (2000) *Tipping Point* uses a business example to explain the difference: Innovators and Early Adopters are visionaries, they have small companies, they are just starting out, they can take enormous risks. The Early Majority, on the other hand, are pragmatists, they run big companies. "They have to worry about any change fitting into their complex arrangement of suppliers and distributors...They will undertake risks when required, but they first will put in safety nets and manage the risks very closely" (198).

Applying this paradigm to parental behavior and school choice, Innovators and Early Adopters are able to imagine integration happening if they take the "risk" and make it happen through their own actions. The Early Majority does not have the same ability to imagine possibilities, and their school-choice hierarchy requires schools that are already on the GP list of acceptable neighborhood schools. Wave 3 GPs have to have heard from someone in their peer group who has firsthand knowledge of a school that the school is a good option. To do otherwise would be outside of their risk-comfort level.

When Wave 3 GPs talk about their school-choice process, they primarily differentiate themselves from Waves 1 and 2 in what they don't say. They aren't focused on networking to solve the collective action problem. They aren't thinking about ways to change the world to fit their ideal. They aren't revealing unique-seeking personality traits or any kind of commitment to social justice. They are simply parents looking for a good school option in their community, and the Stage 2 school in their neighborhood is on their list of possibilities only because GPs in their network are talking about it from personal experience on the inside.

When pressed to talk about their school choice within the context of social justice and how they see themselves within their communities, Leslie's response is typical of Wave 3 GPs. First, she praised the people in her community whom she viewed as being devoted to bettering the world: "Margaret, you met her, she is one of the parents who got involved before her kids even went to P.S.____. She was determined, she was like this is it, this is where we're going, we're going to make it better. She is a great model." Then, when asked if she shared any of Margaret's social-justice zeal, Leslie responded, "To be really, really honest, only in the sense that I know I *ought* to be feeling that, [laughter] you know what I mean? Like, just given my socio-economic and generational grouping. But no, I think ultimately I would go with what I think is best for my kid and my family, and that wouldn't rule my decision making." My conversation with Jackie, another Wave 3 GP, was almost identical. First, she praised Ivy as a parent "with the energy to change things," and then described herself as *not* being that kind of person, just a mom looking for the right school for her child.

Selling a Stage 2 School to the Early Majority

Wave 3 GPs are not interested in changing something or taking risks. Thus, Stage 2 schools have to be sold to them as schools that have already changed *enough*. While Innovator and Early Adopter GPs simply have to convince themselves that what they are doing is the right thing for their child, Early Majority GPs have to be convinced *by others* that what they are doing is the right thing. Gladwell (2000) makes the case that for an idea to spread from the Innovators and Early Adopters to the Early Majority, there has to be someone mediating the leap, someone who can translate. Using both technology and fashion as examples, he explains that "Innovations don't just slide effortlessly from one group to the next. There is a chasm between them. All kinds of high-tech products fail, never making it beyond the Early Adopters, because the companies that market them can't find a way to transform an idea that makes perfect sense to an Early Adopter into one that makes perfect sense to a member of the Early Majority...They were wearing them precisely because no one else would wear them. What they were looking for in fashion was a revolutionary statement. They were willing to take risks in order to set themselves apart. But most of us in the Early and Late Majority don't want to make a revolutionary statement or take risks with fashion at all" (198–199). Nor do most of us want to make a revolutionary statement or take risks with a school for our children. There has to be a GP leader, or several GPs in that early group of white, middle-class families in a school, who are helping the Early Majority, understand why sending their child to this school makes sense.

Any attempt to lure the Early Majority into a Stage 2 school has to make the decision seem the opposite of unique. It must seem completely normal, like this is a great opportunity. Wave 3 GPs must be convinced that they are fortunate to find a great school before it becomes too popular and impossible to get into. In New York City, parents who believe they have choices all feel a sense of scarcity about good schools,[3] and easy entry must be a sign that a school is not good enough. What GPs on the inside of a Stage 2 school have to do is convince Wave 3 GPs that the school is simply a hidden gem, it *is* good enough, and this is their chance to beat the system. Innovator and Early Adopter GPs try to mediate the leap between themselves and the Wave 3 GPs considering their schools primarily through staging spectacular school tours.

School Tours and the Role They Play

For Innovator and Early Adopter GPs to sell a school to Early Majority GPs, they must concoct the appearance of a significant middle-class presence and vibe in the school. GPs are clearly not the numerical majority in a Stage 2 school, but when Early Majority GPs hear that a school is changing, they need to be able to visit that school and actually *see* the change in a tangible way. The easiest way for this to happen is on a school tour. Conversations within the GP network may plant the idea in their head that a school not currently on their list of accepted school options should be placed on the list, but until they are inside the school bearing witness to the change, they won't necessarily believe it. Wave 3 GPs appear to need the affirming experience of looking at a school with other GPs.

As a potential Wave 3 GP on my own kindergarten quest, I took many tours of schools in all stages of integration, allowing me a chance to compare the experiences. School tours appear to take one of two tones: they are either led by parent volunteers in the school (sometimes with the help of enthusiastic students), or they are led by a member of the school staff, possibly the parent coordinator or some other nonteaching member of the school community. The tours led by parent volunteers send the message that the parent community at the school is strong, engaged, passionate, and dedicated. The tours led by school staff give the impression that the parent community isn't particularly active. When Wave 3 GPs are shopping for a school, they need to be assured that there are parents in the school who are like them. They are not unique seekers; they want to be part of a group. If the tour is given by a school aide, they assume that there are no parents like them in the school, because if there were, they would be giving tours. I know this was my impression. In addition, many of the other GPs I interviewed both formally and informally, while not explicitly assessing tours as such, stated that they eliminated Stage 0, Stage 1, or Stage 2 schools from their list repeatedly "because there wasn't an active parent body." This sentiment was often expressed in conjunction with, or in lieu of, the statement that the school "wasn't diverse." Both expressions appear to be code for the same thing: no white, middle-class families.

To ensure that prospective Wave 3 GPs are not left with this impression, the Innovator and Early Adopter GPs in Stage 2 schools who are trying to bring in the Early Majority have to stage school tours that are similar in style and enthusiasm to those schools that are much further along in the integration process. This is analogous to dressing for the job you want, not for the job you have. Since Wave 3 GPs will also be touring the popular Stage 3 schools in their districts, just in case they get lucky or can afford to move to a better zone, Stage 2 schools have to look like *those* schools when they give tours. In practical terms, this means that GPs must be both leading the tours and scheduling few enough tours so that there will be crowds at their tours. They have to create an image of scarcity and a feeling of momentum and buzz. If there are only two tours all year, for example, all of the potential Wave 3 GPs will show up at the same time and see not only the GPs on the inside leading the tours, demonstrating the middle-class presence in the school, but also each other. They will be able to imagine the possibility of what the school would be like if all of those people on the tour also decided to enroll their children. It is a way to transform the school's label in the minds of potential Wave 3 GPs from "changing" to "changed" simply by staging a crowded tour. Avery described one of these kinds of tours at her school as "exciting and interesting, and there were parents coming in and leading them, showing them the excitement, not just administrators parading people around."

Stage 2 schools that offer tours once a week, led by the parent coordinator, may be very convenient for GPs on the circuit, but if GPs are alone on the tour, or part of a very small group, the school suddenly seems not good enough. There is no palpable middle-class energy to meld into. Mia, a potential Wave 3 GP, described the tour process for her as "a Rorshack test." She believes that the tours "have nothing to do with your kids, but have to do with how you see yourself and what kind of community you want to be a part of. You take tours so you can look at who else is on the tour and imagine whether you can see yourself as being part of the same community with those people."

The Innovator and Early Adopter GPs I interviewed who were intentionally trying to bring more GPs into the school understood the importance of creating this feeling of a GP presence larger than their numbers. Sharon organized *one* open house, where the principal would speak to all interested parents, ensuring the crowd would be large and they would see each other. And she spoke at the meeting as well, "because as parents, that makes a huge difference, we don't come out of a bureaucracy." She was consciously ensuring the GPs already in the school "put our face in everything...giving all of the tours, talking to parents, giving out our phone numbers if people had questions, " while also remaining conscious that "it may not have been correct" to do so. She wasn't always comfortable as a GP leader, but she was executing a plan she deemed essential to attract more GPs. Lisbeth and her early GP cohort also consciously worked hard on "the PR machine" and "selling ourselves to the neighborhood," producing T-shirts, mugs, and other paraphernalia with the new school logo designed by a GP who is also a professional graphic artist. They further boosted the school's image with book readings by famous local authors, silent auction fundraisers, and adding comments to websites with school information, explaining how the school had changed. Innovator and Early Adopter GPs can be exceptionally good at creating a flurry of middle-class energy that masks their low numerical presence in a Stage 2 school.

The Early Majority Respond to Well-Executed Boosting

All of this strategic boosting does its job in terms of making Wave 3 GPs feel comfortable entering a Stage 2 school. Wave 3 GPs speak of their decision to enter a Stage 2 school as a rational one, not as a risk. Leslie explained to me that she is "not the urban pioneer," nor is she "the school pioneer. P.S.____ has already been on this course, it made it easy for me to decide and go there." She expanded that "there were definitely people going there, there was a sense or vibe about it, this is the good public school, people want to get in there, this is the acceptable option." Rhonda was similarly convinced that she was not taking a risk in entering a Stage 2 school, the school was a place "everybody was talking about," she had friends there "who really liked it," who would say "what a great community of parents it is, and that it's on the up and up, and the new principal is great, and a lot of parents who want to be involved go there."

Knowing someone personally on the inside of a Stage 2 school was common for Wave 3 GPs who felt confident giving the school a try. In addition to noting the good test scores at her Stage 2 school, Faith commented that she knew people who were going there, who "seemed to like the experience," and she didn't think the decision was risky. Patricia, who entered the same school as Faith, agreed that "everyone was talking about P.S.____, and how they were excited about P.S.____." She "heard a lot of good things" from friends who had older children who were there. Mandy knew "several people in her building" whose children attended her neighborhood Stage 2 school. And even though she wasn't close with them, they were demographic peers, and their reports of being "happy" were enough to make enrollment seem normal.

School Choice as a Socially Charged Process

Wave 3 GPs appear to be much more heavily influenced by their peers than are Wave 1 and 2 GPs, and their positive response to boosting affirms Sunstein's (2006) description of group polarization and its impact on decision making. Sunstein argues that group polarization occurs when members of a group, after going through the process of deliberating with each other about an issue, tend to end up with more extreme positions than they held before the deliberation began. Segregated schools in gentrifying neighborhoods often stay stuck in Stage 0 because there is no GP group pushing the group think in favor of sending their children to the school, instead, the group think pushes in the other direction. The GP who has hesitations about entering the neighborhood school, but is open to the idea, deliberates with other GPs, who also have hesitations about whether to enter that school, and they end up reinforcing each other's fears. The GPs then all move from not being sure about the school to being against the school. When a GP who isn't sure about a school finds out that other GPs, people who are from the same social group and share their values, are *also* unsure, it's now acceptable to be unsure and, if others are unsure, it is probably even wiser to simply be against the school.

By contrast, the views of "out-group members," in this case the poorer families of color who are currently using the school, have little ability to influence the opinions of the deliberating group, the GPs. If these poorer parents speak highly of their school, this opinion has little impact, since these parents are viewed as having a different set of values and/or having no choice but to attend this school. Vera, for example, recalled some African American acquaintances telling her how "great" the neighborhood Stage 0 school is. She probed further, only to find out that their primary criteria was that "they have an after school program that is $40 per week." She clearly did not relate, and didn't even tour the school.

In a Stage 2 school, there are now Innovator and Early Adopter GPs on the inside of the school who are viewed by Early Majority GPs as people from the same social group with similar values and the same freedom to make choices. The group think can now be pushed in the other direction. The socially charged component of school choice can now help facilitate further integration in Stage 2 schools. Reluctant Wave 3 GPs, who are bombarded by Waves 1 and 2 with a dose of enthusiastic boosterism in favor of enrolling in the neighborhood school, now reinforce each other's decision to attend. They don't want to miss out on the opportunity to send their child to a great school while it is still possible to get a seat. Timothy, an Innovator who spearheaded the "cheerleading" at his school, describes "the drastic difference, just over the course of one year" that stemmed from the GP outreach and burst of GP intensity in the school: "Everybody was super-jazzed and excited, and we tried all of these different kinds of clubs. And I wrote a grant, we got $5000 to do a mobile computer cart. And we had a photography exhibit, and we had people donating money and resources and it was, it could have been amazing. And there was enough momentum in the building that we started doing open houses, they had never done open houses or tours, and parents were leading tours. We had tons of people coming from all over because this was kindergarten year so a lot of people had put their kids in private schools or whatever, and people were excited. And the day of pre-K registration, we had like fifty people there at six in the morning to sign up!"

Private Preschools as a Key Component of the GP School-Choice Network

Timothy's description of the drastic difference over the course of a year was common in Stage 2 schools attempting to shift to Stage 3. In a city like New York, where there is such a perceived scarcity of good public school options, group polarization can shift quickly in favor of a school because people are desperate. In one year's time, a school can move from being on nobody's list of options to being on everybody's list of options. Within my own GP network, all it took to move the neighborhood Stage 2 school from not an option to a good option was the entrance of one Early Adopter GP who previously had been sending her children to our preschool.

The preschool community is a very powerful component of the GP network. Even GPs who can't afford private elementary school usually manage to pay for private preschool. It's only two years of financial strain, or one year if the family does public pre-K, and highly educated GPs believe it is their obligation as parents to provide excellent early childhood education since experts believe it is so foundational. Within this private preschool world, there are daily conversations in cubby rooms across the city about the elementary school decision. The conversations are two-tiered. There are private school only families, and public school only families, and they each have their separate conversations about what options are acceptable and feasible. If someone from this group sends her child to a school that isn't on anyone's list, eyebrows are raised, as are hopes. If the reports from this person, *this group member*, are good, the cubby room chatter can explode into group think toward this new public school option. The parents then become polarized into thinking not only that this is now a good option, but also possibly that they may not even be able to get a spot. Buzz starts to generate a sense of scarcity as GPs wonder whether they have missed the window to get a spot at this newly labeled "good" option as non-zone residents. Faye used the term "about to explode" in reference to her changing school. Within a year, the school where interest was sparked in my preschool cubby room "crossed over," as Melanie put it, from not a desirable GP option to a popular option, and "every tour was packed." Friends were suddenly telling Melanie, "Oh, we just want to be at your school so badly!" as they lamented not being in the zone because they lived on the wrong side of the street. Two years prior, Melanie assured me this kind of talk "just wasn't so."

The Impact of Not Boosting the School

There was only one Stage 2 school in this study where the GPs did not engage in intense boosterism and outreach, nor did the school offer group tours to entice the Early Majority GPs to imagine themselves as part of a blossoming community. The Innovator and Early Adopter GPs in the school were primarily white foreigners, whose unusual disposition continued to reveal itself in the lack of "cheerleading" they felt compelled to execute on behalf of their school. Astrid's "thank God for racism" comment best sums up the attitude of the foreigners. They found a great school that wasn't bombarded with GPs competing to get in, which is why they got a spot, and they wanted to keep it that way. They didn't care if there were additional GPs at the school, nor, it seemed, did the principal. One of the few nonforeign GPs at the school, Maggie, offered what she remembered being the principal's explanation of why the school didn't offer tours. At a PTA meeting, Dr. Smith said to the parents: "My school is good. I've been there for 12 years. When I went to that first principal's meeting 12 years ago, people were like, 'Yeah, good luck to you at that school up there.' And now I go to the meetings, and people are like, 'Can we come? Can we do this? We want to see what you're doing!' And I'm like 'No, you can't come.'" Maggie went on to explain that Dr. Smith thinks "this is his property, and he takes a lot of pride in the school, and he doesn't think he needs to sell it to anybody. He thinks the school doesn't need to give tours because it is obviously a good place and they have nothing to prove."

This strategy of not offering tours is clearly slowing down the integration process of this Stage 2 school, making it more difficult for the Early Majority to consider it as an option. Without GP packed tours—a chance to see other GPs to gauge the interest, and be seen by other GPs as a potential school mate—rumors about the school possibly become a primary source of data. I interviewed a GP, Shayla, who told me that when she tried to enroll her daughter in this school, "the parent coordinator kept her out," because, as Shayla recounts, "They saw me as this crazy white lady and they didn't want me there." A couple of weeks later, I was talking to another GP, Vera, about this same school, and how it was starting to integrate, to which she responded, "Oh there are white people there? I'd heard they didn't want white people at that school." This almost verbatim quotation of another GP's impression of the school suggests that the GP grapevine is alive in this community, and it can dominate the school-choice discourse when the GP tour mobile doesn't make a stop and allow people to form their own impressions. The "school is changing" buzz, which has made its way into the neighborhood discourse of all of the other Stage 2 schools where GPs are staging tours and actively boosting the school, does not seem to exist at the same level for this school. While GPs talk about the school as having a good academic reputation and a fantastic principal, they rarely describe it as "changing."

At some level, it appears that protecting people from the hype generated through the school-touring process might be working to the advantage of this school. As the next chapter explores in detail, retaining Early Majority GPs in a Stage 2 school is a tremendous roadblock to tipping in. Part of why they leave is that the hype of the school doesn't match the reality. Thus, an unhyped school that only attracts the Early Majority GPs who do serious homework about a school and thus, perhaps, gain a more realistic picture of the school, might be more likely to retain these GPs, allowing the school to make it to Stage 3 of integration, albeit more slowly.

7

Retaining the Early Majority, A Crucial Step

Attracting Wave 3 gentry parents (GPs), the Early Majority, to Stage 2 schools is fairly easy when compared with the much more difficult task of retaining this group. Changing Schools don't become Diverse Schools, schools that have tipped in, unless the Early Majority stays and becomes a permanent part of the school community. This is a crucial point in the integration process for three reasons: (1) GPs in the Early Majority have different expectations for a school than their GP peers who were part of Waves 1 and 2; (2) Wave 3 GPs have a lower threshold for tolerating the various manifestations of the gentry/nongentry gap (G/NG Gap); and (3) unlike the Innovators and Early Adopters, Early Majority GPs aren't looking for reasons to stay, they are very willing to go if their child isn't getting a *good enough* education. The Early Majority enters the perceived "risky" situation of a Stage 2 school with a "safety net" to "manage the risks very closely" (Gladwell 2000, 198), which for these Wave 3 GPs is the knowledge that they have the ability to exit the school if it fails to meet their expectations.

Like all GPs, the Early Majority believes they have choices about how their children are educated. Innovators and Early Adopters are able to couch this belief within the larger goal of making a difference in their communities, as long as their children are happy and learning, and they can weigh the pros and cons of their situation accordingly, with a fairly high threshold for tolerating their own discomfort. However, Early Majority GPs appear to be far less adept at tolerating their own discomfort, and flee swiftly if the school just doesn't feel like the right fit for their family. They do not enter the school with any larger goal that can serve as a scaffold to support them through their discomfort. Lisbeth, an Innovator GP who was working very hard to improve her Stage 2 school and successfully brought in Wave 3 GPs, only to see them leave, was "very discouraged" by these different orientations, because, as she laments, "I felt like I don't want to be doing this either, this is not something that I think is great, but it's something that I feel needs to happen. I had become invested in other people that were in it, and I wasn't going to leave." She and others like her will persist under less than ideal conditions to achieve the goal of integration, whereas Wave 3 GPs, who are *not* like her, will quickly put in motion a plan to find another school for the following year at the first sign that their child isn't thriving, that there is too much yelling, that the school isn't quite what was promised, and that it "just isn't for them."

When Wave 3 GPs enter a Changing School, they are under the impression that the school has already changed from what it was, and that the G/NG Gap has been bridged. The successful boosting by the GPs on the inside gives the wrong impression of where the school is *really* at in terms of change. Lisbeth explains that "a lot of them expected it to already be done for them" because they had heard that the school was "changing." But, there is only so much that can change in a school in a short period of time, even if there is a vibrant school leader open to change working with an energetic group of GPs. As Timothy's disappointment taught him, "the idea of gentrifying a school is not just about being there in numbers, it's about changing the way the school looks at curriculum and education and discipline. A school can bring in a conflict resolution plan, they can add a lot of supports and enrichments. But you can't fire teachers, and you can't fire school aides, they're all under union protection. So trying to get people to buy into a curriculum that wasn't always there or trying to get them to talk to kids in a different way, that's really hard." Substantive change takes time and patience from the GPs who have different expectations for a school *and* a group of GPs that is large enough that it must be taken seriously. The third wave of GPs is necessary to create this "large enough" GP population.

Innovator and Early Adopter GPs can't be as honest as Timothy in their assessment of change and expect to attract Wave 3 GPs, which is why the school tours and cheerleading described in chapter 6 serve to mask the school's inadequacies so that the school really *can* change with additional GPs and additional time. However, masking problems is a risk. The Early Majority enters a Changing School and doesn't expect to have to deal with the discomfort of the G/NG Gap; their expectations are much higher than Waves 1 and 2, who are very aware of their superminority status and what this might entail. When confronted with many of the same issues that the Innovator and Early Adopter GPs experienced during the earlier stages of integration, Wave 3 GPs need *more* than faith in a competent and effective school leader working to bridge the gap. Oftentimes, they just want out.

Early Majority GPs Compared to Innovators and Early Adopters

The following example of "the recess problem" at a Stage 2 school illustrates the difference in how Wave 3 GPs respond to the G/NG Gap compared to their peers in Waves 1 and 2. In short, the "recess problem" arose because the children were not being allowed to go outside for recess when it got "too cold," which for the GPs was unreasonably defined as lower than 40 degrees. They thought it didn't make any sense for a variety of reasons ranging from the need for children to run around (according to all of the child development experts) to the arbitrariness of 40, since 32 degrees Fahrenheit is freezing. It also bothered them because the substitute activity was watching cartoons and various Disney movies in the auditorium. All of the GPs who told me this story were under the impression that the divide over whether to send kids out to recess when it was cold broke down along gentry/nongentry lines, with the GPs wanting recess all the time and the non-GPs not wanting their children outside when it is cold.

GP responses to "the recess problem" were distributed along the timeline of when they had entered the school. Innovator and Early Adopter GPs were constructively trying to find ways to solve the problem. Early Majority GPs were using the problem as a reason to leave the school. The principal, Dr. Jones, was listening to concerns from all sides, allowing open discussion of the issue, and *trying* to bridge the G/NG Gap. Margaret appreciated the principal's effort, and her response is representative of the mentality of Waves 1 and 2. After ranting to me about the stupidity of showing "Daddy Day Care" 12 times in a row, Margaret went on to explain how she simply purchased a slew of educational videos and gave them to the school, encouraging the principal to show these movies instead. She recognized that she might not win the recess battle right now when the GPs in the school were still a minority, so she looked for an acceptable solution, despite her annoyance.

Rhonda, an Early Majority GP in the same school, told me the same story, but it had a very different ending, an ending common among the Wave 3 GPs I interviewed. After complaining about how her son watched cartoons at school when he should have been moving his body and this simply shouldn't be OK, she said, "Um, so that annoyed me, and I commiserated with the other parents, and then we decided to re-apply to private school and ask our parents to help pay for it." That was it, she was leaving the school. She insisted it had nothing to do with her son being a minority, she wants her son to "feel like its normal" to be one of a few white kids. The recess issue was just some sort of signal to her, and others like her, that the type of education they were giving their children wasn't good enough, and Leslie claims that "if they had gone outside three times a day and nothing else had been different, I would probably have a really different opinion of the school."

Wave 3 GPs cannot tolerate manifestations of the G/NG Gap if they send the signal that a school just isn't "good enough," especially when these Early Majority GPs enter the school thinking that the G/NG Gap has already been bridged and everything is perfectly fine, within the boundaries of their expected norms. The recess example is just one of many stories Wave 3 GPs shared with me to explain why they left or were leaving their Stage 2 schools. Some anecdotes involved the same type of "yelling" described in chapter 5, but with an additional level of complaint about the school's overall system of discipline. The average Wave 3 GP does not like any type of discipline system that involves public humiliation. Classroom charts that tracked daily student behavior with color codes for different levels of goodness were common in Stage 2 schools. Rewards and punishments were attached to the weekly emergent pattern on the chart.

While Innovator and Early Adopter GPs responded to this type of chart with a positive spin—some praised the teachers and principal for having a preemptive and constructive handle on discipline problems; some enjoyed celebrating their child's rewards as a group with other gentry families, viewing the system as one of communal good will—the Early Majority GPs were generally very uncomfortable with the charts and how they perceived them to be impacting their children. Rhonda's son would often come home from school talking about which kids in his class were "good" and which kids were "bad," something she "hated" because she thought it was "divisive," and she didn't want her son "thinking about his classmates like that." Amanda was similarly concerned by what her Stage 2 school's discipline system was doing to her son, who had spent two years at a progressive preschool where "there was no discipline system in place" and "discussing problems" was the norm. Like Rhonda's son, he was now bringing home stories of "rule breaking" and passing judgment on his classmates. Amanda "didn't like the person he was becoming," and she abruptly withdrew him from school mid-year (It was pre-K, so she simply kept him home until he could start kindergarten elsewhere.) Monica also found this type of disciplining to be "hostile" to learning, an intense reaction probably enhanced by what she described as a kindergarten teacher "who screamed all the time." And

Jackie simply found the "red, yellow, green" system "too authoritarian," and unexpectedly harsh for pre-K.

The School Is Too Traditional

Like Jackie, Wave 3 GPs were often surprised by how authoritarian and traditional a Stage 2 school ended up being, and they were disappointed by both pedagogy and school culture. The typical Wave 3 GP expects her Stage 2 school to be different than it ends up being. When I asked Leslie, a Wave 3 GP, what was appealing to her about the other schools she was applying to in an attempt to leave her Stage 2 school, she replied, "These schools seem to be really living the idea of progressive education, not just sort of saying it. Which is sort of what I feel like P.S.____is doing. You go on the tour, you see the school, you hear what the principal has to say, and you think it's like, 'Wow, this is really great energy, they do a lot of field trips, they do a lot of art, and they have a gym. There is definitely a lot in the right direction.' The projects they do, the kids are very involved and they are doing all of these projects, but you know there still just seems to be this pervasive, 'Just sit down and do what I say,' a lot of traditional minded behavior in the classroom where it's like, teachers yelling at kids to sit down. I just hear this shouting going on that really bothers me. And I don't know whether it's just me." Rhonda, also on the way out, shared Leslie's view about the difference between hype and reality in a Stage 2 school. When she decided to enroll her son, she "thought it was all about how everybody was involved, and doing stuff for the school to raise money," but after spending a couple of months there, she concluded that "it didn't feel like anybody really was. There's a different perception of what's going on, and it's... It was more about potential than the reality in the school. I think that the hype was about how great the school *could* be, and how far it had come. It probably *is* a lot better, but I don't know what it was like before, I wasn't there. So, for me it was like, this school that we ended up at, with friends, we all just felt like the school wasn't all there."

Changing a School

While the disappointment over reality not meeting expectations is one of the primary reasons Wave 3 GPs exit their Stage 2 schools en masse, whether they stay or go also seems to depend, in part, on whether Wave 3 GPs think a school can be further changed, or even should be further changed. Innovator and Early Adopter GPs consider changing a school to be precisely the point. They want to change it demographically *and* change the school culture and pedagogy to reflect something more appealing to their GP cohort. They go in and try to slowly push the school toward a GP ideal in order to attract more GPs. Integration will not happen unless they can attract more GPs, and they know they can't easily sell the school as is, they must sell it as "changing," and engage in activities that they think will, substantively, change the school. Wave 3 GPs, on the other hand, enter a school thinking it is a certain way—already more of the GP ideal—and when it isn't, they don't know whether trying to change it is something they want to do, can do, or should do. They were comfortable thinking that the school had already been changed by their GP predecessors, but when faced with having to do some of the uncomfortable work themselves, they question it. They don't appear to see themselves in that role.

Innovator and Early Adopter GPs seem to be quite energized by the idea of changing something. To do so would enhance their status as unique-seeking individuals and benefit their communities. Jeremy's response to meeting with the new principal of his neighborhood Stage 0 school, Dr. Brown, is indicative of how Innovator GPs talk about change and their role in the process. He excitedly described how Dr. Brown told him, "Bring the kids, and you can have any school you want!" Dr. Brown educated her own kids at a progressive school in the city, and that was the model she was aspiring toward. However, as he explained, "she is in a community with a student body, which implies a parent body of a certain type, and she has to work with that parent body. And so if the parent body changes, she'll change. But as long as a certain parent body expects teachers to be called by their last name, and they come in uniforms, and homework is viewed as a sign of true education, she can't on her own change the parent body. She can work with the students, but can't change the parents, and therefore she needs a parent body that is interested in that, and that is where we come in." Jeremy was ready to step into that role of "changing parent" with zest, never doubting that change *could* happen, or that he should be a part of making it happen.

Standing in sharp contrast, Early Majority GPs are usually filled with doubt when it comes to change. They not only don't see themselves as agents of change, as Jeremy does, but also aren't even sure change is appropriate or possible. Carrie was very explicit in her opposition to being a part of change, explaining how, among neighborhood GPs, "there was a lot of talk of, 'We can change the school,' and I just didn't think that was very... you cannot choose a school with the premise that you're going to change it. You need to choose a school believing that it's the right school for your child. Right then. The day you walk in the door." Leslie also reflected openly about change, and how "uncomfortable" she is "as a white parent, to feel like I'm going in saying, 'Do it this way.'"

Whereas Leslie was beset by discomfort, Innovator and Early Adopter GPs appear quite comfortable taking a stance that a more child-centered, progressive school culture is better for children, all the while remaining much more tolerant of a not-so-child-centered school culture as they work to bring in more GPs and move the school in the direction they want it to go. Early Majority GPs, however, aren't as sure that they know one way of schooling is better than another. They know it is better for *them* and what they want for *their* children, but they don't think it is their place to push this way of thinking on a community that may think differently. Maybe because they *aren't* visionaries, they can't see their school as being different than it is because of anything they themselves might do. If the school hasn't already changed, they consider leaving so, as Leslie put it, they "can be more comfortable in a different environment." They never entered a school seeking the thrill of instigating change. They bought into the school as an acceptable choice *as is*, based on incomplete information.

The Eventual Exit of Wave 3 GPs

Wave 3 GPs can be quick to leave Stage 2 schools, usually finding other options for the following school year. For all of the reasons described above, many of these parents aren't happy enough with the quality of the education. More importantly, they often don't think their children are happy enough. Most GP stories of leaving a Stage 2 school ended or began with the fact that the gentry child was believed to be unhappy. Leslie started our interview by telling me that she was seriously considering leaving her Stage 2 school because her son "had a really difficult time adjusting to the school. It went on longer than it seemed to go on for any of the other kids. He really kind of, he went through this hysterical place, he was screaming and crying, by the third week of school, he was still holding onto me, and it was really upsetting." Because her son "had been fine in daycare," and had friends in the class who he knew prior to kindergarten, she attributed his being "miserable for two months" to the school itself.

Lisbeth's observations of the countless Wave 3 GPs who have come and gone from her Stage 2 school suggest that Leslie's reaction is common. Lisbeth attributes the continual leaving to the fact that "there is always something to complain about in public school," and Wave 3 GPs don't have enough confidence in a Changing School to write off a child's problems as not being specifically related to the school. Despite having the resolve of an Innovator GP, she empathized with this fear: "When my kids act up, I don't know whether it's the school, my husband and

I, our parenting? You don't know what it is, you have so many things to choose from that could be the cause, like at least if you've got them in a school you can trust, you can write that off the list—probably not the school. Maybe it's the kid. But you don't know whether the child is running away because of the child or what is happening at school." Wave 3 GPs who leave simply don't have enough trust in a Changing School for them to write off unhappy children as having nothing to do with the quality of the school, nor do they have the same degree of commitment to social justice as Lisbeth to keep working to improve the school in the face of doubt.

Retaining the Early Majority

Wave 3 GPs who persist seem to have found a way to trust in the legitimacy of the institution. This trust appears to be easier to find when the GPs are concentrated in an enclave program that persists past pre-K, and the GP energy feels more like a laser than a 60-watt glow. Schools in this study that have had the easiest time retaining the Early Majority GPs have enclave programs harnessing the group together—both Gifted and Talented (G&T) and Dual Language (DL). The two schools in this study that appear to be stuck in Stage 2 of integration, because Early Majority GPs keep leaving, have enclave pre-Ks, which help bring in GPs to the school, but neither have enclave programs beyond that first year keeping the GPs tightly together.[1] Their energy becomes thinly spread through the multiple general-education classrooms, making the G/NG Gap more difficult to mask. It is also harder for GPs to form a "tight-knit community" when the GP families are not interacting on a daily basis in the enclave classroom. However, despite the success of enclave programs in keeping GPs in integrating schools, they are problematic if the schools are to ever truly be considered "diverse," a dilemma that will be explored in greater detail in chapter 8.

More Than One Enclave Complicates GP Retention

Enclaves are also potentially problematic in the integration process if there is more than one enclave as a point of entry into the school. At one Stage 2 school, a large number of GPs entered the school together in the pre-K program. They reported having a very positive experience, and all of them claim they would have continued in the school if there had not been a G&T program that started in kindergarten. The G&T program ended up dividing the GPs into those whose children tested into the program, and those whose children did not test into the program. As Patricia explains, "It created this whole thing in the school, which was, 'Did your kid get into the gifted program? Did you get the results?' And the school changed from this nice, neighborhood, low-key place to go, to like, 'Did you get into Gifted and Talented? Did you get in?' It changed the environment so much, for me as a parent, that it really started putting me off," so much so that she ended up leaving the school. Her child did not test into the program, and she suddenly felt relegated to second-class status, because "once they had that division, and once you start to get categorized, who doesn't want to be G and T? It's not like you're going to go in there saying, 'Oh no, no, we want general!' You always, it's just human nature I think, just that it existed." Monica had the same experience. Although happy in pre-K, when her daughter didn't test into the G&T, she felt like "this class system was created at the school." She believes the existence of the G&T program is "why this school doesn't work, it really pits people against each other." Even within a family. Brigitta refused to keep her twin sons in the school, despite a positive pre-K experience, because one of them "tested into G&T and the other didn't," and she "couldn't have one boy be the smart one and the other one be the less smart one, which was preposterous to begin with."

GPs whose children didn't test into G&T were further deflated by the fact that the G&T program at this particular school had a class size almost half as large as the general education program. Monica, who kept her daughter in the general education class for a year before finding another option at a different school, explains how she and her GP friend were "freaking out all year, feeling like second-class citizens, because we have 29 kids, they have 15." This stark difference in resourcing made the G&T program clearly the better place to be, and GPs were unwilling to remain in a school where they were obviously "the have nots." Even the GPs whose children tested into the G&T program and happily moved from pre-K to G&T kindergarten acknowledged the divisive nature of the G&T program. Faith, despite benefiting from her daughter's placement in G&T, seemed genuine when she said she'd "prefer they didn't have G and T at the school, that way it would be really integrated, and everyone would move around and get to know each other and learn to grow together." Perhaps they would, or perhaps all gentry children would exit the school, not just those who didn't test into G&T. Every school has its own unique personality, and many factors play a role in determining what exactly happens when a school tries to integrate, and how Early Majority GPs respond to the challenges that integration brings.

Integrated versus Integrating

To summarize, Wave 3 GPs do not have the same kind of tolerance for discomfort compared to Innovator and Early Adopter GPs, and it is very hard to convince Wave 3 GPs that they should stay in the school and tolerate something when they believe they are entitled, by virtue of their level of education and own roots from middle- or upper-middle-class families, to something better. Wave 1 and 2 GPs are able to successfully connect Early Majority GPs to the idea of giving a Stage 2 school a try through their effective school tours and overall boosting, but they are often unable to translate to them why *staying* in a subpar situation (i.e. their school preferences are not being met) makes sense. While both groups want integra*ted* experiences, only one group is able to easily engage in the integrat*ing* process. They think differently. Astrid, an Innovator GP, ranted about the inanity of GPs who "send their child to an Upper East Side school so they can have a Martin Luther King experience" when they could just send their child to the Stage 2 neighborhood school, "where you are actually integrating a school." She can't understand why a GP would "take their white child out of the neighborhood to have an integrated experience in another neighborhood. 'What's the point?'" she asks. "Go and integrate the school in your neighborhood!" She fails to see the difference in the act of *integrating* versus the experience of being in an *integrated* environment. Or, perhaps she refuses to acknowledge the very real difference in experience, possibly so she herself does not waver in her Innovator resolve to integrate her neighborhood school.

8

A Diverse School

Diverse Schools are schools that have successfully tipped in. What it means to be diverse in strict demographic terms varies from school to school, and will be explored in more detail later in this chapter. For the purposes of this study, however, a school successfully reaches Stage 3 of integration and becomes a Diverse School once it retains its Early Majority gentry parents (GPs), and GPs start describing the school to one another as diverse. Since diversity is an important preference for most GPs, the term diverse within the GP network is an important signifier. In this one word, GPs know that their peer group approves of the school, and they can enroll their children in the diverse school with little worry. Even Late Majority GPs—the skeptics who will never try anything until the most respected members of their GP peer group have tried it first and given their stamp of approval—will enroll their children in a diverse school. The word signals both racial diversity—that is, a white child will not stand out—and socioeconomic diversity—that is, the school has a large enough middle-class presence that the school has a middle-class culture.

Ellen, a GP and education activist who has thought a great deal about the integration process, believes there is "clearly a tipping point, a number where everyone identifies, where the feeling changes from it being their school to being our school." The evidence from this study suggests that the "number where people identify" and "the feeling" GPs get from a school differs depending on the type of GP. Thus, a school can only be defined as having tipped in once the most resistant GPs, the Late Majority, decide they are comfortable. *Their* perceptual point of tipping in is key. Since a successful tipping in process concentrates the gentry children in the lower grades first, with the gentry presence expanding a grade each year, a school that is integrating will see each successive kindergarten class with a larger percent of GPs than the previous year. The actual numbers do not provide a definitive measure of diversity, there is a range in what Late Majority GPs will perceive to be an acceptable demographic mix. The numbers reveal some interesting parameters of what it means, in New York City in the year 2010, for a school to be considered diverse.

Characteristics of a Stage 3, Diverse School

The demographic breakdown of public school children in New York City is approximately as follows[1]:

- White: 14 percent
- Black: 32 percent
- Hispanic: 40 percent
- Asian: 13 percent
- Other: 1 percent
- Free and Reduced Lunch Recipients: 75 percent

Within the constraints of this demographic reality, where seven of ten children are black or Hispanic and receive free and reduced lunch, the word diversity, for most GPs, appears to realistically conform to what is possible. An analysis of the Diverse Schools that GPs in this study consistently ranked as top choices on their lists of acceptable public schools shows a wide range of what they are willing to consider as diverse. Table 8.1 specifically looks at the acceptable diversity quotient in a zone school, while table 8.2 delineates what is considered diverse when the school is a progressive school of choice.[2]

The proportion of white children in these Diverse Schools was as low as 13 percent (roughly the same proportion of whites in the city using public schools), and the average white percent was in the mid-30s. Because the Diverse Schools in this study have a healthy racial mix of the nonwhite student population, the perception of school diversity is

Table 8.1 Demographic breakdown of *zone schools* gentry parents consider "Diverse Schools"[3]

	P.S.1003	P.S.1004	P.S.1005	P.S.1006
White	54	13	28	41
Black	17	30	43	40
Hispanic	21	49	24	11
Asian	7	7	5	7
Free lunch	19	65	66	45

Table 8.2 Demographic breakdown of *progressive public choice schools* (PCS) gentry parents consider "Diverse Schools"[4]

	PCS1	PCS2	PCS3	PCS4	PCS5	PCS6	PCS7	PCS8	PCS9
White	47	33	36	34	35	36	32	24	15
Black	19	43	30	13	19	11	18	38	49
Hispanic	25	6	22	36	27	32	23	25	23
Asian	6	2	8	13	13	13	13	5	2
Free lunch	23	30	23	48	42	55	55	62	77

likely grounded partly in the fact that no one racial group dominates the school's culture, with the exception of two Diverse Schools that are majority white. Schools in this study in the early stages of integration that did *not* have a diverse nonwhite population, and instead were dominated by one racial group, seemed to be having a harder time moving from one stage of integration to another. Changing perceptions of a school appears to be harder when the nonwhite diversity isn't there. Jessica, an Innovator GP who was having a fairly easy time attracting the next wave of GPs to her Stage 1 Catalyzed school, thought it was, in part, due to the "healthier mix of kids" than other neighborhood schools that were almost 100 percent black. She uncomfortably described this reality to me: "My school is very Hispanic and a real mix of other things, rather than being...I mean, P.S.____ is very African American. I mean 98%, yeah. Whereas P.S.____ [her school] I think eighty-something percent of the kids are below the poverty line. But they're not all...socioeconomically they're unified, but not in...you know the cultural diversity there is much greater. Which I like."

The average poverty rate in these Diverse Schools, that is, the number of children who received free or reduced lunch, was in the mid-40s, but as high as 77 percent. These free-lunch numbers paint a complicated picture of what it means to be socioeconomically diverse, and do not necessarily support existing research. Kahlenberg's (2001) work on school integration and the benefits of socioeconomic mixing indicates a *majority* nonpoor school is necessary to assure a school culture that is middle class. However, 5 out of the 13 diverse schools mentioned by GPs as acceptable school options have poverty rates significantly greater than 50 percent, suggesting the 50 percent threshold, while perhaps desirable, is not *necessary* to establish a middle-class culture in a school, at least in terms of the average GP comfort zone. A lower number appears to be possible due to the way GPs involve themselves in their children's schools.

GPs Appear to Exert Disproportionate Influence on a School's Culture

My research suggests that GPs exert a disproportionate influence on a school's culture through their assumption of leadership positions in the school and their ability to raise money from the small percent of wealthier families who are there. GPs also have a tendency to act as "helicopter parents," as Margaret described herself and her friends, since they are often hovering protectively around their child's school for a significant period of time, dropping off their kids in the classroom if they are allowed to do so, picking their children up, asking lots of questions, forming close relationships with the teachers, and keeping close tabs on what is actually happening in the school on a day-to-day basis. Brie called GPs "little energizer bunnies," and this description seems quite apt.

Ivy, one of the Innovator GPs in this study who is working to move her currently Stage 2 school toward Stage 3 status, embodies this "energizer bunny" ethos that demonstrates how a very small group can impact a school's culture. When Ivy realized that her school didn't have a fundraising committee, because no one had ever asked *her* for money, she just started one. She saw a void, and she took steps to fill it on her own. Similarly, Timothy, after enrolling his child in the Stage 0 neighborhood school, immediately told the principal he "was willing to write grants and stuff," because he had done grant writing in his last job. GPs are part of a power culture that doesn't question whether asserting their talent is appropriate. They simply insert themselves if they think they can be of value and of service. Joanie, an Early Adopter, described the flurry of activity when she entered her Stage 1 Catalyzed School as GPs got to work inserting themselves: "So that first week, we were starting to get really involved with the PTA, Sunday night, I was working on a survey to the other parents that we were going to distribute in backpacks: are you interested in after school? Would you be willing to pay for after school? How about for classroom assistants? Because they had no infrastructure whatsoever in terms of a parent body."

Melanie, another Early Adopter GP at Joanie's school, described how the first PTA meeting she attended was "kind of not structured...there were no treasurers." She goes on to explain how a GP friend "volunteered to be a treasurer, and another parent from the dual language class also volunteered, and we just kind of took over." Her description of the PTA fundraising difference after the GP "take over" was staggering, if accurate: "maybe $400" before the GPs inserted and asserted themselves, "probably $30,000" the first year after the takeover. By the second year after the GPs took control of the PTA, they raised $50,000 in giving alone, with an additional $17,000 from a raffle. And this was all before the second annual school fair where Melanie thought they would raise close to $30,000. Many GPs referenced the type of fundraising they do for their schools, always coming back to Diverse schools and the kind of money they raise as their benchmark for fundraising success. Marcia's comment best summarizes the general GP sentiment about fundraising in the public schools: "Unfortunately that's how it is in New York City, that it's the parent body that participates is how you get to keep all these extracurricular activities."

Consequences of Diversity: Losing Title I Funding

The type of fundraising GPs are able to do becomes especially important during the tipping in process, as one consequence of a school becoming diverse can be the loss of Title I[5] funding when the school's poverty rate declines. Some of the principals described in chapter 6, who were openly resistant to welcoming the new GP demographic to their school, specifically spoke about their feared loss of Title I status. Timothy described his tour of a Stage 1 school, where the principal, Dr. Caraway, "made these sweeping statements about how white people were coming in and threatening her Title I status." Lisbeth heard the same complaints from Dr. Caraway, but tried to be sympathetic about this "paranoia." Lisbeth could understand the fear of "a bunch of wealthy people dabbling around in her school," leading to the loss of Title I status, without the "wealthy" then being able to make up for it through their own contributions. "Catch 22" was a fitting term used by Lisbeth as she analyzed the problem: "If the school becomes successful enough, you don't get that money anymore, and Title I gives you a lot of money! But you don't necessarily have enough parents to fund raise in a really aggressive way, and so it's, so then you suffer. You have to make sure that the people who are coming in are going to work really hard to raise funds, and if they don't really love the school they aren't going to do that work." Although the fundraising difference described by Melanie upon the entrance of the GPs to her school was hefty, not all schools in the early stages of integration are necessarily going to have as wealthy or committed a GP population as were concentrated in Melanie's school.

It can be a serious problem for principals struggling to meet the expectations of a more vocal group of power parents when their budgets are slashed because of the very presence of these parents. Title I money can buy lower class sizes, something that parents love even if it isn't necessarily a top preference (about 20 percent of the GPs in this study specifically mentioned class size as important, but it was never their central consideration). Astrid, a foreign GP who loved her Stage 2 school, in part, because of the small class size and the fact that "the kids have space," was very aware of the potential downside of more GPs in the school, and she humorously suggested that they needed to keep the neighborhood GPs out of the school for another year, until her second child was in the pre-K, and "then we can integrate and be all lovey dovey."

The Fundraising Dilemma in a Diverse School: How Inclusive Must an Event Be?

Further exacerbating this potential Title I problem faced by principals on tight budgets is the fact that schools going through the tipping in process and becoming more diverse have to be sensitive to *how* they are raising money. While these schools may now have a group of relatively wealthy parents who are able to pay a certain amount for an event or for PTA dues, the poorer families in the school might feel shut out of the school's new culture if they can't afford the ticket price or the dues. At Faith's school, a Stage 2 school, "people were up in arms" when the PTA wanted to raise the dues from $5 to $10. She laughed at how the citywide gifted school's PTA down the street had suggested dues of $500, and her PTA couldn't even ask for $10 without offending people.

Kate, who headed her Stage 2 school's fundraising committee, understood why there was a need to be sensitive to the possibility of seeming exclusive, but also thought those who insisted on making everything "inclusive" were missing the point. "It's the *fundraising* committee!" she said with exasperation. "I'm sorry, but if we're having a charity auction, I want parents there who can pay a lot of money, it's not a social event, it's to raise money for all of the children. My goal is raise money, not entertain people." Kate lost this battle, and was frustrated by the constraints placed on her by the principal and other GPs at the school who "wanted everyone to feel like they're welcome at everything." She didn't think this was necessary, and described a Gospel event at the school that she didn't have any interest in attending. She "didn't go to the organizers and say, 'This sucks, I have no interest in this, don't have it,'" she just didn't go, and "didn't feel unwelcome," because, "You can't please everybody all the time, and I think there are times when that is not necessary."

Kate effectively rationalized the argument for holding exclusive events for the good of the school, but most GPs don't want to be viewed as elitist, and fundraisers that exclude an entire class of people at the school because of their price tag will likely be viewed as elite, potentially exacerbating race and class tensions that are already simmering underneath the surface of schools going through the process of integration. Schools going through the tipping in process may lose Title I funding before they have expanded the middle- and upper-middle-class population in the school *enough* to fill the funding gap through parent contributions. This will most likely happen in due time as the integrating community matures, but the transition can be financially complicated.

Are Apartheid Schools Diverse?

Schools that are integrated at the school level but not at the classroom level, the so called "apartheid schools"—where there is a predominantly white gifted and talented (G&T) program and a predominantly nonwhite general education program—are *not* considered diverse when talked about by GPs. As described in chapter 2, the G&T programs in these schools are merely considered *options* for most GPs if they are unable to secure a spot at a school they consider diverse. Most GPs enter apartheid schools reluctantly, and they would never call them diverse schools, even if they find a happy niche within them. Apartheid schools can potentially go through their own tipping in process and *become* diverse schools, if the general education classes in these schools become diverse as a result of the school becoming a popular G&T enclave.

Evidence from this study suggests that schoolwide integration *can* come from seeding the GPs in a G&T enclave. The middle-class presence that is concentrated in the G&T program can have a palpable effect on the overall school culture, and the school will become more appealing to GPs even if their child doesn't test into the G&T Program. For example, the G&T GPs at one formerly segregated school raise thousands of dollars to pay for classroom assistants in *every* class, not just the G&T classes, reducing teacher/student ratios for all the children. This type of additional resourcing over the years is now making the general education program at this particular school attractive to GPs who are shut out of the G&T program (i.e., their child doesn't test in), but zoned for the school. It is not a *first* choice, but it is now an option whereas before it wasn't.

There are GPs who might be considered "Gen. Ed. Innovators." This type of GP is more similar to Early Majority GPs than to Innovator GPs. They are bucking the trend of their GP peer group by enrolling their children in the general education classroom in an apartheid school, but the move feels much less risky, because the overall school culture has changed due to the large presence of the G&T families. The Gen. Ed. Innovator is thus less committed to change, unique seeking, and social justice, and more committed to convenience within their comfort zone. Karen, a Gen. Ed. Innovator, enrolled her son in the general education program at her zone school because he didn't get a spot in the school's popular G&T program and instead was offered a G&T spot at a school 30 blocks from her house, a school she describes as "a failing school, except for G and T." So, with neither option particularly desirable, she chose the general education spot in her zone school, even though it was considered an apartheid school, because the school was conveniently located and not considered to be a failing school either in or out of the G&T classroom. The overall culture of the school was middle class due to the popular G&T program, and she felt comfortable enough to "see how it goes."

Other GPs take the leap away from G&T into general education through the sibling dilemma. Karen explains this trend: "What I'm finding very interesting and what I'm seeing happen is you have more and more siblings whose older child is in G and T, and the younger child either does not place or does not get a spot at P.S.____, but the parents are sending the younger sibling into Gen. Ed. because (a) it makes your life a little easier, and (b) we have an excellent principal who started last year." Just as an excellent principal appears to be necessary to bridge the gentry/nongentry gap, an excellent principal also seems to be able to help bridge the G&T/non-G&T gap in an apartheid school. The principal in this particular school is described as "wanting her school to be a place like P.S.____ (a wildly popular diverse school)," and is making sure "her teachers are provided with the appropriate resources" so that all of the children in the school are learning and progressing. The principal, thus far, has been able to make the Gen. Ed. Innovators feel just as valuable as the G&T parents.

Gwen, another Gen. Ed. Innovator, also sees the sibling trend happening, and thinks it is great that the parents' attitudes are changing. She explained to me that having a child in both programs "opens up minds" to not seeing G&T as the only option, and thinks this is "really good for the school." Gwen is right that changing perceptions is the first step toward integration. GPs need to be able to visualize their child in an option for it to move onto their list of acceptable choices, and this takes Innovators paving the way. It is very difficult for most GPs to imagine a schooling option that is not currently being utilized by a peer.

In apartheid schools, Gen. Ed. Innovators can easily push the general education classroom onto the list of acceptable options, especially for other families in the school who may have a child in G&T but are struggling with what to do for their second child. Ava, a GP who had serious reservations about sending her son to the G&T program at his apartheid school, but "definitely would not have enrolled him" in the general education program at the school, enrolled her daughter in the general education program three years later. She had a deep comfort level at the school after three years with her son in the G&T program, she knew a few of the Gen. Ed. Innovators at the school, and she was now able to make the mental leap into imagining her daughter in the general education program.

If this type of trend continues, it is easy to imagine this apartheid school losing its reputation and becoming diverse. However, as long as a G&T program is in place, it may prevent a school from ever achieving the label, "diverse." As explored in chapter 2, if a school has a hierarchy, no GP wants to be at the bottom. The Gen. Ed. Innovators I interviewed, despite their happiness in the non-G&T program, were all still planning to retest their child for G&T. As Ava explained, "I don't want one kid in G&T and one kid not in G&T, because once they figure it out, I am afraid of how that will impact their relationship as siblings, with one always thinking he is smarter than the other." Lucy purposely kept her third child, a sibling of two G&T enrollees, out of the school's general education program, even though she "saw nothing different about it" except the demographics, because she didn't want to be put in the position of feeling like she had to retest her child every year, and she knew she would feel that pressure, based on her impressions of the parents who had kids in both programs. As she describes: "They are spending all their efforts prepping their kids for testing, and I didn't want to be in that position where every year, I'm stressed over testing her, and then I'm either happy that she got in, or upset that she didn't get in, and praying that her friends didn't get in either so that we can all still stick together. I've seen enough people in that boat that I didn't want to be that person. And I didn't want to put that pressure on her. I wanted her to be set and be happy where we are and not do that to her."

G&T Programs create a division that can be very uncomfortable both within families and between families. Even a principal providing equal resourcing cannot erase the negative stigma of not being G&T in a school with this hierarchy. Thus, while it appears that G&T programs can be helpful in seeding a middle-class culture in a school and putting the resources in place to eventually lure in GPs to the general education program, an apartheid school will never be considered diverse until it eliminates its G&T program. Schools with large numbers of Gen. Ed. Innovators should consider eliminating their G&T program, removing the G&T scaffolding that helped move the school to a viable middle-class option, allowing these schools to become diverse.

Are Schools with Dual Language Programs Also Apartheid Schools?

Dual language (DL) programs, while also responsible for creating somewhat exclusive enclaves of GPs, do not create as stark of a race/class division in their schools, and thus do not seem to inspire allegations of apartheid. None of the GPs in this study spoke disparagingly of schools housing DL programs as apartheid schools, even if the DL enclaves tended to be much whiter than the rest of the school. Since the ideal DL program requires a 50/50 mix of native and nonnative speakers, Spanish DL programs will have a large number of Hispanic children in the class, making them almost impossible to label as white enclaves, like G&T programs. French DL language programs will likely be whiter than Spanish DL programs, but still much more diverse than a typical G&T classroom. Melanie, when asked about the diversity of the French DL class at her Stage 1 school, responded, "You know what, at first I was like, 'Oh, wow, it's really white, I mean, compared to the rest of the school.' But I think it's actually just a better balance. We have at least five or six African American children in there. There are kids of mixed race, for example Asian and black parents. There's just, there's a good mix in there, I must say. I mean, I don't feel like it's all of one." Her phrase, "compared to the rest of the school," is very important. If there is a significant percentage of white children in any one class, of course it will stand out. But DL classes appear to be far more mixed than G&T classes, and this mixture, in addition to a screening process viewed by GPs as far more reasonable than G&T screening programs, prevents DL classes from causing the same peer allegations of apartheid. In a DL school, there is less of an implicit hierarchy.

That said, schools where the GPs will *only* enroll their children in the DL program, and not in the general education program, cannot yet be called diverse. Just like in schools where there are G&T programs, schools housing enclaves of GPs in DL programs must go through their own within-school tipping in process to be considered diverse. Like their counterparts in G&T schools, these "Monolingual Innovators" are the first in their peer group to venture outside of the DL enclave into the monolingual classroom to help set the stage for a school's complete integration. Trista might be considered a Monolingual Innovator in her school where the GPs have primarily congregated in the DL enclave. She recognizes the "definite divide" between the DL enclave and the monolingual classes (or "English stream" as she likes to call them), demographically, but when she didn't get a DL placement for her son, she enrolled him in the monolingual program without worrying about any kind of stigma because he was non-DL, telling me, "I was fine with it. I was like, 'You know, okay. You know what, we'll just go. Because I really like the school.'"

A demographic divide is different from a hierarchical divide, and G&T is clearly hierarchical in a way that DL is not. The school itself was giving off a "great vibe," due to the GP explosion in the DL programs. The GPs were giving tours and attracting crowds at the tours, and this was enough to make Trista feel comfortable about the school as a whole. And she called her son's class "diverse," describing it as "diverse in every sense of the word. We're talking about nationality, ethnicity, socio-economic, the whole gamut."

Because there is not a stigma attached to being a non-DL child, schools that successfully attract GPs to their DL enclaves appear to be able to go through a within-school tipping in process fairly quickly. Although she only entered her Stage 1 school because of the DL enclave she was able to be a part of, and never would have enrolled her daughter in the monolingual program, Melanie saw a tremendous shift in GP attitudes after only a couple of years. She described her school, today, as place "where people didn't care if they were in the dual language program, they just want to be in the school."

Diversity Is Fraught

Diverse Schools, despite being the goal of the tipping in process, and despite their desirability to GPs, are not without problems. As Shawn reminded me during our interview, "Diversity is fraught!" Schools that are truly diverse force contact between people from very different backgrounds, and that can be uncomfortable. Even if GPs perceive a middle-class school culture and a desirable environment for their children because they have come to dominate the vibe of the school, non-GPs do not necessarily welcome the changes, and there can still be some of the kind of gentry/nongentry tension that was manifest in schools in the earlier stages of integration. In a Diverse School, the tension loses its power to heavily influence the school-choice decision-making process of GPs, but it remains. A handful of GPs I interviewed who had eventually transferred from early stage integrating schools to Diverse Schools, shared anecdotes in the course of our conversation that clearly had them pondering the meaning and impact of diversity.

Sondra, whose son attends Public Choice School (PCS) 2, recalled going to the open house for the school, and feeling so "appreciative" that the school's director acknowledged that "diversity is our greatest strength, but also our greatest challenge." She explained, "I appreciated that she was honest about it. Because that *is* our biggest challenge here, but nobody talks about it. Nobody. It's the huge elephant in the room, nobody talks about it." It wasn't clear to her why no one talks about it, beyond the obvious fact that conversations about race and class are not easy. Karen told me a story about her son coming home from his Diverse School and telling her, "Johnny's daddy is in prison. He was tricked, Mommy." To which she responded, "Oh! I see." She then earnestly asked me, "How do you, what do you do with that?" She didn't know what answer would best help her son and herself deal with the diversity of life experiences. She didn't have the language.

Monica, whose daughters are at PCS 4, vividly remembered an interaction she had with an African American grandmother who volunteers frequently at the school. The grandmother said to her, "Well, you know, when the school first started I was in the neighborhood and I was protesting it because I knew there was gonna be too many white people," which left Monica speechless. As a comedian, her instinct was to joke with the woman and say, "What's wrong with white people? You got a problem?" But instead, she recognized, for the first time, the genuine fear the nongentry have of losing their school, and she didn't say anything. So the grandmother continued, "Well, don't you realize that is looks like there's a lot of white kids in the lower grades?" To which Monica replied, "Well, you know, it's truly diverse. Like, we have a Chinese kid, we have an Indian kid, we have a Greek kid, we have white kids, but we have European kids...We have black kids...Um, it's truly diverse. That's what diversity is. It doesn't mean there are no white people there." She didn't know if this argument had any effect on the grandmother's thinking, but she was still, clearly, somewhat unsettled by the interaction.

Ellen had a similar experience at PCS 5 while interacting with the security guard who worked for the more traditional, segregated public school that shared the building with PCS 5. When Ellen questioned the security guard about whether a lunch sack Ellen had found in the cafeteria might belong to one of their students, that is, did the guard recognize the initials on the bag, the guard replied, "Ugh. That belongs to PCS 5." Ellen responded with, "Well, you didn't even look at the initials. How do you know?" And the guard said, directly, "Because our kids don't bring their lunch." This moment crystallized the meaning of diversity for Ellen, and she remembers thinking, "'Oh, right. Right. Right there. You take the free school lunch. You don't pack organic tofu and hummus. Right. Oh, right.' Those are the things that no matter what we talk about, you know, people know the difference."

9

Tipping In

Tipping in—the integration of a segregated school in a gentrifying neighborhood through the school-choice patterns of gentry parents (GPs)—happens through a chain of actions and reactions of different types of GPs, each with a different threshold for tolerating their own minority status, each with a different idea about whether they *can* and *should* try to change a school to better match their preferences. To summarize, tipping in starts when the district public school options that match GP school preferences—schools that are diverse and progressive—all reach capacity. In response to the scarcity of preferred options, Innovator GPs—GPs who enjoy being different from their peers and/or have a strong commitment to social justice—find a neighborhood school that is not considered a failure by any measure other than being segregated, and that has some sort of enclave program where they can congregate—a Gifted and Talented (GT), Dual Language (DL), or preschool program—and they use various strategies to solve the collective action problem so that their children are entering the school as a small group, not alone.

If the Innovator GPs perceive that they are a welcome addition to the school community by the principal, and the principal appears to be willing to listen to their suggestions for school change and can successfully bridge the gentry/nongentry culture gap (G/NG Gap) that exists between the new type of parents who are coming in and the existing parent community, Innovator GPs will keep their children enrolled in the school. They will work hard to raise money for the school, volunteer their time in the school, and do outreach to other neighborhood GPs to bring more gentry children into the school the following year. Early Adopter GPs—similarly unique and committed to social justice—will quickly join their Innovator GP peers in the school, and together these two groups of GPs will create a flurry of activity and outreach, primarily through staging impressive school tours, all of which will give the school the label "changing" in the GP neighborhood network.

Once a school acquires this label, the third wave of GPs, the Early Majority, will feel comfortable enough to enroll their children. Early Majority GPs are not interested in a unique experience nor are they committed to righting societal wrongs through their own actions. They enter a Changing School because it appears to have already changed enough to match their school preferences. In contrast to Innovator and Early Adopter GPs who are able to tolerate their own discomfort as minorities while working toward the goal of an integrated community, Early Majority GPs must feel at ease in the Changing School *as is* to keep their children enrolled. *If* they stay, their presence will attract additional GPs, and the tipping in process will soon complete itself with Late Majority GPs finally secure enough to enroll their own children in what is now perceived and talked about as a "diverse" school. Diverse Schools have successfully integrated to the extent that is possible in a gentrifying/gentrified neighborhood.

At each stage in the integration process, there is the potential for reversion back to the previous stage of integration if the GPs decide to exit the school. Retaining GPs in an integrating school is almost more difficult than attracting them in the first place. The differences in attitudes and expectations about schooling that exist between the gentry and their non-gentry neighbors are often unexpected by GPs, and they can be hard for GPs to negotiate and tolerate without an able school leader bridging the two groups. Early Majority GPs have an especially low tolerance threshold, as they entered a Changing School with no intention of changing

---

- **Wave 1 GPs: "Innovators"**—GPs willing to be the first of their peer group to try a school that peers consider risky, able to imagine something different and take action.
- **Wave 2 GPs: "Early Adopters"**—GPs willing to be the first of their peer group, but because of the timing of their child's age, they end up in a second wave of school entry instead of the first.
- **Wave 3 GPs: "Early Majority"**—GPs who are not risk takers and will only try a school once other GPs have proven its viability.
- **Wave 4 GPs: "Late Majority"**—GPs who are not risk takers and will only try a school that is popular among peers and has made the official lists of "good" schools.

Figure 9.1 Types of gentry parents.

it themselves, and they are particularly uncomfortable, as a minority group, imposing their ideas about what they think makes a great school if their ideas are not already a part of the school's culture. Retaining Early Majority GPs in a Changing School is a crucial point in the tipping in process.

The ability of a principal to bridge the different expectations of gentry and nongentry parents is the key factor in retaining GPs at all stages of integration. Two variables can make it easier for the principal to be successful in this shepherding role. First, a school with a diverse *non*gentry composition appears to be more welcoming of gentry families, as there is not a single, dominant culture that already exists in the school beyond the school culture. The principal is already skilled in managing a diverse constituency, and adding GPs to the mix is not jarring in the way it is when a school is primarily one ethnic/racial group. Second, a school that is in a neighborhood much further along in the gentrification process has a surrounding community much more accepting of school change, which gives the principal political room to adjust the school's culture to better match the preferences of the GPs.

A more thoroughly gentrified neighborhood also has a larger group of Early Majority GPs poised to enter a school once it becomes a Changing School. This can lead to a very fast tipping in process as the larger group of GPs provides its own, automatic comfort zone during a crucial stage of integration. The pent-up GP demand for a new neighborhood school

---

- **Stage 0: A Segregated School**—no white, gentry children enrolled, or there is a perception by neighborhood gentry parents that there are no white, gentry children.
- **Stage 1: A Catalyzed School**—either one gentry child or a small handful of white, gentry children enrolled in the early grades who have gentry parents that are very active in outreach to other neighborhood gentry parents.
- **Stage 1: A Stagnant School**—either one gentry child or a small handful of white, gentry children enrolled who have gentry parents that are not interested in engaging in outreach to other gentry parents.
- **Stage 2: A Changing School**—a solid, stable presence of gentry children enrolled in the early grades who have gentry parents that are very active in outreach to other neighborhood GPs.
- **Stage 3: A Diverse School**—a solid, stable presence of gentry children enrolled in all grades who have gentry parents that are very active in the school community. In New York City, a diverse school would be considered integrated, a school that has completed the integration process.

Figure 9.2 Stages of school integration.

option can be like a dam breaking with the right leadership and outreach effort. In neighborhoods less far along in the gentrification process, however, the Changing School may have skillful leadership and conduct effective outreach, but the stream of Early Majority GPs entering will be a trickle simply because of their relatively small population numbers in the community, thus making it harder for them to feel comfortable in the school, because there are never quite enough of them to *clearly* set the tone of the classroom. Without a large enough group of Early Majority GPs available to enter a school, the tipping in process is likely to get stuck in Stage 2, and remain there until the neighborhood further gentrifies and provides an adequate number of gentry children to solidify their presence.

A Difficult Process

Ellen called the integration process "a planet aligning situation." Paula offered "aligning of the stars" to try to explain how everything came together to integrate her neighborhood school. Both women, through their ethereal references, make the important point that no one element can guarantee the successful tipping in of a school. Neighborhood circumstances and school circumstances might suggest change can happen, enticing Innovator GPs to take action. However, after enrolling their own children in a Stage 0 school, and tirelessly volunteering in the school and boosting the school throughout their GP network, these parents might find that the school gets stuck in an early stage of integration because the school leader can't successfully manage the G/NG Gap and hold onto its Early Majority GPs. The process is a complicated intertwining of many individuals, each with their own perceptions of reality, each with their own sets of priorities. These ethereal references also highlight the fact that the New York City Department of Education (NYCDOE) does not seem to be doing all that it could to harness the potential that exists for school integration in diverse neighborhoods. If there is residential integration, it shouldn't take a celestial miracle for there to be school integration.

Although school integration efforts have been essentially abandoned in most of the country due to legal restrictions,[1] flagging political will, and the reality of segregated housing patterns, gentrifying neighborhoods have the requisite residential diversity to create integrated schools. If city governments are implementing housing, business, and zoning policies that encourage neighborhood reinvestment and renewal in poorer neighborhoods, then the next step should be to implement education policies that are poised to capitalize on the intended influx of wealthier families into a neighborhood. Deconcentrating the poor isn't meaningful unless there is substantive social mixing, and schools are ideally situated to be the pivotal institution in a gentrifying neighborhood for interaction between residents new and old.

Meaningful Social Mixing

The social mixing that was described by GPs in this study indicates that tipping in *does* bring with it this desired outcome, though much more so for children than for adults. Leslie described the racial separateness of the adults in her school, something that confounded her, because it didn't seem to quite fit with her image of who she wants to be. As she recounts: "I have noticed at school, I find it easier to meet and talk to other white parents, now what is that? Is that, am I more open to them? Are they more open to me? But I do perceive that happening. The black parents talk to each other, the white parents talk to each other, and why? I am left sitting there going, 'Why do we do this?' But we do." Avery also described the reality of racial cliques that seemed to naturally happen for the adults in her school, and how "it is easier to stand on the playground and talk to the people you already know than to introduce yourself to someone new." But, Avery also ran the class email list as class parent, and had a surface level form of interaction with nongentry families on a regular basis.

The adult relationships between gentry and nongentry seemed to generally take on this more superficial form, though a couple of GPs *did* describe more substantive interaction. Sharon, whose service on the PTA forged a close working relationship between her and the copresident, described this copresident as, "a Title I parent, a woman who comes from an extraordinarily different background from me," but someone who "understood exactly the value of what we were all doing, and was there 100%, in her own way. Great resource, wonderful team player." Sheila, too, worked closely with non-GPs while raising money for her school, describing them awkwardly as "really low-SES and really very international," and talked about the benefit the social mixing was having for her. She described her own personal evolution: "I have to say, working with these women who are so wonderful and dedicated to the school...I mean, I feel like, just my own perceptions of race and demographics...I mean, I have really, sort of, changed...since my daughter has been going there. I mean, it really has sort of become a much less divided kind of world for me, which has been very nice."

While that type of adult interaction was rare, the descriptions of gentry children easily interacting with nongentry children were common.

Loren best summed up the contrasting behavior of adults and children, observing: "It's the grownups who are all screwed up. We're the ones who can't mix!" The children didn't seem to have a problem; mixing came naturally. Recall Karen's son, who had a friend with a father in prison who had been "tricked," or Margaret's daughter, whose best friend lived in the "scary" apartment building. Recall also the GPs who tied their desire for diversity in a school to the way this experience seems to be preventing their children from developing the same race and class constructs that they themselves have: Laura, whose kids "don't know the difference," or Astrid, whose daughter "has no concept." A few GPs made reference to the fact that their children's best friends were usually the one or two other white children in the class, and a couple expressed frustration with attempting play dates, as this type of interaction seems to be much more common for gentry families than nongentry families. But with only a couple of exceptions, the GPs in this study witnessed nothing but positive interaction between their children and nongentry children, and the issues of school culture that drove many GPs out of their neighborhood schools had to do with the behavior of the adults, not the other children.

Hurdles to Tipping In

These findings of substantive social mixing are promising for the futures of the children living in gentrifying neighborhoods, and better policies need to be in place to help facilitate tipping in. Tipping in appears to be quite possible for more than just a handful of schools if various roadblocks are removed. The two primary *logistical* hurdles to tipping in appear to be: (1) solving the collective action problem for interested GPs, specifically within the parameters of restrictive zone lines and the lack of a guarantee that children will be in the same classroom unless there is an enclave program binding them together, and (2) not having effective, broadly appealing school leadership in place to bridge the G/NG Gap once GPs enter a school.

If overcoming these two impediments wasn't challenging enough, policy solutions that might help lower these logistical hurdles to tipping in or eliminate them entirely must *also* take into account the politically contentious landscape of a gentrifying neighborhood, and the self-awareness GPs have about the controversy of their existence. How GPs respond to policies intended to help bring them into their neighborhood schools will depend, in part, on whether the policies are perceived as having the potential to further exacerbate the tension caused by gentrification. Policy solutions also have to be mindful of the fact that the social hierarchies that exist in gentrifying neighborhoods can't be eliminated simply by disregarding them. GPs can't be forced into a segregated school by giving them no other options outside of their zone school, because they are a group of people who perceive themselves as having choices, and actively integrating a school must thus be viewed as a choice they are making.

Exit, Voice, and Loyalty

Hirschman's (1970) classic exploration of the rise and decline of organizations, *Exit, Voice, and Loyalty*, provides a helpful framework for understanding the many factors that will influence whether policies designed to facilitate tipping in will be successful. Operating within the existing school-choice framework, GPs can either enter their segregated zone school and exercise their *voice* to try and change the school to better match their school preferences and expectations, something this study suggests causes a great deal of tension due to the G/NG Gap and the difficulty of social mixing, or they can *exit* their segregated zone school and try to find another option, preventing even the possibility of effective social mixing. Even if the practical and political roadblocks to tipping in are removed, voice remains a less likely choice than exit because, as Hirschman explains, voice depends "...on the willingness to take the chances of the voice option as against the certainty of the exit option and on the probability with which a consumer expects improvements to occur as a result of actions to be taken by himself or by others with him" (38).

Joanie's behavior while looking for a public school for her twin boys provides a good illustration of this tension between the *chance* of voice versus the *certainty* of exit, even for someone inclined to live their expressed values of diversity and integration. When her preferred public option—a diverse lottery school—didn't pan out, in part due to the complication of finding two slots instead of one, she ventured into her Stage 1, Catalyzed School. This school had very active GPs who enticed Joanie with their enthusiastic outreach, and the principal of this particular school is consistently described as an excellent leader, so both practical hurdles to tipping in were basically taken care of, and Joanie went to work exercising her voice to make the school better. She described the first week of school and the energy and optimism she put toward improving this Stage 1 school, also recounted in chapter 8 on the disproportionate influence GPs can have on school culture: "So that first week, we were starting to get really involved with the PTA. Sunday night, I was working on a survey to the other parents that we were going to distribute in backpacks: 'Are you interested in after school? Would you be willing to pay for after school? How about for classroom assistants?' Because they had no infrastructure whatsoever in terms of a parent body. And I was like, 'OK, this is going to be good, we're going to be building an elementary school and I'm really committed to public education, and this is going to be great.'"

Then, two spots opened up at another neighborhood public school, and Joanie was offered the option to exit the Catalyzed School for something she perceived as much more *certain* to give her children the kind of education she wanted for them. The desirable systems were already in place in this other school, and she quickly left, despite having felt that working to improve another public school was "going to be great." Her description of the contrasting picture of the two schools was her justification: "So we show up to P.S.____ on Tuesday, and there are like 100 people in the lobby, and we're like, 'What is going on here?' It was the registration for their after school program. So the comparison of, here I am, working on a survey asking parents if they'd even be interested, what kind of programs, what kind of money are they willing to spend, and then I walk into P.S.____ where there are literally like 50 programs of after school activities for my kids to choose from. And it's all there, it is all set up, there is a huge infrastructure. I then go in the next day to register them for the after school, and there are 15 parents sitting in the room, registering kids, they have it all worked out, they have a full time director of the after school program. I mean the comparison was huge."

Joanie's decision is not surprising. Exit "…requires nothing but a clearcut either-or decision" (Hirschman 1970, 43). Voice, on the other hand, "is costly and conditioned on the influence and bargaining power customers and members can bring to bear" (40). The image of Joanie dutifully compiling a mailing to other parents on a Sunday night, hoping to acquire school improvements, vividly illustrates the cost of voice. She is giving up her time with no guarantee that she will benefit from this investment of time. Thus, the situation GPs face in deciding between exit or voice is clearly biased in favor of exit if a viable exit option presents itself.

The choice between exit and voice, however, isn't always as starkly contrasted as it was for Joanie, a single mother who needed a good after school program, and Hirschman's third variable, loyalty, which "holds exit at bay and activates voice" (Hirschman 1970, 77), also plays a role in the GP school-choice process. The more heavily involved GPs are in a school in the early stages of tipping in, the more loyal they are to the idea of keeping their children there. The important function of loyalty in facilitating the tipping in process can easily be seen in the comparison of

Early Majority GPs with Innovator and Early Adopter GPs. Innovators and Early Adopters are typically loyal to the idea of integration as social justice, and this keeps them motivated to exercise voice over exit. Or they have successfully organized to solve the collective action problem, and group cohesion keeps them loyal to friends and commitments made. The Early Majority does not typically share these loyalties, and they are much quicker to exit when issues surrounding the G/NG Gap arise and challenge their comfort zone. Loyalty to a school is quite limited for *all* GPs, however, if a child is unhappy, or if a school leader is perceived as unable to appreciate the contributions of GPs. Chapters 5 and 7 on the challenges of retaining GPs at the various stages of integration make clear that when it comes to school loyalty, even the most social-justice oriented GPs have their limits. Notwithstanding these limits of loyalty, it would seem that policies that bolster GP loyalty for a school can best facilitate the tipping in process, because it at least *postpones* exit and gives the integration process chance to take root.

Nongentry Voice

While the nongentry may lack the same number of exit options available to the gentry, they do not lack voice, and the voices of the nongentry can easily derail integration efforts if they exacerbate gentrification's tensions. Nongentry voice appears most likely to be activated if a school reform effort exudes racism. Despite evidence that suggests the G/NG Gap is primarily about class, that the differences found in parenting styles and attitudes about schools stem from a *class* divide rather than a *race* divide (Lareau 2003, 240–241) race remains an important construct in majority nonwhite communities, especially those dominated by African Americans (Henig et al. 1999, Wells 1996), and policies designed to facilitate tipping in have to take this construct seriously, and be cognizant of how white actors might be constrained. Any criticism of a black dominant institution, like a zone school comprised primarily of black administrators, teachers, and students, could be seen as a criticism of the black community in general, and a potential threat to the economic security of the black employees, who are viewed as playing a critical role in the overall health of their neighborhoods (Henig et al. 1999, 277). Even if a black institution is not being criticized, African American families may simply not be interested in integration, preferring to remain insular in a culture that feels comfortable, familiar, and secure (Wells 1996; Henig 1996). In short, urban school reform efforts must not fail "...to take into account the way communal identities and personal interests shape responses" (Henig et. al. 1999, 277).

Within the context of a gentrifying neighborhood, where communal identities are already being threatened, this warning is particularly salient to crafting policies designed to help facilitate tipping in. Many of the frustrations expressed by Innovator and Early Adopter GPs as they described the challenges of starting the school integration process stemmed from what these GPs viewed as issues of communal identity, usually stemming from race. Members of Our Neighborhood, Our School (ONOS), for example, found that racial dynamics were undermining their efforts, as the neighborhood perceived them to be a "white group," despite its racial mix, and this triggered friction. Margaret explained to me, "We were a mixed race group, it's not like we were all white parents. In many ways it was much more of a class issue than a race issue, though Kevin and I are both white so sort of as the leaders of this group, the spokespeople of this group, it certainly looked like a very white group. And that caused, definitely caused tensions." In response, Margaret tried to counteract the white group perception by encouraging black members of ONOS to take on leadership roles, which they did, helping to ease the tension, but it never fully diffused the racial discord. Because there were many white members in the group, it was perceived by the resistant nongentry as white—not diverse, not mixed. And the efforts of ONOS were now perceived as some sort of white takeover of the school.

This perception of a white takeover led to false rumors that the black principal was going to be replaced by a "white Jew," almost causing a complete breakdown of integration efforts. Paula's recollection of this time is instructive of how delicate racial politics are in gentrifying neighborhoods. She described the nongentry parents at her Catalyzed School as "really believing that you just should not get rid of a black woman, period. That there is no good reason." She went on to share her belief that the ultimate selection of another black woman "has done a lot to diffuse things." Her concluding thoughts on this matter were, "Don't underestimate the power of racial politics. If they had put a white principal in there, I think the outcome would have been very different." The outcome has been mostly positive in terms of tipping in, with the school's new leader shepherding the community to Stage 2, Changing, where it currently hovers. But the power of communal identities is clearly a daunting force, and it is possible that tipping in efforts might be best seeded in schools that are not majority one ethnicity, but a diverse group of nongentry. The schools that seem to have the easiest time evolving from one stage of integration to the next are schools that are not racially homogenous prior to the entry of gentry families.

Policy Recommendations

Working within the constraints of all of the pieces in play in the process of tipping in—solving the collective action problem, the need for school leaders with wide appeal, ameliorating the conflicts stemming from gentrification, GPs believing they have choices—crafting policies that might help facilitate the tipping in process is daunting. Thus, in addition to identifying a way to possibly transform schools from Stage 0 integration to Stage 3 integration through Urban Education Cooperatives (UECs), I will also explore the possibility of avoiding the tipping in process entirely through the creation of new charter schools that start diverse. Both ideas will be explored below.

Urban Education Cooperatives

I propose the creation of UECs. As conceived, UECs would be groups of parents, formally organized by a school district (in the case of New York City, the Community Education Council would likely be the organizing force), who are committed to public education, but who don't feel comfortable with their zone school, and are willing to enter a district school that is underutilized by zone families if they are guaranteed two things: (1) that their children will be in the same kindergarten classroom with other members of the UEC, and (2) that they get to decide, as a group, which school they would like to attend after meeting with the principals and parent leaders of each school in the district that is identified as an option. Because I believe school integration in gentrifying neighborhoods is desirable, and because GPs appear to have more exit options that their nongentry neighbors, UECs are designed to keep more gentry families in their neighborhoods for elementary school by providing them with a clear path toward helping to create a diverse school. UECs are not a policy solution that has, to my knowledge, been tried before, and thus each step in the formation and implementation of UECs, as I recommend they unfold, will be described in detail below, accompanied with an explanation of how the step attempts to addresses the barriers to tipping in.

Step One: Gauging Interest
All families in a district are mailed information about UECs, and are invited to attend a meeting where they will spend the day engaging in workshops designed to elicit their trepidations about their current zone options, and determine their desires for what it is they want in an elementary school

for their child. Then, depending on the size of the group, families will either all be grouped as one or subdivided into smaller groups by similar school desires, geographic proximity, or however it is they want to subdivide. Families will leave this first session with a sense of who the other UEC participants are in their district, and will be signed up in an online group where they will be able to continue their conversations with the UEC members they have coalesced with.

School districts encompass many neighborhoods, zone lines divide neighborhoods, and social capital can be widely dispersed within a relatively small geographic region. When GPs in this study have tried to network to solve the collective action problem, even if they live two blocks from each other, or attend the same nursery school, their children can be zoned for different schools. Principals in underutilized schools can let nonzone families in, and often do, but it adds a level of stress and uncertainty to the process that can make GP organizing difficult. Evidence from this study suggests that seeding middle-class energy in a school does not require a large number of middle-class families, it is just a matter of figuring out how to get them together in the same place at the same time and provide them with the necessary comfort zone for action.

UECs solve the collective action problem and do so in a way that gives the group institutional support for expressing concerns about the perceived limits of some zone schools. If an arm of the school system is sanctioning organizing efforts and acknowledging that parental reservations about particular zone schools are valid, *and* they are providing a space to discuss these reservations, there can be a "broad public dialogue" (Henig et al. 1999) about what is important in a school. The sooner the gentry and the nongentry can discuss their competing values and identify their shared values, the better the chance integration efforts will take hold and progress. A well-mediated, open dialogue could strip away some of the false assumptions of racism and classism hovering above a gentrifying neighborhood's diverse group of families, and help these families identify what it is they actually do or do not have in common.

By inviting all community members to these meetings, and posing them as a forum for *any* parent unhappy with their zone school to organize for something better, UECs can't legitimately be accused of privileging GPs. While UECs are obviously conceived as a way to solve the collective action problem for GPs to facilitate tipping in in gentrifying neighborhoods, the benefits will not be limited to only GPs. Any parent unhappy with their zone option will have the chance to discuss their reservations about a particular school, and potentially find a way to network prior to entering that school or another underutilized district school to improve their child's situation. UECs give enhanced voice and more choice to all participating families.

At a practical level, GPs participating in UEC organizing meetings will not have to rely on their own limited networks to find other GPs interested in giving their neighborhood school a try as long as others are also interested, nor will they be restricted to only networking with families living in the same zone. The meeting will be set up for them, they can network with whoever shows up from the district regardless of which school they are zoned for, and they can do an initial assessment of whether there is potential within their neighborhood for integrating a segregated school. While chapter 4 describes in great detail the networking efforts of Innovator GPs who successfully brought small groups of GPs together to enter a school collectively, these Innovators were not the only people I interviewed who could see how a path to school integration was quite possible if a large number of GPs in the neighborhood just did it. Many of the Early and Late Majority GPs in this study who had a strong preference for diversity and who had thoughts about what their neighborhood school *could* be, simply couldn't imagine figuring out how to devise such a change in a school by themselves. They didn't feel like the kind of people who could orchestrate such an undertaking. They were not Innovators by nature, but they *were* open to possibilities.

Several Early and Late Majority GPs made comments throughout the course of my research that suggested all that might be necessary to start the tipping in of a school is for someone to ask, "Who wants to do this? We're organizing it." I overheard Lara, in the nursery school cubby room amid anxious chatter about kindergarten, saying, "If a bunch of families are going to go in together and try to change P.S.____ and make it better, I don't want to miss out on that!" But, that was all I ever heard from her about it, despite seeing her every day. She never tried to organize it; she just wanted to be a part of it if it were somehow happening. Zoe was another GP who casually wished for "fewer public school choices," so that she "would be forced to improve P.S.____." These two *non*-Innovators could imagine tipping in, could imagine being part of it, but not under their aegis. Elizabeth was the same. Although an Early Majority GP in *behavior*, she *spoke* with an Innovator's commitment to social justice. She was not a part of any tipping in process with her son, sending him to a popular neighborhood GT program. But because she seemed so open to the concept of tipping in during our interview, I posed the UEC idea to her as something for her younger daughter, to which she responded, "Yes, I think that would be a way to get people, if a group, if every parent in our nursery school, in the graduating class, said, 'OK, we are all going to stay as a unit, and stay strong, and all go to P.S.____,' I would *definitely*, you know, I think I would do it. I think I would do it. I think I would feel good about doing that. But…on your own…" The daunting nature of doing something on one's own repeatedly came up, and having the initial

UEC meeting organized by an arm of the school system could instigate non-Innovator GPs like Lara, Zoe, and Elizabeth to act, simply by asking them, "Are you interested?"

Step Two: Targeting Underutilized Schools
After the initial UEC organizing meeting, the UEC Choice Facilitators, who listened to the families during this initial meeting and helped them organize their groups, will then figure out which schools in the district are underutilized, and target several that seem like good potential schools for a UEC kindergarten group, keeping in mind that every school in this study that is in some stage of tipping in was not considered a failing school by any measure other than being segregated, and that schools with a diverse *non*gentry population also seem easier to tip. The UEC Choice Facilitator will then meet with the principals of these schools to gauge their interest in the UEC program and their openness to taking on the challenge of working with a more racially and socioeconomically diverse school community.

This meeting with school leadership might be considered a strategy of "co-opting the institutional elite" (Wells and Serna 1996, 110), which is a way privileged families have fought successfully to prevent detracking initiatives, but could also be a way to start an integration initiative. The institutional elite, that is, school leaders at all levels, generally don't want to lose elite families from their schools, and likewise would also want to attract elite families. Elite children typically help boost broad public support for a school and make it a more politically viable institution (108). In gentrifying neighborhoods, however, the elite are stained with scarlet Gs, and not all principals will be interested in being co-opted into integration. Thus, at this juncture, school principals who do not want to participate in the UEC program will have the opportunity to opt out. Leaders who are happy with the way things are in their school and are not interested in having to work with a group of vocal families, a more diverse community, or who have other reservations about the program, can decline to participate. This "opt out" provision should ensure that principals not well equipped or not interested in managing the G/NG Gap will select themselves out of the program.

Principals who *are* interested in welcoming a UEC at their school will meet with their school's parent leaders to explain UECs and determine whether there is parent support for a school diversification effort of this type. This could be considered gaining the "buy-in of the 'not-quite elite'" (Wells and Serna 1996, 112), another successful tactic for fighting detracking also applicable for bringing in elite families. The not-quite elite often believe there is value in having the elites in their institutions, and can be persuaded to support policies that keep them around. However, in poor, urban schools, there may not be any "not-quite elites" available to help create the breathing space for the elites to find a comfortable niche. Gentrifying neighborhoods are lands of stark difference, not fluid gradation, and this could be a point where UECs fail. But, if the parent leaders in a targeted school agree to give the UEC a try, the school will become a potential site. UEC groups will then visit each targeted school, tour the school, and spend time with the principal and parent leaders discussing what they would like to see happen in the school's kindergarten the next year, and what they are willing to bring to the table to make that happen, continuing the broad public dialogue started at the initial UEC organizing meeting.

Giving GPs voice about a particular school *prior* to entering that school, instead of forcing them to wait to exercise their voice until they are already in the school, should allow more space and time for building GP loyalty to a school, delaying exit, giving integration efforts more time to take hold. In Hirschman's (1970) paradigm, the choice between exit and voice starts from a point of already being a part of something. A third option needs to exist, where GPs have the possibility of exercising their voice *prior* to entrance. UECs offer the possibility that someone can be a part of something and have a voice about that thing as an incentive to enter in the first place.

Step Three: Choosing a School
After these initial conversations, principals and parent leaders will be invited to post reflections on their meetings with UEC families on the UEC website and make a pitch to the families about why they should choose school X. UEC members will then vote on which school they would like to attend, offering their reasons why. The majority vote would rule. If there is no majority, there would be a second vote between the schools with the top two vote totals. Once the school is selected in this fashion, UEC families would either commit to joining their UEC cohort at the school the following year, or decline, providing a final count to the principal and the group. Those families who choose not to join their UEC cohort would be back on their own, following the Department of Education's established rules for all of their other public options. The goal is to build loyalty for the chosen school prior to entry to increase the chance that parents in the UEC will stay in the school and not exit at the first sign of imperfection and discomfort. Through the voting mechanism, GPs would be empowered to choose a school they think is the best fit for their family, and not be restrained by zone lines. The simple act of choosing should give GPs more of a stake in the school.

Step Four: Building School Community Prior to the Start of School
The principal of the selected school would be notified, and provided with conflict resolution training to help them hone the skills they will likely need to work with a diverse group of families with different demands and expectations. Then, the UEC cohort would start meeting with the principal and parent leaders in the selected school about specific goals for the following school year. The broad public dialogue about what constitutes "good" education would now be a community specific dialogue where "winnable victories" (Henig et al. 1999) could be devised and implemented fairly early in the school year, if not on day one. Groups trying to build sustainable coalitions to reform a school (in this case the reform is integration) need to build confidence and trust in one another, and this is more easily done when some kind of positive change comes quickly, and all can see the benefit in trying something new.

When GPs in this study talked about manifestations of the G/NG gap, many of their complaints were about small details in the day to day operation of a school that were very important to them, and a lack of these things contributed to their losing faith in the school and their eventual exit. It is easy to imagine how simply giving GPs some small victories could make a very big difference in whether a school successfully retains GPs and continues on the path of tipping in. Several GPs who exited their early stage integrating schools made this very point to their principals, but were not listened to, erasing any chance of a necessary early victory. Timothy, for example, kept telling his principal, "Just let the parents walk the kids to class. It makes it seem so much more open and progressive, that's all you have to do." But it was never done. And Frederick, who simply wanted to volunteer in his son's class, was told he could only volunteer in the school if he went into another classroom, because the principal was afraid he "would focus entirely on my kid the whole time." Frederick tried to explain to the principal that he "wanted all kids' boats to rise," but the principal "couldn't wrap his mind around this," and the policy was never changed. And Frederick never volunteered, eventually leaving the school instead.

Those principals who took seemingly small suggestions from GPs built up a reservoir of GP loyalty, like the support of Margaret, who gushed about all of the little changes her new principal had made that were extremely important to her. Margaret describes the contrast between old and new leadership, and how quick action on the little things by a new leader changed everything for her: "We fought for three years over whether we could drop off and pick up in the classroom. I mean when Jenny started in Kindergarten, she had to line up in the cafeteria, I'll never forget her crying her first day, they had to line up, it's a uniform school, she had to line up in the cafeteria and be marched to school, you know, marched up to the classroom, and back down, very rigid, the old principal. The homework in Kindergarten and first grade, now it's, it used to be every night they had a ton of homework, now they only get it once a week, it's basically optional, you decide if you want to make your child do it or not. These were kind of across the board changes that made it very comfortable for us." While the issue of how much homework is appropriate is likely to stoke a prolonged discussion among a newly integrating community over what is "good" for a child's development, the issues of drop off and pick-up in the classroom and allowing parents to volunteer in their own child's classroom are much less likely to be philosophically divisive, and could be early victories given to UEC members if that is what they verbalize as important. Evidence from this study suggests that Timothy is right in his assessment that "little things make parents seem so much more welcome that it doesn't matter, everything else just falls away," and these early UEC community meetings prior to the start of school set these little things in place.

UEC cohort members who show up for X percent of these meetings (to be determined by the group) will be guaranteed a kindergarten seat for their child in the school, regardless of whether they live in the zone, and also be guaranteed that their child will be in the same classroom as the other UEC cohort members that kindergarten year, up to 50 percent of the class. If the UEC cohort is larger than 50 percent of one class, the UEC members will be spread throughout more than one class in roughly equal sized groupings. This enclave guarantee, while potentially problematic in that it will spark backlash against the perceived privileging of an already privileged group, is necessary to prevent GPs from choosing GT programs over UECs, simply to have an enclave guarantee. As already explored in detail in chapter 2, many GPs are against GT programs, they merely utilize them because they want a choice beyond their zone school, specifically a *classroom* where they know their child will be with other middle-class children. GT programs offer this guarantee, and UECs must also offer this guarantee if GPs are to view UECs as equally able, if not better able, to address their concerns about classroom diversity. GT programs have been an effective detracking "bribe" (Wells and Serna 1996), and UECs will not be a similarly effective bribe if they do not provide the same enclave privilege. However, UECs will not create the same kind of hierarchical divide within the school that GT programs create, since children are not being screened for entry, with one group being labeled as superior to the other group. And, with UEC members only guaranteed up to 50 percent of the spots in the classroom, there should be a much larger degree of social class mixing occurring within the classroom than typically happens in a GT classroom.

Step Five: Time to Anchor
The UEC seeding year will be followed up with additional seed years, up to five years so that UEC parent groups will be placed in all grades K-5, after which time the UEC parents inside the school should be well positioned to generate their own PR machine, stage spectacular tours, and continue the schools transition toward maximum utilization by neighborhood families. If the school reaches capacity due to increased demand that comes from only a year or two of seeding, no additional UEC groups will be placed there, and instead new district schools will be targeted. With up to six years total of seeding efforts, there should be enough parents who have had the opportunity to engage in a dialogue about what "good" schooling looks like prior to entry, building up a deep reservoir of loyalty to the school, and ensuring that these discussions will lead to actual changes in school culture so that the school successfully tips in and is considered diverse.

Pitfalls
UECs attempt to address all of the issues preventing tipping in, but they will undoubtedly still fall short in terms of gentrification's conflicts. Despite all of the conversations hosted through the UEC apparatus that will attempt to allow a civilized voicing of what schools should look like and why it matters, with all interested groups invited to the table, UECs are still likely to be perceived as privileging the gentry, especially when all of their children are initially allowed to congregate in the same classroom (assuming all GPs join the UEC). It isn't clear, however, within current policy and societal constraints, how else the elites can be enticed to choose to be integrators outside of privileging them in some way. Even the harshest critics understand that elite parents "are in many ways victims of a social system in which the scarcity of symbolic capital creates an intense demand for it among those in their social strata" (Wells and Serna 1996, 117). It is not enough to tap into the elite parents' sense of justice when equality of opportunity is more American myth than American reality. Nevertheless, that doesn't mean we can't incrementally move toward integration and slowly take apart the walls that separate us. UECs are potentially a realistic tool to facilitate such a dismantling, especially when the alternative is continued segregation and lack of social mixing. Though distasteful, it may simply be necessary for the privileged to be sequestered in *some* way before they can be completely integrated into a less privileged community. The enclaves used by the GPs in this study on their paths to creating Diverse Schools suggest that sequestering is, indeed, a necessary stage. UECs are at least somewhat more palatable than GT programs.

Rationale for UECs versus Controlled Choice

UECs have never been tried, and a case could be made for attempting a controlled choice plan in New York City instead as a better way to solve the collective action problem. In a controlled choice model, the school district spreads the children from impoverished backgrounds throughout the entire district so that all schools share the burden of educating a more challenging group of pupils. All families entering the public school system rank their top school choices, and the district then places families in one of their choices, balancing each school socioeconomically so that no school exceeds X percent poverty rate, typically 50 percent or lower. The model has historically been used in America as a way to distribute children racially, but has more recently been employed as a tool of socioeconomic manipulation in response to the Supreme Court's prohibition of using race as the sole factor in determining public school assignment.[2] The socioeconomic controlled choice model has been shown to effectively distribute children without causing massive exit from the system by the privileged. A 1995 survey done in Boston by Bain and Company found that 80 percent of parents were reportedly satisfied with controlled choice, and 72 percent said they preferred having a choice to being assigned to a neighborhood school (Bordas 2006). Controlled choice is generally hailed by integration advocates as a necessary tool for preventing the return of segregation. Grant (2009) devotes an entire book to attributing the lack of "bad" schools in Raleigh, North Carolina, to its socioeconomic controlled choice policy. Kahlenberg (2001) is similarly passionate in making a case for socioeconomic controlled choice as the way to substantively improve education for poor children. These programs are not without controversy, however, and Raleigh's recent decision to return to a neighborhood based model of school assignment was met a mix of support and dismay (Zucchino 2011), a reminder that all policies have the potential to hurt or anger some individuals even if they arguably improve society as a whole.

Controlled choice, with its focus on more equitable socioeconomic distribution, is a potential tool to be used as a way to force tipping in to occur in one fell swoop at multiple schools. In New York City, however, the use of this tool is problematic, primarily because of current NYC public school demographics, with overall poverty rates hovering around 75 percent. This high number makes controlled choice completely unfeasible in terms of guaranteeing a low enough poverty rate in each school to guarantee families that no school will exceed a reasonable poverty threshold of 50 percent. Implementing a controlled choice plan in NYC community school district by community school district instead of citywide, as appropriate, is another possible option, since *some* community school districts are much more socioeconomically diverse than others. However, this option would likely run into political problems if the district houses schools where popular, middle-class dominant, diverse zone schools already exist, and people have bought property purposely to reside in zone lines. Families in the zone would not want to lose their guaranteed option to attend P.S.____if a controlled choice plan were implemented, and would likely organize to resist such a proposal. The neighborhood school remains an ideal for many (thus the dismantling of controlled choice in Raleigh), and disrupting something that is already working well for *some* would be politically challenging, especially when the *some* tend to be politically active, engaged, regular voters. UECs would only target underutilized schools, and thus popular zone schools that are at capacity would not be impacted.

There is plenty of underutilized school social capital in New York City—families exiting for the suburbs when their preferred public school situation doesn't pan out for kindergarten, families utilizing private schools—but there is not *enough* latent social capital currently within the public school system for it to realistically employ controlled choice. Engaging the surrounding suburbs in a controlled choice plan would be another way to alter the demographic mix and bring down poverty rates to a feasible level; but considering the already mammoth size of the NYC School system, 1.1 million children, this doesn't make logistical sense, irrespective of political concerns. UECs shrink the size of the target reform area instead of expanding it, and harvest latent social capital neighborhood by neighborhood, seeding one underutilized school at a time. Gentrifying neighborhoods are unique demographic islands, and policies that aim too large will fail to focus intently enough on the people whose housing choices and attitudes toward diversity make them especially susceptible to willing participation in school integration efforts.

Target New Charter Schools in Gentrifying Neighborhoods

Alternatively, since tipping in is so difficult, it might be a better investment of political capital to avoid the tipping in process altogether, and simply create new charter schools in gentrifying neighborhoods that start off as diverse, since school diversity is the ultimate goal of tipping in. Charter schools are not restricted by zone lines, and are instead able to use a lottery system to select their student population. If a charter school can successfully recruit a diverse pool of lottery applicants through a carefully crafted marketing campaign, the school will start as diverse from the beginning. And if school diversity can be achieved without communities having to undergo the wrenching process of change, this option should be explored.

Opening charter schools in gentrifying neighborhoods and designing them to be appealing to a diverse group of parents is completely feasible under existing charter law. Despite the challenges of integration described, especially those stemming from the G/NG Gap, it *is* possible for schools to meet the preferences of both groups. Regardless of their general preference for progressive education, GPs will accept a more academically traditional and less progressive school *as long as* the extreme, outdated vestiges of traditional education aren't present—primarily the yelling, the group punishments, and the ban on parents dropping kids off in the classroom—and as long as the schools do not posit a deficit model of instruction. As explored in chapter 2, typical urban charter schools that offer extended school days and school years to ostensibly make up for what the children are not getting at home are *not* appealing to GPs. But, evidence from this study suggests that GPs will enthusiastically enroll in new charter schools if the conditions just described are met. Charter schools appeal to the GP sense of entitlement to have a choice about how their child is educated.

I learned of several new, diverse charter schools in gentrifying neighborhoods while conducting this research; and these schools were typically top choices for GPs. They liked that the school culture was new, and thus tremendously open to the voices of the parents. Everybody was working to build something together; nobody was working to change anything that was already there. The newness and the entrance based on lottery and choice for all families seemed to prevent some of gentrification's tensions from manifesting. And *non*-GPs, because of the excessive media hype that typically portrays charter schools as saviors of the inner city, are drawn to these schools as well. A well-designed charter PR campaign, with different types of targeted ads in a variety of venues, seems to be able to attract a diverse set of children. And if the first year proves to meet or exceed GP expectations, word of mouth will take care of the rest. Critics of expanded school choice believe that a school marketplace can lead to greater race and class isolation, because the choice process "... will lead to 'skimming'—where the best and brightest students exit traditional neighborhood schools and locate in the newly created and higher performing alternative schools" (Schneider et al. 2000, 204). Indeed, one school in this study that was in the early stages of integration struggled to tip in part because of the creation of a new charter school in the neighborhood. The charter school was perceived as better meeting the preferences of the typical GP, and GPs who won the lottery chose the new charter school over the neighborhood zone school that was changing, but not yet diverse. GPs were skimmed away from the zone school and into the charter school, leaving the zone school stuck in Stage 2 of integration. One Innovator GP I interviewed, Margaret, specifically blamed the new charter school for hurting her efforts to integrate the neighborhood zone school, and was very angry that I was suggesting more charter schools might benefit a gentrifying neighborhood. She asserted that charter schools "destroy any hope of improving the neighborhood public school by creating a consumer culture and draining neighborhood schools of important parental resources, because where do they go except these charter schools."

Margaret's critique is shared by many scholars who fear that skimming can further intensify the disparities in student socioeconomic background across schools (Wells 1993; Moore and Davenport 1990), but these critiques do not take into account what happens without these additional school choices. Not all GPs are Innovators, able to withstand the potentially searing integration process, and many will simply opt out of the system entirely instead of allowing themselves to be forced into the zone school, even if they might be able to improve it with their resources. Schneider et al. (2000), in *Choosing Schools,* answer the question of whether choice increases segregation and stratification with a fairly confident, "We think not" (222). Their argument is worth repeating: "If, for example, 80 percent of the population attending alternative schools is white, which schools would these children have attended before school choice was implemented? In many school districts, especially in central cities, we suspect the answer would be either private schools or a small number of neighborhood schools. In this case, the neighborhood schools are highly segregated and the absence of alternative schools does not produce more integrated schools. Indeed, if many of the white students in alternative schools had chosen private schools, the entire school system would be *more* segregated" (205).

Their line of reasoning is supported by evidence from this study, which shows GPs' preferences taking them away from their segregated neighborhood schools and into whatever diverse public option they can find. Or, when faced with the choice between polarized extremes if no diverse option is available, they choose the segregated white GT programs over the segregated nonwhite neighborhood school. Only a handful of Innovators were committed to starting the integration process in their neighborhood school regardless of their other options, with most starting the process out of necessity when more desirable options reached capacity. Margaret was one of the rare Innovators whose social-justice commitments trumped all other choice factors, and thus her belligerence toward charter schools is to be understood. But, as I argued with her and will reiterate here, if the *goal* is diversity, why must we take the most difficult path there? The charter school she was disparaging is Public Choice School (PCS) 2, with a demographic breakdown as follows:

- White: 33 percent
- Black: 43 percent
- Hispanic: 6 percent
- Asian: 2 percent
- Free Lunch Recipients: 30 percent

This is a truly diverse school. While the free lunch numbers are well below the citywide average, and the white percent is double the citywide average, this is still a diverse school by any reasonable standard. By proposing the creation of more charter schools in gentrifying neighborhoods, my hope is that more schools with this type of diversity would be formed.

The political challenges of creating additional charter schools in gentrifying neighborhoods could be as difficult as forming UECs, so they are not offered as an easy alternative. A recent article in the *New York Times* provides a good snapshot of the resistance that would mount in opposition to *any* policy proposal seen as benefiting an already privileged group of people. Reverend Taylor from *Church of the Open Door* is quoted as sermonizing against the expansion of PCS2 into a middle school, saying, "We're going to have some fights ahead, including fights about creating special schools for white children" (Santos 2011). If PCS2 is able to be rendered into nothing more than a special school for white children, despite the fact that a significant majority of the students in the school are not white, the prospects for creating both new charter schools and UECs are dim. Integration might be a value shared by most Americans, but there is little consensus on how it can or should be achieved.

There is a fear of school flipping that accompanies integration, a fear that schools will become all white. This fear morphs diversity into whiteness. Reverend Taylor is not alone in wearing these distorting glasses. But complete school flipping does not seem to happen in New York City. Perceptions do not match reality. None of the schools I examined that were currently in gentrifying neighborhoods, or even fully gentrified neighborhoods, had this problem. Perhaps NYC and New York State housing laws do a much better job of protecting low-income tenants from rent increases than other cities, as even the most thoroughly gentrified neighborhoods still have a significant population of low-income families of color, usually concentrated in housing projects. Further, even the whitest public schools in New York City are not *all* white, and these schools are located in neighborhoods that have historically been predominantly white and upper-middle class (e.g. the Upper East Side of Manhattan). I think the bigger concern in New York City is the *perception* by some that schools that become diverse (e.g. are only 30 percent white) are "white schools," as seems to have happened in the case of PCS2. This misperception threatens diversification efforts.

A Better Bound Place?

If our society is to continue toward a place where diversity is lived and not just talked about as a national value, communities will have to change, and gentrification is one of the ways change can happen. The GPs actually doing the small bore gentrifying—buying relatively affordable apartments, taking advantage of lower rents, slowly altering a neighborhood with different consumption demands—are responding not only to their own economic needs, but also to their expressed desire to live in diverse communities. If their behavior leads to meaningful social mixing for the next generation of urban dwellers, the gentry and nongentry children, the arrival of GPs in cities should be welcomed. I reiterate, if city governments are implementing housing, business, and zoning policies that encourage neighborhood reinvestment and renewal in poorer neighborhoods, then the next step should be to implement education policies that are poised to capitalize on the intended influx of wealthier families into a neighborhood, policies that will actually increase social mixing between gentry and nongentry residents.

This should be done despite the risk that improved schools might accelerate the gentrification process, which could end up displacing some neighborhood families who are among the intended beneficiaries of tipping in and social mixing. This is a potential consequence of tipping in that Kevin spent some time dwelling on, and his conclusions perfectly capture the complexity of this issue, a complexity that will not be easily resolved with any policy: "I suspect that, although the neighborhood may have gentrified just as much, whether or not it had good local schools, you know, the gentrifying parents had ways of getting other options, but will it maybe happen faster and more thoroughly now because there is also a good local public school? It may well be the case that in the end, what we intended to be a binding process that would help to make the neighborhood a better bound place, that that will, in the end, have helped to speed up gentrification. It was certainly not the intent, but I don't know what the alternative is. Everybody has a right to a good public school, both the new parents and the older parents."

Appendix A: Research Methodology

Using the grounded theory method of qualitative research (Charmaz 2006; Glaser and Strauss 1967; Strauss and Corbin 1998), this paper identifies and analyzes the circumstances that enable gentry parents (GPs), through the compounding effect of their many individual choices, to integrate their neighborhood school. Integration, a term I use interchangeably with tipping in, is a process that unfolds in multiple stages, and is driven by the decision-making process of the GPs in gentrifying neighborhoods who, in the integration equation, are the demographic with a greater ability to choose a school option outside of the neighborhood school. The grounded theory method is designed to elicit study participant's perspectives about a process and to explore how they construct a particular phenomenon—in this case, their contribution or noncontribution to the integration process of their high-poverty, racially segregated neighborhood school—without imposing a priori assumptions or theories.

Sensitizing concepts (Blumer 1954), ideas that do not prescribe what to see, but "suggest directions along which to look" (p. 4), were present throughout my involvement in this study, primarily those ideas from the gentrification literature that describe how a neighborhood goes through the process of change (e.g., Clay's [1979] Model of Gentrification), as this was the same type of phenomenon I hoped to identify and explain about schools in these neighborhoods. I fought against these preconceptions, believing a public school community to be a very different type of interacting space than a neighborhood community, and carefully examined my data to discover how school integration can happen in a gentrifying neighborhood. However, I was never far from the gentrification literature as an orienting framework for trying to understand how change happens when dissimilar groups attempt to coinhabit a contested space.

The process of grounded theory research can be conceptualized as a spiral insofar as cycles of sampling, data collection, and analysis are intertwined and proceed in a reinforcing manner. The analysis of each interview guides the next sampling target (known as *theoretical sampling*, explained in more detail below) and is used to generate new questions for subsequent interviews. The process of continuous analysis, using a structured coding system and memos (described in more detail in the "data analysis procedures" section) permits researchers to incorporate new relevant data into building theory as the study progresses.

Grounded theory is particularly well suited to this study, as the method is intended to construct abstract theoretical explanations of social *processes*. School demographic change is, fundamentally, a social process, a collection of individual actions. Schools cannot be changed by a simple legislative directive; they must transform through the actions of the various actors who comprise the school organism. In the setting of gentrifying neighborhoods, the school-choice decision-making process of GPs drives the change. The action of each individual GP has the potential to impact the actions of other neighborhood GPs and the actions of non-GPs, school leaders, and teachers, rendering the concept of school change interdependent and dynamic. It is a process that is not easily captured in a single snapshot of data. Developing a comprehensive understanding of tipping in requires a thorough analysis of individual perceptions, a full data set of what has been happening, from multiple perspectives, over a period of time. Perceptions are an important part of the integration process, because part of what must change to change a school *is* GP's perceptions of a segregated school, so that prior negative perceptions don't continue to be self-fulfilling prophecies.

Appropriately for this study, grounded theory is rooted in the school of *symbolic interactionism* (Blumer 1962), a theoretical perspective that assumes society, reality, and self are constructed through interaction and thus rely on language and communication. Interviews capture the communication of each person's interpretation of reality, and intensive coding and comparison of these interviews reveal how the various players in a process create, enact, and change meanings and actions (Charmaz 2006). My attempt to understand the tipping in process in a school focuses on the perceptions of the GPs who are choosing to enter, or not enter, their neighborhood schools, where their perceptions come from, how they transmit their perceptions to one another, and to what extent they can influence their GP peers through the ways they communicate their own choice.

Researcher Bias

I am a GP who has been through my own school-choice process for my daughter, most of which was happening simultaneously with conducting interviews of other GPs, and thus my role as an investigator is biased toward understanding GPs and sympathizing with GPs. Group membership enabled me to ask the kinds of questions of my interviewees that non-GPs might not have felt comfortable asking—exploring the sensitive topics of race and class for example. By authentically admitting my own reservations about integrating a school and enrolling my daughter as a white minority, I was able to provide a safe space for honest conversations about the parameters of social justice and one's own efficacy and responsibility. Making sense of social life requires both closeness *and* distance (Lofland and Lofland 1995), however, and thus, in addition to effectively utilizing my ability to intimately interface with GPs, I also sought "mechanisms for distancing" (23). To dissociate myself from my own bias as a GP, I employed regular self-reflection in my field notes to ensure that I was separating out my personal feelings from those of my interviewees. I also employed a line-by-line coding technique, described in detail later in this chapter, which forces the researcher to look at what each interviewee actually said, and does not allow the researcher to simply recall the major points that were taken away from an interview. While I did record my impressions of each interview in descriptive memos, these thoughts were supplemental to a meticulous analysis of the words used by my subjects.

Selecting GPs to Interview

To explore the tipping in process using grounded theory, I formally interviewed 52 GPs—both those who contributed to the integration of their neighborhood school and those who did not. GPs, as opposed to the nongentry parents who are also living in these newly integrating neighborhoods, are the center of this study precisely because they are considered a more privileged group with the ability to exit their neighborhood school if they deem it unacceptable. If school integration is a desirable societal goal, as I believe it is, and if some groups have more exit options than others, then analyzing the actions and beliefs of the more privileged parents in the integration equation should provide the kind of data necessary to craft policies designed to get the privileged to choose to integrate.

It is important to note that I am defining GPs as those *white* parents who are middle- or upper middle class, highly educated, and are contributing to the gentrification of their neighborhood with their presence and relative wealth. While middle-class black and Hispanic families can be, and usually are, part of the gentrification process, it is the entrance of white families into a neighborhood that overtly signals a neighborhood's gentrification, and causes the nongentry residents to take note and react.

Freeman (2006) discovered that "the role of race as a marker of socioeconomic status and as a determinant of who gets what is a recurring theme in the gentrification discussion. More specifically, the perceptions that whites command and obtain better services and amenities wherever they live is a source of appreciation, resentment, and resignation" (14). Thus, I confine my definition of GPs to the white parents in gentrifying neighborhoods, since the entrance of white gentry children into a segregated school would also be a much more overt marker of a school starting to integrate than the entrance of gentry black or Hispanic children. Even if an interviewee's child was biracial due to an interracial marriage, as long as one parent was white, I accepted that GP in my sample. I also interviewed a handful of Asian Americans, and consider them to be GPs for the purposes of this study, as they stood out in their schools as racially and socioeconomically different, and themselves closely identified with the white families in the neighborhood.

To select GPs to interview, I first had to figure out where to focus my attention by finding elementary schools in gentrifying New York City (NYC) neighborhoods that were actually in some stage of tipping in. My own GP network was mostly filled with parents like me who were avoiding their local school, and I wasn't sure if there actually were schools currently in the process of tipping in, or if there were just random white kids, like my neighbor's son, interspersed here and there in what remained, for all intents and purposes, segregated schools. I focused on elementary schools for two reasons: (1) the school-choice process in New York City has actual choice built into it at all levels of education, but for the elementary years, there are zone schools that most students attend by default since they are unlikely to land a spot in the small handful of choice options. For the middle school years, some districts still have zone schools but some have almost all choice schools; and at the high school level, all NYC students participate in a choice system where they rank their top 12 choices and go through a matching process. Without default zone schools for neighborhoods, the question of school choice for GPs would be much different. (2) Five-year olds are less likely to be engaged in stereotypical inner-city problem behavior—drugs, gangs, violence, teen pregnancy—and having a child as a the only white 5-year-old in a school likely feels different than having a child as the only white 13-year-old in a school.

To identify potential schools to research, I first quantitatively identified elementary schools in New York City that had undergone some degree of integration over the past ten years to increase the chances that the GPs who either were or were not part of that change were still living in their neighborhoods with school age children, and the memories of their school-choice process would be fairly fresh. I specifically looked for schools that started with essentially no white children, and increased their percent of white children by some noticeable degree over the decade. To quantitatively identify schools that have undergone some degree of integration over the past decade, I used the Common Core of Data (CCD), from the National Center for Education Statistics, which has detailed demographic data about every NYC public school through the 2004–2005 school year. For the years 2005–2008, I used the New York State Testing and Accountability Reporting Tool, merging this data base with the CCD using each school's unique 12 digit state identification code.

I then identified NYC elementary schools that were no more than 10 percent white a decade ago as a starting sample, as I wanted to examine what it takes to get GPs to send their children to what is essentially a nonwhite school. Anything greater than 10 percent white would be considered by some as already integrated. Ellen (2000), in her book *Sharing America's Neighborhoods*, settles on the following definition: "'Racially integrated neighborhoods are taken to be those in which the black population constitutes between 10 percent and 50 percent of the total population. This definition reflects the general feeling that integration should be about sharing spaces on relatively equal grounds, but also takes into account the fact that blacks make up just 13% of the total population of metropolitan areas around the country" (17). I am most interested in perceptions, and how GPs approach the idea of sending their child to a school that they perceive to be nonwhite. Thus, the less than 10 percent threshold made sense for the purposes of this study.

Next, I identified those schools that have since increased their white student population by some measureable amount over the past decade. Schools that had a surge of white enrollment over the past ten years would be indicative of a school possibly having tipped in. Schools in the early stages of the integration process would show less dramatic increases. An uptick in white attendance, however small, *could* signal that more significant change is coming, that the tipping in process had started, and I was looking for schools in various stages of integration. I didn't quantify exactly how much of a white student increase was necessary for a school to be considered as having gone through a complete tipping in process. Prior to conducting research, it wasn't clear what would be the various racial thresholds for signaling to GPs that integration was happening in their neighborhood school. I wanted to remain open, as the literature suggested I should, to the idea that integration is a concept difficult to define because different distributions of race and class can be *perceived* as integration depending on the context where the term is being used. In

New York City, the race and poverty status breakdown of public school families is approximately as follows:

- White: 14 percent
- Black: 32 percent
- Hispanic: 40 percent
- Asian: 13 percent
- Other: 1 percent
- Free and Reduced Lunch Recipients: 75 percent

Considering these numbers, it might be realistic to consider a school as having tipped in if the white students in the school comprise at least 14 percent, their proportion in the system. However, since whites still comprise the majority of citizens in America, the psychological threshold for GPs to perceive integration in their schools might be higher. Accordingly, I simply looked for schools that had some increase in white enrollment, and waited for a more official definition of tipping in to emerge from the analysis of my GP interviews. While I was never able to determine an exact percentage of white enrollment that would define a school as having tipped in, these schools were talked about in GP circles as "diverse," and white enrollment in a Diverse School could be as low as 13 percent, with an average white percent in the mid-30s (see tables 8.1 and 8.2 for a demographic breakdown of schools GPs consider diverse).

After identifying NYC elementary schools that had some increase in their white student enrollment over the past decade, I then determined which of these schools also had a reduction in their poverty rates, as defined by students receiving free and reduced lunch. While race is the most visible indicator that a public space is gentrifying, it is the comparably greater wealth and education level of the gentry that ultimately plays a role in changing the space—changing the types of goods and services that are demanded and provided, changing the aesthetics and the culture of expectations. A school may *look* different with an influx of *poor*, white families and cause a stir within the school community, but change in a school's social class composition is what is more likely to *substantively* change the school in terms of parental involvement, parental expectations, fund-raising ability, and so on. Thus, both a change in a school's racial composition *and* a change in a school's socioeconomic composition are necessary for a school to integrate in a way that could be beneficial for the poor children of color in the school.

As with race, I didn't set a specific poverty level as indicative of a school having tipped in. The number of children in New York City who receive free and reduced lunch is approximately 75 percent. Thus, a school with fewer than 75 percent of its students living in poverty might be considered socioeconomically integrated. However, research done by Kahlenberg (2001) on the benefits of socioeconomic integration for poor, disadvantaged children makes the claim that schools must be at least 50 percent middle class for the school to have a predominantly middle-class culture and thus impart the benefits of mixing. Accordingly, a 50 percent threshold to quantify a school as having tipped might have the most substantive meaning in the lives of poor children. A smaller threshold of 26 percent, though more realistic, would likely have less of a positive impact on the school's culture. Again, I simply looked for schools that had some decrease in poverty, in addition to having an increase in white student enrollment, and waited for a more official definition of tipping in, and what this means in terms of a school's poverty rate in New York City, to emerge from the analysis of my GP interviews. My results suggest that the average poverty rate (percent of students receiving free and reduced lunch) in schools that are considered diverse, schools that have tipped in, is in the mid-40s, but could be as high as 77 percent (see tables 8.1 and 8.2 for a complete picture).

Out of the approximately 724 NYC elementary schools that had complete demographic data, my selection process yielded 11 schools that appear to be in some stage of tipping in. I placed these schools on a map of New York City to determine whether any of the schools were located in neighborhoods that are continually described in the media and in scholarly research as being gentrifying or gentrified neighborhoods. There were nine schools in four neighborhoods that met this criterion. I then further narrowed the selection process by identifying gentrifying/gentrified neighborhoods that contained at least two schools from my remaining list of nine that are in some stage of tipping in, ensuring more data would be available for within neighborhood comparison of attitudes about schools. I chose to use the neighborhood as a GP catchment instead of the individual schools identified to ensure that I would capture the thought processes of GPs whose children were either enrolled in their neighborhood school, were not enrolled in their neighborhood school, or had been enrolled in the neighborhood school at some point but were not currently enrolled. All perspectives are necessary to build a comprehensive theory of tipping in. This approach also makes allowances for the fact that some schools may have started the tipping in process since 2008, the last year for which there was complete demographic data when I started this research, and this change could be identified through talking to parents in the neighborhood even if the schools were not identified through quantitative data analysis. This process resulted in the selection of three neighborhoods: Neighborhood A contained three schools,

Neighborhood B contained two schools, and Neighborhood C contained two schools. Neighborhoods are not specifically identified as per the confidentiality agreements signed by the GPs that I interviewed. I promised to deidentify them, their schools, and their neighborhoods so that they would feel free to speak openly about their school-choice process and the experiences they had in early stage integrating schools. Each neighborhood's gentrification looked and felt slightly different.

Neighborhood Context

Gentrification, like tipping in, is a process, and neighborhoods undergoing this type of transition go through several stages. Clay's (1979) early model of gentrification starts with Stage 1, pioneer gentrification, where the "...risk oblivious people move in and renovate properties for their own use." These "pioneers" are typically artists, design professionals, or homosexuals, and they use a lot of sweat equity to improve their properties. Stage 2 brings more of this same type of person, the neighborhood's name may change, and housing starts to become more desirable and scarce. Stage 3 is characterized by media interest in the neighborhood, the entrance of real estate developers into the market, the beginning of significant price escalation, and an influx of young middle-class professionals who now view the neighborhood as safe. Stage 3 is typically when tensions between old and new residents intensify, and displacement is perceived to be underway. Stage 4, mature gentrification, has arrived when the business and managerial class now view the neighborhood as a desirable place to be. Retail, restaurant, and commercial activities explode, as do housing and rental prices, making it impossible for anyone but the well off to enter the neighborhood as buyers or renters (Clay's [1979], 57–59).

Neighborhood A would be considered Stage 4, and possibly even as a neighborhood undergoing super-gentrification (Lees 2003), a situation where the simply affluent are displaced by the extremely wealthy. However, it still contains segregated schools, due to the effectiveness of public housing projects and rent control laws that have maintained some of the neighborhood's racial and socioeconomic diversity throughout the gentrification process. The nonwhite population, a minority of roughly 20 percent in this neighborhood, is a mix of black and Hispanic residents. Neighborhood A started Stage 1 gentrification in the early 1970s, and has steadily gone through the four stages of gentrification over the decades, with the process continually creeping northward, block by block, and the boundaries of what is considered the "safe" part of Neighborhood A continually changing.

Neighborhood B is in an earlier stage of gentrification than Neighborhood A, Stage 3, and is far grittier. The nonwhite population comprises a significant majority, and is predominantly African American. It is important to note that even though a neighborhood may be in Clay's (1979) Stage 3, with middle-class professionals feeling comfortable, shops and restaurants for the affluent patron springing up, and real estate prices skyrocketing, that doesn't mean that the gentry comprise a majority in the neighborhood, or even come close. Neighborhood B's white percent is roughly 20 percent according to 2000 census data. Stage 1 gentrification happened in pockets throughout the 70s and 80s, but it wasn't until the 90s that the neighborhood started moving through the gentrification process into Stages 2 and 3. Neighborhood B is known to be especially hospitable to interracial couples, and to have a fairly strong black middle-class presence. Like Neighborhood A, there are numerous housing projects in the neighborhood that will ensure the neighborhood remains both racially and socioeconomically mixed, no matter what happens with the private real estate market.

Neighborhood C is also in Stage 3 of gentrification, with some pockets that have crossed over to Stage 4, and some pockets that remain in Stage 2. The nonwhite population, the majority, is predominantly Hispanic and recent Asian immigrants, and the white population is only around 30 percent. (Asians are a difficult group to place in this study. The Asian Americans I interviewed as GPs clearly identified with the other neighborhood GPs in terms of income, education level, and being perceived by non-GPs as "white," whereas recent Asian immigrants who are poorer and do not speak English do not fit into the GP mold.) Neighborhood C's gentrification took off in the late 1980s, and has been the site of particularly fierce battles over public space, and who the neighborhood belongs to. The park in the heart of the neighborhood has been effectively used as a place to wage war on gentrification, with homeless encampments and heated protests standing firmly against displacement. These public tensions, however, haven't stopped the gentrification process, and the neighborhood continues to slowly expand its boundary line of safety, block by block. Housing projects are also in abundance in this neighborhood.

Neighborhoods A, B, and C are contained within school district boundaries that extend beyond their neighborhood lines. The district line is an important one in the NYC public school search process, as families can often access extra seats in schools outside of their zone if they live within that school's district. Lotteries for charter schools and other choice schools also give priority to families living within a school's district lines. Thus, as this study evolved, I sometimes expanded my discussions with GPs outside of loosely defined neighborhood lines to include families within the same school district as the gentrifying/gentrified neighborhood, since the schools in these neighborhoods were part of a larger network of school options based on district. I also discovered other schools that were in the early stages of integration, schools not on my initial list of eight, by talking to GPs within these neighborhoods and the larger school districts and listening to the latest buzz.

To identify GPs to interview about their school-choice process, I used newspaper articles and personal connections to identify an entry point into the GP world of each neighborhood, that is, an individual GP who was willing to be interviewed and educate me about the schools considered options by the GPs in each neighborhood. After identifying a GP entry point into each neighborhood, I subsequently used both snowball sampling and theoretical sampling to identify additional interviewees, and conducted interviews until theoretical saturation was reached. Rather than sampling on a predetermined theoretical framework, "theoretical sampling" in grounded theory involves a type of purposive sampling to collect the most relevant data to construct a theory. Who to sample is intricately tied to and guided by the ongoing analysis of interview data, and is determined in response to the developing conceptual model. While I limited my sampling target to GPs in three different neighborhoods, my developing model of tipping in, arrived at through an extensive coding process, suggested that there were different types of GPs who were willing or not willing to enter schools at different stages of integration. The different stages of integration appeared to be breaking down as follows:

- **Stage 0 Integration: A Segregated School**—no white, gentry children enrolled, or there is a perception by neighborhood GPs that there are no white, gentry children
- **Stage 1 Integration: A Catalyzed School**—either one gentry child or a small handful of white, gentry children enrolled in the early grades who have GPs that are very active in outreach to other neighborhood GPs
- **Stage 1 Integration: Stagnant**—either one gentry child or a small handful of white, gentry children enrolled who have GPs that are not interested in engaging in outreach to other GPs
- **Stage 2 Integration: A Changing School**—a solid, stable presence of gentry children enrolled in the early grades who have GPs that are very active in outreach to other neighborhood GPs.
- **Stage 3 Integration: A Diverse School**—a solid, stable presence of gentry children enrolled in all grades who have GPs that are very active in the school community. In New York City, a diverse school would be considered integrated, a school that has completed the tipping in process.

My emerging theory suggested that for a school to transition from one stage of integration to the next, it had to first retain each new wave of GPs, who would then attract the next wave. Pivotal to understanding each stage of integration was the identification of different types of GPs: those who were willing to enroll their child in a school as the first white student or as part of a small group of white students, and those who were not willing to enroll their child in the school until it had an established group of gentry children already there. The size of the group of gentry children necessary to entice them also varied, and further differentiated the different types of GPs. For example, there were those who would enter a Diverse School, but not a Changing School. Or those who would enter a Changing School, but not a Segregated School. Thus, as I used snowball sampling to seek out additional GPs to interview, I also employed theoretical sampling by asking each of my GP interviewees if they knew, specifically, GPs who were part of the first group of GPs in a school, GPs who entered a school in later years, or GPs who were still reluctant to use the neighborhood school. By using theoretical sampling, I was able to identify and interview enough of the different types of GPs in each neighborhood to fully develop my theory of tipping in. I eventually categorized the GPs into four categories, borrowing terminology from Malcolm Gladwell's (2002) *The Tipping Point*:

- **Wave 1 GPs: "Innovators"**—GPs willing to be the first of their peer group to try a school that peers consider risky, able to imagine something different and take action
- **Wave 2 GPs: "Early Adopters"**—GPs willing to be the first of their peer group, but because of the timing of their child's age, they end up in a second wave of school entry instead of the first.
- **Wave 3 GPs: "Early Majority"**—GPs who are not risk takers and will only try a school once other GPs have proven its viability.
- **Wave 4 GPs: "Late Majority"**—GPs who are not risk takers and will only try a school that is popular amongst peers and has made the official lists of "good" schools

Interview Procedures

While conducting interviews with GPs, I used a semistructured interview guide (see Appendix B). Each interview lasted between 30 and 90 minutes. Questions were open ended, probing parents about their decision-making process when choosing an elementary school for their child. GPs who sent their child, or were planning to send their child, to a school that was either still segregated or in the early stages of integration were asked questions about their decision-making process and the circumstances that allowed them to be sufficiently comfortable with this decision. GPs who did not send their child to the neighborhood elementary school, or who had no plans to do so, were asked questions about their decision-making process, and the circumstances, if any, that might have made them more comfortable and open to sending their child to a school that is segregated or in the very early stages of integration. Interviews were conducted in person, by me, either at the GP's home or a mutually convenient public location, like a coffee shop or restaurant. Interviews were voluntary and obtained through informed consent. Since all GPs were literate, they were guided through a written consent process, and asked to read and sign the written consent form prior to starting the interview.

Additional Data Collection through Observations

In addition to conducting extensive formal interviews with 52 GPs, I also spent time observing GPs at the local playground in my own gentrifying neighborhood, observing them on public school tours, and observing them in my preschool cubby room. As a GP myself, I was able to blend into these environments and listen to what they told one another and asked one another about various neighborhood schools. Utilizing eavesdropping provided me with an authentic window into how GPs talk about schools, their "perspectives in action"—accounts or patterns of talk formulated for the purpose of accomplishing a particular task in a naturally occurring situation (Snow and Anderson 1987). This mode of communication is different from "perspectives *of* action," where, in this example, GPs are talking about their school-choice process in response to the queries of a researcher, and framing their school-choice process to make sense to someone else. While listening to GPs talk to *each other* about school choice instead of to me, I was able to add additional data points to my emerging theory of tipping in, affirming, for example, that natural GP dialogue involves the use of the words "changing" and "diverse" to indicate the stage of a school and GP comfort level with that school.

Through regular eavesdropping in GP venues I was also able to keep tabs on the rapidity or sluggishness of change in the schools in my own gentrifying neighborhood, as my informal observations continued long after I had completed my formal observations. These regular updates forced me to revisit my data and question whether I had appropriately labeled each school's stage in the integration process. In one instance, a school I had identified as Stage 1, Stagnant had to be moved to Stage 2, Changing during the early stages of writing up my results, simply because the buzz on the playground was suddenly that the school was "changing," with current pre-K parents offering specific demographic numbers to each other that suggested something had indeed shifted in the school. My first year of research didn't initially pick up on the change that was to come in the pre-K, but keeping my eavesdropping ear open brought new information that allowed me to more fully develop my theory of how schools move from Stage 1 to Stage 2. The same thing happened with a school initially identified as Stage 2, Changing that had to be moved during my initial writing stage to Stage 3, Diverse. My theory was constantly being refined as I analyzed and reanalyzed my data in light of new information that continually streamed in.

The information obtained through eavesdropping was mentally recorded and quickly written into my field notes as soon as I arrived home. Particularly fascinating quotes were texted to myself so that I wouldn't forget the verbatim reference to a school. But most overheard conversations were a summary of what was talked about and how it was talked about. See Appendix C for an example from my field notes of how observations were recorded. Sometimes I participated in the overheard conversations, telling the GPs who were talking that I couldn't help but overhear what they were saying about P.S._____, and could they tell me more about X. Sometimes I identified myself as a researcher, sometimes I simply inhabited my role as GP and asked questions to help inform my own school search for my daughter. Both approaches brought a wealth of information that would have been missed had I simply relied on formal interviewing to capture the GP perspective of school choice.

Data Analysis Procedures

The in-depth interviews were transcribed, my observational field notes were meticulously maintained, and data analysis was performed using ATLAS Ti, a computer software program designed to facilitate the management and analysis of qualitative data. The grounded theory approach first requires assigning descriptive codes to chunks or lines of text, such as "GPs networking," every time this idea is discussed. Focused coding was then used to identify the most significant and/or frequent line-by-line codes, and to choose codes that best categorized the emerging themes and patterns. Axial coding was subsequently used to identify relationships between the different codes and how the data could be rearranged to effectively describe observed patterns of behavior. Different kinds of memoing —for example, analytic, reflective, descriptive, summative— were used throughout the process, first to define and describe various codes, and then to conduct theoretical coding, which is a way of rebuilding already coded data and establishing a conceptual framework by exploring the relationships between categories and subcategories. Theoretical sampling, as described earlier in this chapter, was used throughout the research process to identify the next batch of research participants, individuals who helped elaborate and refine the emerging categories constituting the theory, until no new properties emerged (Charmaz, 2006). Details of my own coding process will be described below.

Line-by-Line Coding

I started coding my data as soon as each interview was transcribed. Continuous coding while data was still being collected allowed me to effectively employ theoretical sampling, as I identified frequent codes, data patterns, and emerging theoretical ideas early in the process. Line-by-line coding led to the creation of approximately 300 codes. Charmaz (2006) recommends using action words whenever possible when ascribing codes, as this forces the researcher to think critically about the process being described by the participants as they saw it. Action words create a time line of events that reveal a process as it unfolded. Since my guiding interview question was about the school-choice process, my initial active codes included lists of what GPs believed about school, for example, "GPs believing they have a choice," "GPs having more interest in a school if other GPs are interested," or "GPs believing diversity is important." Eventually, I discovered that coding everything as a belief cluttered my ability to analyze the data, so I went back and changed many of the codes to a simple summary of what it was that the GPs believed, since all of the data was essentially a belief—an individual's perspective about reality, some that would be challenged by others, some that would be confirmed by others—and there was no need to preface each code with this fact.

The simpler line-by-line codes were a compilation of school-choice preferences, such as, "Convenience an important component of school choice," or "Emotional component of school choice," and school-choice complicating factors, such as, "Child not happy," "Progressive parenting style," or "Considering new options, the difficulty." In vivo coding, where the interviewee's own words are used as a code, was used only twice, for the code, "Drift," which describes the act of students travelling from one zone school to another zone school considered to be superior, and "Free-K," which describes public preschool programs that are chosen by

GPs precisely because they are free, a reminder that economic concerns are typically important for GPs.

Focused Coding

After completing the line-by-line coding process, I then did focused coding, determining which codes were the most frequent and/or significant, and whether any of the other codes could be folded within them (Charmaz 2006). This process winnowed down approximately 300 codes to 200 codes. (See Appendix D for a list of the most frequent codes.) Most of the collapsing of codes was in the realm of problems with a principal or support for a principal. The specific complaints were merged into one code, "Principal Problem," and the specific stories of support were merged into one code, "Principal key to changing a school." Other coding collapsing was done to unite specific GP concerns about high-poverty schools into one code, "Poverty concerns: exploring the boundaries of socio-economic comfort," and "Racial politics and their role in school change" was a compilation of the variations ways race was perceived to be negatively impacting GP efforts to integrate. The one area where I chose not to collapse codes was in the area of GP thoughts about gifted and talented programs (G&T programs). The number of times a G&T program was referenced by an interviewee and coded was approximately 240, under 33 subcategories about G&T programs. As will be explored throughout this study, G&T programs play a very complicated role in the school-choice process of GPs and whether schools are able to go through a tipping in process, and differentiating between the many ways GPs talked about G&T programs was a key aspect of this study.

Axial and Theoretical Coding

Focused coding was followed by axial coding, where I reassembled my fractured data (Charmaz 2006) to start building a theory of tipping in. I made index cards of all of my codes, and then shuffled the cards about in many configurations to figure out how the ideas fit together. I first divided them into three major ideas, "Reasons for avoiding the local school," "Reasons for entering the local school," and "Reasons for exiting the local school." This process revealed that there are different kinds of GPs with different thresholds for tolerating their own minority status, and different stages of integration, as was already described in the section on theoretical sampling.

Using the principles of constant comparison (Strauss 1987), I further extricated these differences by comparing codes—within the same interview, between and among interviewees in the same emerging category, and between interviewees in the different emerging categories—to find consistencies and differences. I then sketched out the relationship between the various groups and schools (see Appendix E for a recreation of the sketch and how I put the pieces together), and then went back and reorganized the index cards based on which stage of integration each code is related to. My theoretical codes emerged from this process, which were further developed and refined through memoing.

Memoing

The memoing process allowed me to explore my emerging theory of tipping in, and then follow up on my thoughts with additional memos that ensured my ideas were actually grounded in the data. For example, I wrote an extensive memo on different types of GPs and different stages of integration, playing around with what the properties might be of each category of GP and school stage (See Appendix F for a copy of this early memo). I then added GP categorizations to my descriptive memos of each GP, where I had previously summarized each interview, my impressions of each GP that may not have been captured in the interview, a brief physical description so I could better remember each individual, and a short summary of what I thought to be this person's most important contribution to the study. The new categorization information was an analysis of which type of GP I thought each person was, and why. I then sorted the memos by GP type and meticulously went through the interviews and codes for each GP to further develop the properties of each type of GP, and relabel each GP if I determined that my initial assessment of their type wasn't accurate. Again, I utilized constant comparison as a tool for fine tuning GP types.

I went through a similar process to define the properties of the different stages of integration in a school. I first did descriptive memos of each school that was utilized or discussed by the GPs I interviewed, and identified which stage of integration the school appeared to be in based on my emerging theory. I then resorted my school memos so that I could analyze each group of Stage 0, Stage 1, Stage 2, and Stage 3 schools to determine what these schools had in common, and where they differed. Schools are dynamic in a way that individual GPs are not, and placing an integration stage label on a school was much more challenging than identifying a GP type. An initial assessment could easily be challenged as the new public school-choice cycle started for different families than were in my early data pool. For example, I interviewed several GPs who had gone through the choice process a year earlier than I started my own choice process for my daughter, and the buzz I was hearing about which schools were changing or diverse was sometimes different from what my interviewees had heard a year earlier. Likewise, the buzz on the playground among parents going through the choice process a year later than me were having different conversations than I had had only one year prior. To fully understand the evolution of a school, I made sure that I interviewed GPs at many stages in a school's time line to capture how the story of a school changes over time. This was the core strategy of my theoretical sampling technique—identifying and interviewing GPs who entered the same schools but in different years.

Member Checking

I also employed "member checking," a strategy of sharing preliminary theoretical findings with the research subjects to verify the results and bolster the credibility of the research (Creswell 2007). Member checks were done with both GPs who were interviewed for data collection purposes, and with new GPs to test the transferability of my findings. The responses from these members were all very affirming. Eduardo (a pseudonym, as are all names throughout this book as per the confidentiality agreement signed by my interviewees), for example, would finish my sentences during our member checking conversation. I would tell him the beginning of some aspect of my theory, and he would finish the summation before I was able to get the words out, an end that was almost identical to my own. Jeremy emailed his reaction, and despite his concerns about whether *any* individual's experience could be fully captured as part of a larger theory, he thought I described the GP reality as well as I could. He wrote: "This process is so nuanced and individual for each family that it's hard from me, a statistical cynic to begin with, to readily subscribe to a clean sterile theory. Obviously it can't reflect my views precisely, but I also don't think it can reflect my linear/temporal experience, but rather some amalgam that sort of, kind of, gets the average of the idea of me (the generic GP) across. In all fairness, you have been able to put large parts of the experience into a written form that informs and explains all, (and I do think all,) of the questions and concerns that people have. So I guess I'm saying that I think it's amazing." Lisbeth, who also provided written feedback, was similarly supportive, using the words "spot on" and "marvelous" to describe her overall reaction to my theory of tipping in. She thought I captured "the difference between the gentry 'sidewalk dance' and what it means to invest deeply in the institutions of a neighborhood" particularly well. She also agreed that figuring out how to retain the third wave of GPs is crucial to the tipping in process. A couple of the GPs who participated in member checking did offer a few suggestions for improvement, their perception of a more precise assessment of reality. These suggestions were taken into account and incorporated into the final draft if appropriate. Since my findings reflect 52 perceptions, I weighed individual critiques within this framework.

Study Limitations and Areas for Further Research

While this study was able to capture the viewpoint of GPs about their own role in the process of school integration, the findings are limited to this perspective. Despite my belief that the perspective of the GP is the most important one for understanding how tipping in can happen, due to the fact that GPs are the neighborhood parents with a greater ability to choose and thus have a more developed capacity for avoiding the neighborhood school or exiting the neighborhood school if it fails to meet their preferences, other points of view would provide greater insight into the complicated race and class politics that are perceived by GPs to impede tipping in.

Nonwhite GPs are one group that likely holds considerable insight into how uncomfortable manifestations of class differences can be better moderated. I did interview a handful of black GPs who clearly held a different kind of knowledge about tipping in than white GPs. In the early stages of conducting interviews, I had not yet decided if I wanted to limit this study to white GPs, and I sat down with a total of five black GPs, having discussions with them that were remarkably frank. We delved into issues that most of the white GPs in this study were hesitant to explore without considerable prompting. These five black GPs were not afraid to describe what they saw as the issues preventing smoother assimilation by themselves and their white GP counterparts into segregated schools. They had confidence that they know what the nongentry community needs to thrive, a confidence decidedly not shared by the white GPs. This confidence made them fundamentally different from white GPs, as did their greater ability to mask their difference. Because of the marker of race, white GPs and their children were never able to assimilate into these newly integrating schools in the same way black and Hispanic families could, making their experience uniquely different from the nonwhite GPs.

The black GPs I interviewed also all shared with me their belief that most of *their* peers do not consider public schools an option, explaining, "If a black family is successful, they send their children to private school." Because of the widely available scholarships at private schools that are openly used to promote diversity, nonwhite GPs have a greater variety of school options for their children than white GPs, and according to the black GPs I interviewed, most of them take advantage of these opportunities and stay out of the public school system when possible. I believe nonwhite GPs can effectively serve as a bridge community in integrating schools, and if they comprised a larger presence, segregated schools would have an easier time going through the tipping in process. A principal can more easily bridge the gap between gentry and nongentry if there are nonwhite GPs helping to make the connections. But, due to time and resource constraints, I decided to eliminate them from my study and pursue the sole perspective of white GPs. The nonwhite GP community is worthy of its own study.

Another serious limitation of this research is that it lacks the viewpoint of the principals who are charged with the difficult task of managing the gentry/nongentry culture (G/NG) gap. From the perspective of the GPs, school leadership was vital to whether they felt welcome to bring themselves, their children, and their ideas to a school. Because of the responsibility placed upon this one person to skillfully facilitate the integration of two disparate parenting and school philosophies under one roof, the principal's voice is needed for a more complete picture of how the tipping in process can be successful. Interviewing principals would have required approval from the New York City Department of Education (NYCDOE), which was not necessary for me to acquire to interview parents identified through neighborhood networks. This extra hurdle would have greatly extended the time necessary to complete this study. Further, I believed that if I opened up the study to the voice of the principal, then it would also be necessary to expand it to include nongentry parents and their thoughts on what was happening in their integrating schools, since all three voices would encompass the entire school community. It made sense to do an intensive study of one component of the school community, or a study of all components, but including only two out of three voices would have diluted the analysis of GPs without providing a complete picture. Again, because of time and resource constraints, I chose to limit the study to the GP point of view instead of trying to capture all perspectives. But, further study of both the principal's role in facilitating tipping in and the reaction of the nongentry to the change happening in their schools would be valuable additions to the gentrification literature.

This study could also be enhanced by research on what type of learning environment actually works best with children. I have chosen not to take a clear stand on whether poor children might actually *need* a stricter, more traditional, more skills focused environment, as this question goes beyond the scope of my book. I focus on GP perceptions, and many of them do openly question whether what they want for their children is necessarily good for all children. What is "good" for different types of children is an open debate that would be enhanced by further research on the impact of progressive education on poor children of color. Deborah Meier, the founder of the very progressive Central Park East elementary school in East Harlem, has written extensively about progressive education in poor communities, and building upon her work with additional research would be valuable for informing the progressive versus traditional education debate.

Appendix B: Gentry Parent Interview Guide

Question 1

First, how long have you lived in this community? Can you tell me a little bit about what brought you here?

- Probe 1: How old were you when you moved here?
- Probe 2: What was the neighborhood like then?
- Probe 3: What is it like now?
- Probe 4: Did you have kids when you moved here
- Probe 5: Is this where you plan to make your life or do you have plans to leave?

Question 2

Can you tell me a little bit about your child/children?

Question 3

When the time came to choose a kindergarten for _____, what did you do? Can you walk me through the process?

- Probe 1: Did you do much research about your options? Walk me through the research process.
- Probe 2: Did you consult with anyone about your options before choosing? Can you tell me about those conversations?
- Probe 3: Did you know other parents who were contemplating schools outside of their neighborhood zone school? What did they choose?
- Probe 4: Did the decisions of other parents you know impact your decision-making process?

Question 4

Other parents in this neighborhood have chosen not to attend the local school, where your child goes. Why do you think that is?

OR

Question 5

Can you describe for me a scenario where you would choose to send your child to your local, neighborhood, zone school?

Appendix C: Examples of Observations Recorded in My Field Notes

October 22, 2009

I overheard some GPs talking in the playground today about P.S._____, and one of them was talking about how they were moving and she was taking her kid out of the pre-K. The other mom didn't have a child in P.S._____. I told them I couldn't help but overhear, and that I was doing research, and asked her why she was pulling her son out (the other mom didn't ask why, perhaps she already knew, and I had to find out!). Finally, I found a mom who is not happy with the program and not happy with the school for the reasons I theorized most white, middle-class parents would not be happy! She is pulling her kid out of the school at the end of the week. They are moving to Brooklyn, so she would be pulling him out anyway, but they aren't moving for another month, and she is pulling him out early. She said the school was too traditional with too many rules. The whole rules/punishment system just didn't work with the way they had been heretofore raising their kid. He was used to discussing things and was coming from two years at a progressive preschool where there was no rules/punishment system. Now, she said he was picking up things at school she didn't like, coming home and talking about rules they had to follow, it was a negative interaction at home, and she just didn't like how he was becoming. She said the parents might be changing but the teachers weren't, they taught in a very traditional, inner-city way. She said something about how the school was going to be great eventually, because the principal was a hard charger who was pushing for this school to be the best. But, the teaching staff would have to change. So she attributed the school culture to the teachers, not to the principal. Interesting. But, she was clearly not happy with the place and the effect it was having on her kid.

November 16, 2009

Met another mom in the park today who does NOT send her kid to P.S._____ but is zoned for this school. She is friends with a woman in my building whose son goes to _____, one of the progressive choice schools in the neighborhood, and I overheard them talking about how things were going for their children in kindergarten. This woman's son also ended up at a progressive choice school, but not the same one as my neighbor. Her son goes to _____. I forced my way into their conversation, having an easy opening since I had already interviewed my neighbor. I asked neighbor's friend why she chose _____ over P.S._____. She said it was because of the pedagogy at _____, and that they seriously considered P.S._____. But they were concerned about the intense test prep at P.S._____, didn't want their child subjected to intense test prep. So, in a sense, it's like P.S._____'s high rankings on test scores are turning off some parents. An unintended inverted consequence of doing well on tests? They know the only way "these" kids can do well on these tests is through intense test prep, and they don't want their own kids to be a part of it. I'm assuming this is the stereotype, this woman didn't say this of course. When I asked if P.S._____would have been their back up plan, she hesitantly said yes, as if it wouldn't have been. She acknowledged what a great job the school was doing and how impressive it was how far the school had come over the last decade, but it was all said with a tone of that's great that has happened for that school, but that school still isn't a good fit for my family, because of the pedagogy. I have my own prejudices about P.S._____'s pedagogy, so I know exactly what she is saying, but it is always good to have confirmatory data point, to know I am not the only one with this perception.

September 19, 2010

Overhead some GPs at the playground today talking about P.S._____. The dad was describing the demographics of the pre-K class, and it sounded like they were at something like 50 percent white, 25 percent black, 25 percent Hispanic. Shocking! Well, not really, the question is, are they retaining the pre-Kers? I think the school is Stage 2, Changing, and the question is, will these new folks stay or go? I obviously can't wait to write my dissertation until all of these things unfold; I need to say this is where the school is at now, and these are my findings, something to watch for in the future.

Appendix D: Codes Most Frequently Identified

Black culture versus white culture
Changing a school
Choices limited by competition
Class versus race
Community as an important value
Convenience component of school choice
Diversity: Meanings and challenges
Dual language desire drives the choice process
Exit
Foreigners, the role they play in changing a school
Gentry parent leadership
Gentry parents networking to address myriad concerns about schools
Gentry parents believing they have choices
Gentry parents characteristics
Gentry parents more interested in a school if other GPs are
Gifted and Talented: 33 different subcategories
Hierarchy: perceiving which cohort of schools one belongs to
Insider/Outsider dynamic of demographic change
Judging other parents
Middle class bringing more resources to the school
Minority status: does or doesn't bother me
Momentum and Buzz
Neighborhood Choice
Perfectly fine school
Poverty concerns, exploring the boundaries of socioeconomic comfort
Principal problem, including resisting integration and change
Principal key to school change, positive comments
Private school option as a component of school choice
Racial politics and their role in school change
School tours, the role they play

Teachers yelling at kids
Teachers, their role in the process of changing a school
White counting
Word of mouth as an important component of school choice

Appendix E: A Visual Overview of Tipping In, Recreated from My Notebook Sketches

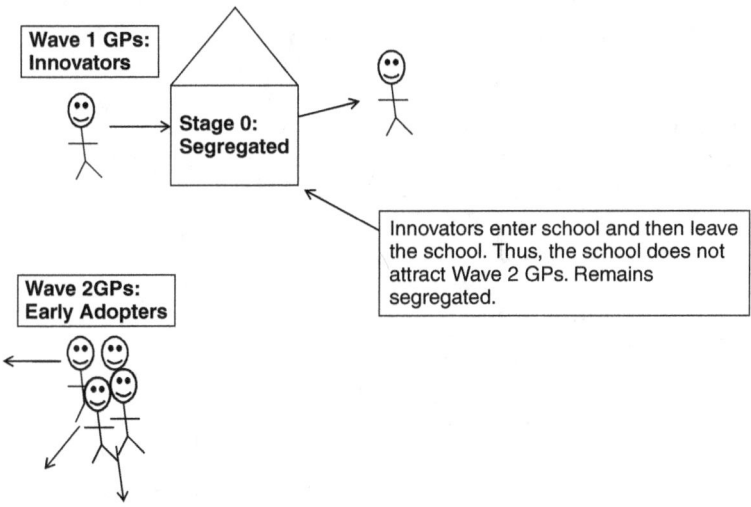

Figure E.1 Stage 0 of integration: the school is segregated.

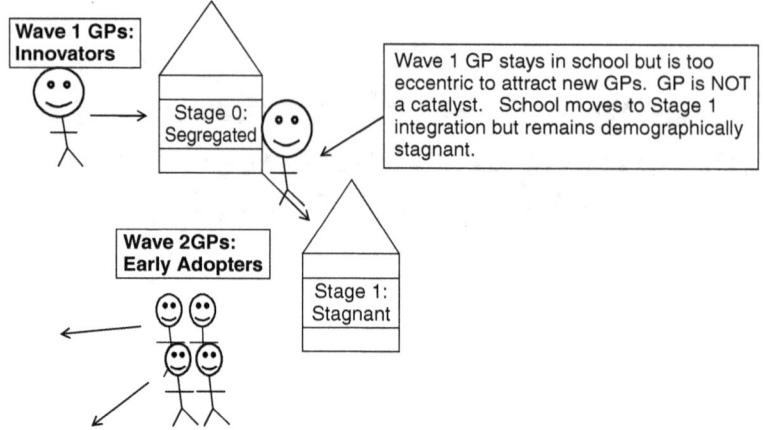

Figure E.2 Stage 1 of integration: the school is stagnant.

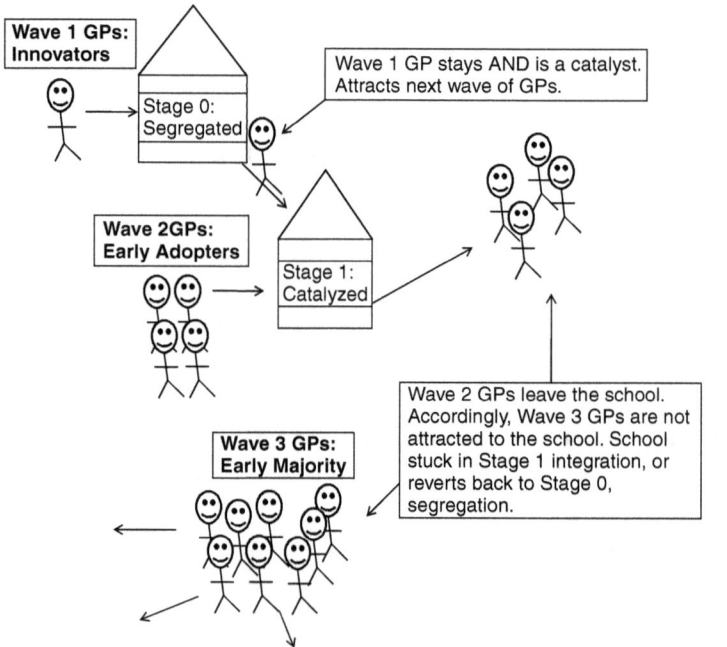

Figure E.3 Stage 1 of integration: the school is catalyzed.

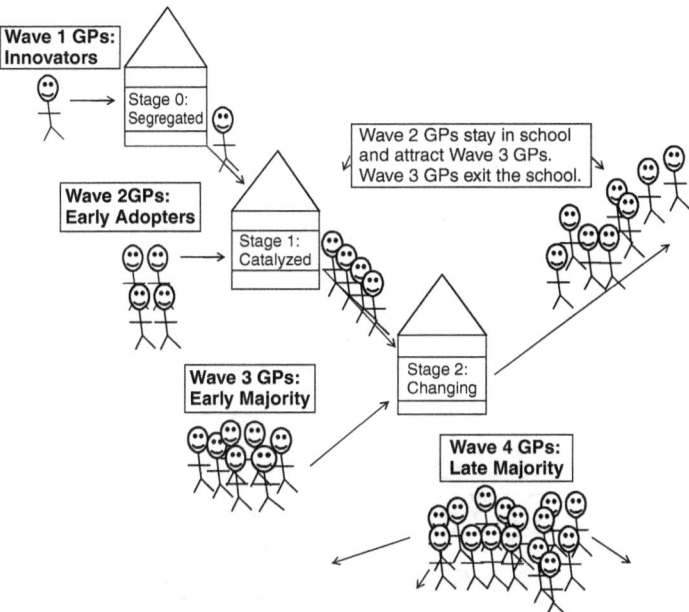

Figure E.4 Stage 2 of integration: the school is changing.

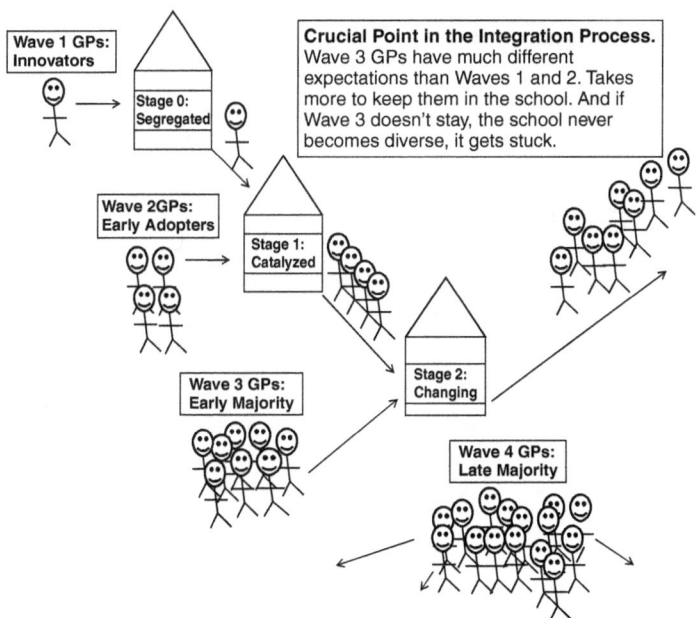

Figure E.5 Retaining the early majority gentry parents: a crucial point in the integration process.

180 APPENDICES

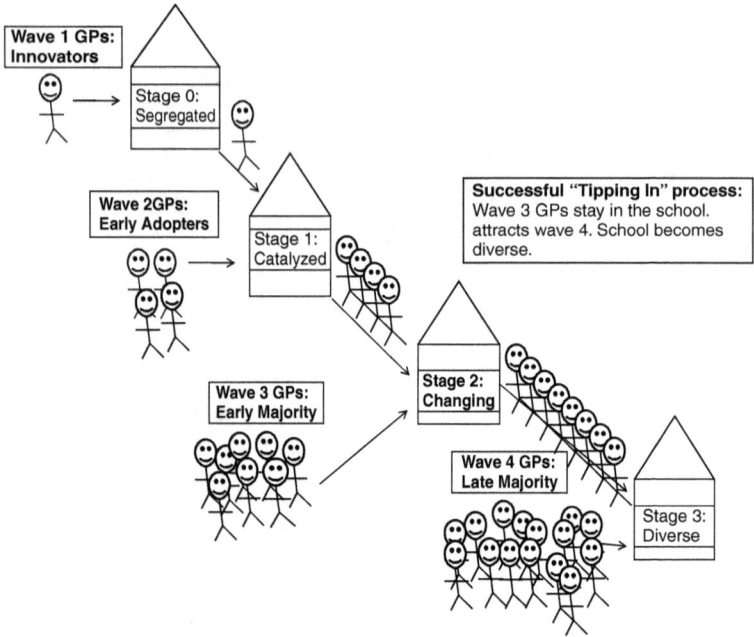

Figure E.6 Successful tipping in process: the school is diverse.

Appendix F: Early Memo on the Properties of Different Types of GPs and Different Stages of School Integration

Looking over my notes, reflecting on some of the things Margaret and Paula said during our second interview, which was affirmed by Lisbeth. Margaret said that the new parents coming in are "not coming in with good will." Likewise, Paula said "the principal needs to understand that these parents are choosing between private school and P.S____." These two comments reflect the difference that M and P see between their own motivations and the motivations of newcomers. Likewise, Lisbeth, a distinct wave-oner, said of the newcomers, "A lot of them expected it to already be done for them." There are those who commit to a new project for social justice reasons and are willing to do the hard work. Then there are those who are willing to take a chance on something that is up and coming, but they don't want to do the hard work still required of them, because they heard the school was good, and changing, and their expectations are much different from the Wave 1 folks. However, at a school like P.S.____ in Neighborhood A, the process of change was much different, the expectations were different. The wave-oners came in not with a desire to change anything, they were just tolerant cosmopolitans who thought they already found a good school. They were foreign GPs. And now the Wave 2 folks who saw Wave 1 white folks in the school as a sign that it was OK for them to enter are now tinkering around with trying to change the school because it wasn't what they thought it would be. Maybe? I need to find more pre-K P.S.____ folks. Think about the different wave mentalities, and whether they are always so distinct.

Maybe it needs to be less about a Wave 1 versus Wave 2 mentality and more about white counting or the presence of any GPs in the school who are clearly active and making a difference. Or not necessarily making a difference, but their presence is obvious in a way that a Wave 2er doesn't enter thinking she is alone as *the* minority.

I think it is important for me to distinguish between who is Wave 1 and who is Wave 2 and who is Wave 3 in each of my interviewees so that I can build the properties of each of these categories using examples, and figure out how one wave impacts the next. For each person's memo, start with a 1, 2, or 3 before the GPs name for effective sorting purposes.

Also thinking about people who *could* have been Wave 2 but instead opt to be Wave 1. Specifically the P.S.____/ P.S._____ split. Its seems that most of my P.S. _____ folks also considered P.S._____, and would have been Wave 2 there, but not Wave 3, and instead opted to be Wave 1 at P.S._____. Buzz coming out of P.S._____ from the Wave 1'ers not good enough to attract Wave 2'ers who are being lead by another force (Timothy in this case).

I'm thinking a Wave 2 person usually enters as a second/third/fourth choice. If they are Wave 2, the school is not their first choice, but an acceptable choice. What makes a school Stage 3 is that it could be considered a first choice, no big deal. When a school is in Stage 1, a gentry parent who chooses that school raises eyebrows in a big way among the social group. They have to explain themselves. When a GP enters a Stage 2 school, they have less explaining to do, the school is usually a second choice or third choice, but they are not totally crazy to give it a try. If it were their first choice, they might need to do some explaining, but if they are only going if they don't get X, Y, or Z, then they don't necessarily need to explain. Stage 3, no explanations necessary.

Do the Waves correspond with the stages? Yes. A Wave 1 parent goes into a Stage 0 school making it a stage 1 school. Wave 2 parents go into Stage 1 schools making them Stage 2 schools. And Wave 3 parents go into Stage 2 schools making them Stage 3 schools. So the Wave comes before the stage. A wave must come to create the stage.

What is another name for Stage 0: Segregated School? I need to come up with better names. Though to call Wave 1 "innovators" is sort of the same as calling them pioneers. Early adopters and early majority sounds much more civilized and less loaded, somehow. Though maybe not. Though, if my goal is integration, then saying, "The school is segregated" (Stage 0), now it is in Stage 1 of integration, Stage 2 of integration, Stage 3 of integration, which is arguably... Integrated!!!

I'm actually now thinking that there needs to be a Stage 4 school: Integrated. The Wave 3 GPs have been entering the school for enough years that the school is finally integrated throughout, not just in the early grades. P.S._____, P.S. __ maybe. Though if someone chooses a G&T program over a Stage 4 school Gen. Ed. program, then maybe the school isn't really Stage 4. Or maybe a school that has a G&T program can never be a Stage 4, because there will always be a class system within the school that prevents it from becoming the first choice. So, presence of a G&T system prevents a school from being Stage 4. Presence of a dual language may not, however, especially a Spanish Dual Language program. P.S._____ is arguably Stage 4, there is no G&T, but there is a Dual Language. I'm not sure if the middle class is concentrated in that program or not. P.S. _____ might be a good Neighborhood B example of Stage 4, that and P.S _____. This might be something worth putting in policy recommendations. Noting that G&T programs must be eliminated if the school is to transform to a Stage 4 school.

Properties less about numbers and more about the buzz in the school and who is going to that school, which wave of parents is being attracted to the school. If Wave 3 parents are coming in, then the school is Stage 2, Changing, even if a pure numerical breakdown would suggest Stage 1, Catalyzed. Maybe.

Notes

1 School Integration in Gentrifying Neighborhoods

1. Research suggests that racial isolation and concentrated poverty contribute to lower average student achievement levels in these schools. Socioeconomically and racially integrated schools have been shown to produce better results for poor children of color, reflecting some combination of peer effects, access to social networks, enhanced parental involvement, and additional school resources, including higher quality teachers (Kahlenberg 2001; Lankford, Loeb, and Wyckoff 2002; Rumberger and Palardy 2005; Wells and Crain 1994). Additional evidence suggests that teachers in high poverty, high minority schools have lower expectations that lead to less challenging work, further disadvantaging poor children of color (Ferguson 1998). Further, a recent school integration study found that children from a high socioeconomic status *also* do not learn as much in schools dominated by children from low socioeconomic backgrounds as they do in schools dominated by children from high socioeconomic backgrounds (Rumberger and Palardy 2005).
2. I use the terms "nongentry" and "gentry" throughout this book to refer to the different groups living in what the media and scholarly communities have labeled "gentrifying neighborhoods." This term, gentrification, was coined by the British sociologist, Ruth Glass, in 1964, "deliberately ironic and tongue in cheek...designed to point to the emergence of a new 'urban gentry,' paralleling the 18th and 19th century rural gentry familiar to readers of Jane Austen who comprised the class strata below the landed gentry, but above yeoman farmers and peasants" (Lees, Slater, and Wyly, 2008).
3. Carrie is a pseudonym, as are all of the names used throughout this book to protect the identities of the parents who allowed me to interview them. Pseudonyms are also used for school names and neighborhood names as per the confidentiality agreement signed by my interviewees.
4. While middle-class black and Hispanic families can be, and usually are, part of the gentrification process, it is the entrance of white families into a neighborhood that overtly signals a neighborhood's gentrification, and causes the nongentry residents to take note and react. Freeman (2006) discovered that "the role of race as a marker of socioeconomic status and as a determinant

of who gets what is a recurring theme in the gentrification discussion. More specifically, the perceptions that whites command and obtain better services and amenities wherever they live is a source of appreciation, resentment, and resignation"(14). Thus, I confine my definition of GPs to the white parents in gentrifying neighborhoods, since the entrance of white gentry children into a segregated school would also be a much more overt marker of a school starting to integrate than the entrance of gentry black or Hispanic children. Even if an interviewee's child was biracial due to an interracial marriage, as long as one parent was white, I accepted that GP in my sample. I also interviewed a handful of Asian Americans, and consider them to be GPs for the purposes of this study, as they stood out in their schools as racially and socioeconomically different, and themselves closely identified with the white families in the neighborhood.
5. Whether or not gentrification is causing widespread displacement of poor families remains an open question. It is clearly a widely held belief about gentrification, but it is not easily supported by the data. Freeman and Braconi's (2004) quantitative study of gentrification and displacement in New York City in the 1990s found that poor people generally move more often than the nonpoor, regardless of where they are living, and they are actually *less* likely to move from a gentrifying neighborhood. But, displacement can mean more than physical movement. Having one's culture and comfort zone quashed by overpriced coffee and upscale cafes can also be a form of displacement.
6. There are different types of GPs who are willing to enroll their children at different stages of integration. To explain the four types, I borrowed terminology from Malcolm Gladwell's (2002) *The Tipping Point:* Innovators, Early Adopters, Early Majority, and Late Majority.

2 School Preferences and the Process of Choosing

1. This BSRA test is an individual cognitive test designed for children, pre-K through second grade, assessing six basic skills: colors, letters, numbers, sizes, comparisons, and shapes.
2. The OLSAT test is a test of abstract thinking and reasoning ability of children pre-K to 18. The Otis-Lennon measures verbal, quantitative, and spatial reasoning ability. The test yields verbal and nonverbal scores, from which a total score is derived, called a School Ability Index (SAI).
3. The Stanford Binet IQ test measures fluid reasoning, knowledge, quantitative reasoning, visual-spatial processing, and working memory.
4. See table 8.1 in chapter 8 for a detailed demographic breakdown of schools GPs consider diverse.
5. Six of my 52 formal interviewees were foreign GPs. While this is a small number, many other nonforeign GPs I interviewed made reference to the impact foreign GPs were having on integrating their schools. Their presence has been noticed and noted.

3 Starting the Integration Process

1. There was only one Stage 0 school in this study that was considered "failing," and still attracted GPs due to the outreach efforts of a new principal who is very charismatic and clearly wanted to do things differently in the school. Understanding the importance of *insideschools.org*, the small group of GPs entering this "failing" school convinced the Inside Schools staff to come and meet with the principal and rewrite their description of the school to reflect the potential that now seemed to exist.
2. The NYC Department of Education (NYCDOE) uses progress reports to evaluate the schools. The reports give each school a letter grade—A, B, C, D, or F—based on the academic achievement and progress of students as well as the results of surveys taken by parents, students, and teachers last spring. Each school's grade is based on its score in three categories: school environment (15 percent), student performance (30 percent), and student progress (55 percent).
3. Neighborhood P is a pseudonym for a neighborhood adjacent to Margaret's neighborhood, a neighborhood not considered diverse, but very white and wealthy.

4 Solving the Collective Action Problem

1. I was invited by Jeremy to join the group so that I could follow the discussion.
2. After learning about this connection tool, I joined the neighborhood kids listserve in two of the three neighborhoods in my study to follow the school buzz. I have since seen more postings of this nature. I was unable to identify a formal kids listserve in the third neighborhood.
3. *Sunshine Bear Academy* is a pseudonym. No preschools in New York City currently have this name, and any future schools that might use this name are in no way connected with this research.
4. ONOS is a pseudonym, and there is currently no group of parents, to my knowledge, in New York City with this name. If a group in the future takes this name, it is in no way connected to this research.

5 Retaining the Innovators and Early Adopters

1. It is possible that Dr. Carson was restricted by union rules on teacher transfers, teacher certification requirements, and she couldn't simply hire the teachers Anna was recommending. If this was the case, she did not effectively communicate her constraints to Anna.
2. According to www.renzullilearning.com, "The Renzulli approach to differentiation starts with the *The Renzulli Profiler*, a simple online tool for

conducting individualized strengths-based assessments that identify a student's interests, learning styles, and expression styles. Educators can then use the *Differentiation Engine*, a lesson-planning tool that differentiates over 25,000 Enrichment Activities—automatically. The result is a highly engaging learning environment that empowers students to achieve more in the classroom, and enables schools to attain better academic results. *Grouping and Reporting Tools* make it easy for teachers to group profiled students by their shared strengths and interests and to compile custom reports on those groups. As a result, students help other students to learn more and take on new challenges."

3. *Bowling Alone* is a book by Robert Putnam, Simon and Schuster (2000), New York, on the "Collapse and Revival of American Community."

6 Attracting the Early Majority

1. Pseudonyms are used in accordance with confidentiality agreements to protect the identities of GPs in this study.
2. Demographic data comes from the 2008 New York State Testing and Reporting Accountability numbers, which would have been the numbers referenced by the families I interviewed primarily during the 2009–2010 school year.
3. The competition among wealthy families for desirable private school spots brings with it its own madness. See, for example, the film documentary, "Nursery University." And both "Waiting for Superman" and "The Lottery" highlight the competition among poor children of color for spots in desirable charter schools.

7 Retaining the Early Majority, A Crucial Step

1. One of the two schools stuck in Stage 2 of integration *had* a G&T program, but it was eliminated only a few years after the commencement of the integration process, reportedly at the behest of the GPs in the school.

8 A Diverse School

1. Data retrieved from www.schoolmatters.com
2. Demographic data comes from the 2008 New York State Testing and Reporting Accountability Tool numbers, which would have been the numbers referenced by the families I interviewed primarily during the 2009–2010 school year.
3. Pseudonyms are used in accordance with confidentiality agreements to protect the identities of GPs in this study.

4. Pseudonyms are used in accordance with confidentiality agreements to protect the identities of GPs in this study.
5. Title I, Part A, of the Elementary and Secondary Education Act, as amended, provides financial assistance to local educational agencies and schools with high numbers or high percentages of children from low-income families to help ensure that all children meet challenging state academic standards. Federal funds are currently allocated through four statutory formulas that are based primarily on census poverty estimates and the cost of education in each state. Definition from the Department of Education's website, ed.gov.

9 Tipping In

1. The Supreme Court's ruling in *Miliken v. Bradley* (1974) hindered the ability of state governments to orchestrate social mixing and break up concentrated district poverty and racial segregation by deeming interdistrict integration plans as unconstitutional, except when the state or suburban districts are proven to have pursued policies that helped create the concentrated racial patterns. Thus, wealth and the ability to live in certain neighborhoods or pay for private school continue to dictate school demographics. Even diverse school districts that constructed effective intradistrict integration plans suffered a setback with the recent Supreme Court ruling in *Parents Involved in Community Schools v. Seattle School District No.1* and *Meredith v. Jefferson County Board of Elections* (2007), with school assignment based explicitly on race deemed unconstitutional. However, Justice Kennedy's concurring opinion emphasizes a state's compelling interest in ensuring that students are not racially isolated, and leaves room for states to strive for diverse student bodies as long as the use of race is not explicit, and is only one component of many being considered for diversity.
2. See *Parents Involved in Community Schools v. Seattle School District No. 1 and Meredith v. Jefferson County Board of Education (2007)*.

References

Allen, I. L. (1984). "The Ideology of Neighborhood Redevelopment." In *Gentrification, Displacement and Neighborhood Revitalization* (pp. 27–40). Albany, NY: State University of New York Press.

Anyon, J. (1980). "Social Class and the Hidden Curriculum of Work." *Journal of Education, 162*: 67–92.

Arcury, T. A., and Quandt, S. A. (n.d.). "Participant Recruitment for Qualitative Research: A Site-Based Approach to Community Research in Complex Societies." *Human Organization, 58*(2): 128–133.

Blomley, N. (2004). *Unsettling the City: Urban Land and the Politics of Property.* New York: Routledge.

Blumer, H. (1954). "What is Wrong with Social Theory?" *American Sociological Review, 18*: 3–10.

———. (1962). "Society as Symbolic Interaction." In A. M. Rose (Ed.), *Human Behavior and Social Process: An Interactionist Approach.* Boston, MA: Houghton Mifflin.

Bordas, H. (2006, Summer). "Desegregation Now. Segregation Tomorrow?" *Ed. Magazine.* Retrieved from http://www.gse.harvard.edu/news_Events/ed/2006/summer/features/resegregation.html

Brantlinger, E. (2003). *Dividing Classes: How the Middle Class Negotiates and Rationalizes School Advantage.* New York: Routledge.

Butler, T., and Robson, G. (2001, January 2). *Negotiating the New Urban Economy—Work, Home and School: Middle Class Life in London.* Paper presented at The Royal Geographical Society—Institute of British Geographers Conference, Plymouth, UK.

Byrne, J. P. (2003). "Two Cheers for Gentrification." *Howard Law Journal, 46*(3): 405–432.

Caulfield, J. (1994). *City Form and Everyday Life: Toronto's Gentrification and Critical Social Practice.* Toronto: University of Toronto Press.

Charmaz, K. (2006). *Constructing Grounded Theory: A Practical Guide through Qualitative Analysis.* Thousand Oaks, CA: Sage Publications.

Clay, P. (1979). *Neighborhood Renewal: Middle-Class Resettlement and Incumbent Upgrading in American Neighborhoods.* Lexington, MA: D.C. Heath.

Clotfelter, C. T. (2004). *After Brown.* Princeton, NJ: Princeton University Press.

Creswell, J. W. (2007). *Qualitative Inquiry and Research Design: Choosing Among Five Approaches.* Thousand Oaks, CA: Sage Publications.

Davila, A. (2005). *Barrio Dreams: Puerto Ricans, Latinos, and the Neoliberal City*. Berkeley, CA: University of California Press.

Delpit, L. (1995). *Other People's Children: Cultural Conflict in the Classroom*. New York: The New Press.

DeSena, J. (2006, October). "What's a Mother To Do? Gentrification, School Selection, and the Problems for Community Cohesion." *American Behavioral Scientist*, 50(2).

Ehrenreich, B. (1990). *Fear of Falling: The Inner Life of the Middle Class*. New York, NY: Harper Perennial.

Ellen, I. G. (2000). *Sharing America's Neighborhoods*. Cambridge, MA: Harvard University Press.

Ellen, I. G., Schwartz, A. E., and Stiefel, L. (2008). "Can Economically Integrated Neighborhoods Improve Childrenj's Educational Outcomes?" In *Urban and Regional Policy and Its Effects* (pp. 181–205). Washington, DC: The Brookings Institution.

Ferguson, R. F. (1998). "Teachers' Perceptions and Expectations and the Black-White Test Score Gap." In C. Jencks and M. Phillips (Eds.), *The Black-White Test Score Gap* (pp. 273–317). Washington, DC: Brookings.

Florida, R. (2002). *The Rise of the Creative Class: And How It's Transforming Work, Leisure, Community and Everyday Life*. New York: Basic Books.

———. (2004). *Cities and the Creative Class*. London: Routledge.

Freeman, L. (2006). *There Goes the 'Hood: Views of Gentrification from the Ground Up*. Philadelphia: Temple University Press.

Freeman, L. and Braconi, F. (2004). "Gentrification and Displacement: New York City in the 1990s." *Journal of the American Planning Association*, 1(70): 39–52.

Gladwell, M. (2000). *The Tipping Point: How Little Things Can Make a Big Difference*. New York: Little Brown and Co.

Glaser, B. G., and Strauss, A. L. (1967). *The Discovery of Grounded Theory: Strategies for Qualitative Research*. Chicago, IL: Aldine Transaction.

Goetz, E. G. (2003). *Cleaing the Way: Deconcentrating the Poor in Urban America*. Washington, DC: The Urban Institute Press.

Grant, G. (2009). *Hope and Despair in the American city: Why There Are No Bad Schools in Raleigh*. Cambridge, MA: Harvard University Press.

Hardin, R. (1982). *Collective Action*. Baltimore, MD: Johns Hopkins University Press.

Headden, S. (2006, February 20). "Two Guys...and a Dream." *U.S. News and World Report*.

Henig, J. R. (1996). "The Local Dynamics of Choice: Ethnic Preferences and Institutional Responses." In B. Fuller and R. Elmore (Eds.), *Who Chooses? Who Loses?: Culture, Institutions, and the Unequal Effects of School Choice* (pp. 95–117). New York: Teachers College Press.

Henig, J. R., Hula, R. C., Orr, M., and Pedescleaux, D. S. (1999). *The Color of School Reform: Race, Politics, and the Challenge of Urban Education*. Princeton, NJ: Princeton University Press.

Herszenhorn, D. (2003, December 10). "Mixed Signals over Fate of Gifted-and-Talented Program." *The New York Times*.

Hirschman, A. O. (1970). *Exit, Voice, and Loyalty: Responses to Decline in Firms, Organizations, and States*. Cambridge, MA: Harvard University Press.

Holme, J. J. (2002). "Buying Homes, Buying Schools: School Choice and the Social Construction of School Quality." *Harvard Educational Review*, 72(2): 177–205.

Jacobs, J. (1961). *The Death and Life of Great American Cities*. New York: Random House.

Kahlenberg, R. D. (2001). *All Together Now: Creating Middle-Class Schools through Public School Choice*. Washington, DC: Brookings Institution Press.

Kelly, S. P. (2008). "Social Class and Tracking Within Schools." In L. Weis (Ed.), *The Way Class Works: Readings on School, Family, and the Economy* (pp. 210–224). New York: Routledge.

Kohn, M. L. (1963, January). "Social Class and Parent-Child Relationships: An Interpretation." *The American Journal of Sociology*, 68(4): 471–480. Retrieved from http:/www.jstor.org/stable/2774426?seq=10

Kozol, J. (1992). *Savage Inequalities: Children in America's Schools*. New York: Harper Perennial.

Lankford, H., Loeb, S., and Wyckoff, J. (2002). "Teacher Sorting and The Plight of Urban Schools: A Descriptive Analysis." *Educational Evaluation and Policy Analysis*, 1(24): 37–62.

Lareau, A. (2003). *Unequal Childhoods: Class, Race, and Family Life*. Berkeley, CA: University of California Press.

Lees, L. (2003, May). "Super-Gentrification: The Case of Brooklyn Heights, New York City." *Urban Studies*, 40(12): 2487–2509.

Lees, L., Slater, T., and Wyly, E. (2008). *Gentrification*. New York: Routledge.

Ley, D. (1996). *The New Middle Class and the Remaking of the Central City*. New York: Oxford University Press.

Lloyd, R. (2006). *Neo Bohemia: Art and Commerce in the Post-Industrial City*. Chicago, IL: University of Chicago Press.

Lofland, J., and Lofland, L. H. (1995). *Analyzing Social Settings: A Guide to Qualitative Observation and Analysis*. Belmont, CA: Wadsworth Publishing Company.

Lukas, J. A. (1986). *Common Ground: A Turbulent Decade in the Lives of Three American Families*. New York: Vintage Books.

Lydersen, K. (1999, March 15). "Shame of the Cities: Gentrification in the New Urban America." *Lip Magazine*. Retrieved from http://www.lipmagazine.org/articles/featlydersen_7.shtml

Matthews, J. (2006, April 2). "A Miracle in the Making? KIPP Turns Its Efforts towards Elementary Schools." *The Washington Post*.

Mitchell, D. (2003). *The Right to the City: Social Justice and the Fight for Public Space*. New York: The Guilford Press.

Moore, D., and Davenport, S. (1990). "School Choice: The New Improved Sorting Machine." In W. Boyd and H. Walberg (Eds.), *Choice in Education*. Berkeley, CA: McCutchan.

Olson, M. (1965). *The Logic of Collective Action: Public Goods and the Theory of Groups*. Cambridge, MA: Harvard University Press.

Patterson, O. (1998). *The Ordeal of Integration*. New York: Basic Civitas.

Powell, J., and Spencer, M. (2003). "Giving Them the Old 'one-two': Gentrification and the K O of Impoverished Urban Dwellers of Color." *Howard Law Journal*, 46(3): 433–490.

Rumberger, R. W., and Palardy, G. J. (2005). "Does Segregation Still Matter? The Impact of Student Composition on Academic Achievement in High School." *Teachers College Record*, 9(107): 1999–2045.

Santos, F. (2011, April 11). "Where School System's Toughest Battles Are a Reality, Support for a New Leader." *The New York Times*, p. A22.

Saporito, S., and Lareau, A. (1999). "School Selection as a Process: The Multiple Dimensions of Race in Framing Educational Choice." *Social Problems*, 46: 418–435.

Schelling, T. C. (1972). "A Process of Residential Segregation: Neighborhood Tipping." In A. H. Pascal (Trans.), *Racial Discrimination in Economic Life* (pp. 157–184). Lexington, MA: Lexington Books.

———. (1978). *Micro Motives and Macro Behavior*. New York: W.W. Norton & Company.

Schneider, M., Teske, P., and Marschall, M. (2000). *Choosing Schools: Consumer Choice and the Quality of American Schools*. Princeton, NJ: Princeton University Press.

Semel, S. F., and Sadovnik, A. R. (Eds.). (1999). *Schools of Tomorrow, Schools of Today: What Happened to Progressive Education*. New York: Peter Lang.

Smith, N. (1996). *The New Urban Frontier: Gentrification and the Revanchist City*. New York: Routledge.

Snow, D., and Anderson, L. (1987). "Identity Work among the Homeless: The Verbal Construction and Avowal of Personal Identities." *American Journal of Sociology*, 92(6): 1336–1371.

Strauss, A., and Corbin, J. (1998). "Grounded Theory Methodology: An Overview." In N. Denzin and Y. Lincoln (Eds.), *Strategies of Qualitative Inquiry*. London: Sage.

Strauss, A. L. (1987). *Qualitative Analysis for Social Scientists*. New York: Cambridge University Press.

Sunstein, C. R. (2006). *Infotopia: How Many Minds Produce Knowledge*. Oxford: Oxford University Press.

Wells, A. S. (1993). "The Sociology of School Choice: Why Some Win and Others Lose in the Educational Marketplace." In E. Rasell and R. Rothstein (Eds.), *School Choice: Examining the Evidence* (pp. 29–48). Washington, DC: Economic Policy Institute.

———. (1996). "African-American Students' View of School Choice." In B. Fuller and R. Elmore (Eds.), *Who Chooses? Who Loses?: Culture, Institutions, and the Unequal Effects of School Choice* (pp. 25–49). New York: Teachers College Press.

Wells, A. S., and Crain, R. L. (1994). "Perpetuation Theory and the Long-Term Effects of School Desegregation. *Review of Educational Research*, 4(64): 531–555.

Wells, A. S., and Serna, I. (1996, Spring). "The Politics of Culture: Understanding Local Political Resistance to Detracking in Racially Mixed Schools." *Harvard Educational Review*, 66(1): 93–118.

Wilson, J. Q. (1975). *Thinking About Crime*. New York: Basic Books, Inc., Publishers.

Winerip, M. (2010, July 25). "Equity of Test is Debated as Children Compete for Gifted Kindergarten." *The New York Times*.

Zucchino, D. (2011, February 5). "End of Diversity Policy Leaves a Southern School District Divided." *The Los Angeles Times*.

Index

apartheid school, 25–26, 36, 121–123
authoritarian parenting style (*see also* yelling adults), 67–69
authoritarian schools (*see also* yelling adults), 21–22, 70, 109, 147, 170, 173

boosting a school, 49, 100, 102–103
buzz, 94, 98, 99, 101–103, 160, 163, 167, 182

Catalyzed School (*see* Stage 1, Catalyzed School)
Changing School (*see* Stage 2, Changing School)
charter schools, 15, 21–22, 146–149, 159, 188
choice (*see* school choice)
class v. race (*see* race v. class)
class size, 55, 113, 119–120
collective action problem, xiv, 36, 49, 51–63, 94–95, 127, 132, 135, 137–140, 145–146, 187
Common Ground, Lukas, J. Anthony (1986), 52–53
controlled choice, 145–146
culture shock (*see* gentry/non-gentry culture gap)

The Death and Life of the Great America City, Jacobs, Jane (1961), 27
discipline (*see also* yelling adults), 73–76, 106–109

displacement, 2, 6, 7, 41, 158, 159, 186
diversity
challenges of (*see also* gentry/non-gentry culture gap), 27, 125–126
definitions of, 19–20, 37, 115–117, 149–150
as a value, 13, 15–18, 38, 44, 52, 139, 143, 146–147, 150, 169, 189
Diverse School (*see* Stage 3, Diverse School)
drift, 34, 40–42, 83, 164
dual language programs, 37–38, 40, 53, 91, 112, 118, 124–125, 127, 183

Early Adopter Gentry Parents
definition of, 48–49, 128
attracting them to Stage 0 schools, 49
retaining them in Stage 1 schools, 66–91
Early Majority Gentry Parents
definition of, 94–96, 128
attracting them to Stage 2 schools, 96–101
retaining them in Stage 2 schools, 105–114
elitism (*see also* privilege), 6, 21, 37, 42, 140–141
enclave programs (*see also* dual language programs; gifted and talented programs; pre-K programs), 35–40, 112–113, 132, 143, 144

exit, 90–91, 133–135
Exit, Voice, and Loyalty, Hirschman, A.O., 133–135
foreign gentry parents, 18–20, 37, 43, 49, 73, 83, 85, 89, 102, 120, 181, 186
Free-K (*see also* pre-K programs), 39, 164
Friends of the Mackey, 52–53, 57–58, 60
fundraising, 118–121

Gen. Ed. Innovators, 121–123
gentrification
  arguments in favor (*see also* social mixing), 2
  arguments against (*see also* gentry internal conflict), 2
  definition of, 1
  housing issues, 3, 186
  stages, 158–159
  street tensions, 27
gentry internal conflict, 1–7
gentry/non-gentry culture gap (G/NG Gap)
  definition of, 66
  different parenting styles, 67–69
  examples of, xi–xii, 70–77, 107–109
  managing the gap, 77–85
gentry parents (GPs)
  career choices of, 12
  definition of, xiii, xiv, 3, 185–186
  foreign (*see* foreign gentry parents)
  relativity of their wealth, xiv, 12–13, 30
  types (*see* Early Adopter Gentry Parents; Early Majority Gentry Parents; Innovator Gentry Parents; Late Majority Gentry Parents)
ghetto families, 71
gifted and talented programs
  attitudes against them, 15–16, 23–24, 85
  as segregated white enclaves (*see* apartheid schools)
  choosing them anyway, 24–25, 26–28, 34
  dividing parents (the dual enclave problem), 112–113
  non-white programs as GP enclaves, 28–29, 36–37, 112
  testing process, 15
group polarization, 100–101

Innovator Gentry Parents
  definition of, 33, 42–48, 128
  attracting them to Stage 0 schools, 33–42
  retaining them in Stage 1 schools, 65–91
insideschools.org, 28, 35, 77, 187
integration (*see* tipping in)
integrated v. integrating, 114

Late Majority Gentry Parents, 115, 128
listserv, 54–55, 60, 187

middle-class culture/ethos, 6–7, 14, 67–75, 77, 88, 97–98, 115, 117, 121, 123, 138, 157
momentum (*see* buzz)
Monolingual Innovators, 124–125

"new" parents v. "old" parents (*see* gentry/non-gentry culture gap)
networking (*see* collective action problem)

"old" parents v. "new "parents (*see* gentry/non-gentry culture gap)
Other People's Children, Delpit, Lisa (1995), 74–75
Our Neighborhood, Our School (ONOS), 57–61, 62, 136, 187

pacts, 61–63
Parent Teacher Association (PTA), 40, 47, 58, 59, 73, 83, 102, 118, 120, 131, 133

parenting styles (*see* authoritarian parenting style; progressive parenting style)
peer effects, 6, 7, 117, 185
physical discipline, 75–76
power culture, 13, 30, 118
pre-K programs, 39, 57, 74, 80, 90, 93, 101, 108–109, 112–113, 163, 173, 174, 181
principals (*see* school leadership)
private school, 12–13, 86–87, 101, 148, 169, 181, 188
privilege (*see also* elitism), 1–7, 45–46, 86–87, 90, 140, 143–144, 145, 149, 153
progressive education, 20–21, 23, 34, 53, 70, 88, 91, 109, 110, 111, 116–117, 127, 147, 170, 173
progressive parenting style, 40, 67–69, 75, 164
public school (*see also* dual language programs; charter schools; gifted and talented programs)
   districts as important boundary lines, 14, 15, 28, 31, 34, 39, 42, 91, 97, 127, 137–139
   lotteries, 14–15, 24, 25, 30, 34, 39, 42, 133, 146–147, 188
   October enrollment numbers, 30, 62, 91
   options in New York City, 13–15
   public choice schools (PCS), 14–15, 116–117, 125, 126, 149–150
   as a value, 12
   zone schools and lines, 13–14, 21–23, 30–31, 34, 40–42, 116, 132, 137–139, 159

racial divide (*see also* apartheid school) 2, 5, 58, 74, 135–136, 154–156, 165, 168–169
race-based stereo-typing hypothesis, 31
race v. class, 55, 58, 66–69, 135–136, 154–156, 168–179, 185
recess, 71, 74, 79, 88, 107–108
Renzulli method, 85, 88, 187

safe diversity, 37
school choice(*see also* school tours)
   behaving like the herd, 28–29
   bureaucratic loopholes, 30–31, 91
   difficulty of considering new options, 29–31
   failing school, 40, 122, 187
   group polarization, 100–101
   hierarchy of choice, 29, 40, 78
   not a failing school, 35, 39, 140
   preferences, 15–28
   Rorshack Test, 98
   school cohort theory, 28–29
   as a socially charged process, 99–101
   waitlist, 30, 62
   word of mouth (*see* buzz)
school culture (*see* authoritarian schools; progressive education; school leadership)
school leadership
   co-opting the institutional elite, 140
   negative perceptions, 40, 58–60, 78–81, 119
   positive perceptions, 35, 52–53, 61, 82–85, 107, 110, 122, 133, 142–143
   racial politics, 79–80, 136
school tours, 25, 28, 59, 83, 97–99, 100, 101, 102–103, 106, 109, 114, 119, 125, 128, 141, 144, 162
Segregated School (*see* Stage 0, Segregated School)
selling a school (*see also* school tours), 49, 94, 96–99, 100, 102, 110
sidewalk ballet, 27
Social Class and the Hidden Curriculum of Work, Anyon, Jean (1980), 69
Social Class and Parent Child Relationships, Kohn, M.L. (1963), 67
social justice, commitment to, 47–48, 49, 65, 86, 94, 95, 112, 121, 127, 135, 139, 148, 153, 181
social mixing, 5, 7–8, 131–132, 150, 189

Stage 0, Segregated School (*see also* collective action problem), 33–50, 160, 177, 182, 187
Stage 1, Catalyzed School, 48–50, 65–91, 160, 166, 178, 182
Stage 1, Stagnant School, 48–50, 160, 166, 178, 182
Stage 2, Changing School, 93–103, 105–114, 160, 166, 179, 182
Stage 3, Diverse School, 115–126, 160, 166, 180, 182
Stagnant School (*see* Stage 1, Stagnant School)

tight-knit communities, 89–90
tipping in
  circumstances that make it easier, 82–83
  definition of, 1, 8, 11, 115–117, 127–130
  hurdles, 11, 18, 21–23, 26–28, 29–31, 130–131, 132–136
  policy recommendations, 137–150
  summary of the process, 127–130
  tolerance for the process, 85–89
  visual overview, 177–180
  within-school tipping in, 121–125
Tipping Point, The, Gladwell, Malcolm (2000), 95–96, 161, 186
Title I funding, 55, 59, 119–121, 131, 189

traditional education (*see* authoritarian schools)

Unequal Childhoods, Lareau, Annette (2003), 67–69
unique seekers, 43–46, 90, 94–96, 110
Urban Education Cooperatives (UEC), 137–146

verbal abuse (*see* yelling adults)
volunteering in schools, 45, 56, 58, 59–60, 68–69, 72, 75, 97, 118, 126, 127, 130, 142–143

white avoidance (hypothesis of), 18
white counting, xiii, 16, 19, 181
wave 1 gentry parents (*see* Innovator Gentry Parents)
wave 2 gentry parents (*see* Early Adopter Gentry Parents)
wave 3 gentry parents (*see* Early Majority Gentry Parents)
wave 4 gentry parents (*see* Late Majority Gentry Parents)
word of mouth (*see* buzz)

yelling adults, 73–75
yo people, 89
yuppies, 2

GPSR Compliance

The European Union's (EU) General Product Safety Regulation (GPSR) is a set of rules that requires consumer products to be safe and our obligations to ensure this.

If you have any concerns about our products, you can contact us on

ProductSafety@springernature.com

In case Publisher is established outside the EU, the EU authorized representative is:

Springer Nature Customer Service Center GmbH
Europaplatz 3
69115 Heidelberg, Germany

www.ingramcontent.com/pod-product-compliance
Lightning Source LLC
LaVergne TN
LVHW012100070526
838200LV00074BA/3835